Kite-Flying
and Other
Irrational Acts

Kite-Flying and Other Irrational Acts

🍂 *Conversations with Twelve Southern Writers*

Edited by JOHN CARR

Louisiana State University Press
Baton Rouge

ISBN 0–8071–0242–3
Library of Congress Catalog Card Number 72–79328
Copyright © 1972 by Louisiana State University Press
Manufactured in the United States of America
Printed by Kingsport Press, Inc., Kingsport, Tennessee
Designed by A. R. Crochet

The Editor gratefully acknowledges permission
to reprint the following interviews:

Shelby Foote, *Contempora*, July–August, 1970.

Walker Percy, *Georgia Review*, Fall, 1971.

Doris Betts, *Red Clay Reader*, 1970.

Reynolds Price, *Shenandoah*, Summer, 1966.
(Copyright 1966 by *Shenandoah*, reprinted from *Shenandoah:
The Washington and Lee University Review*
with the permission of the Editor.)

Marion Montgomery, *The Southern Review*, Autumn, 1970.

This book is dedicated to
My mother and my brother, with love
and gratitude, and to the memory of
my grandfather Albert Clarence Anderson
and my father Curtis Washington Carr
Servants of the people of Mississippi

Contents

The Making of an Interview Book   ix

It's Worth a Grown Man's Time
SHELBY FOOTE Interviewed by John Carr   3

Rotation and Repetition
WALKER PERCY Interviewed by John Carr   34

Makar
MARION MONTGOMERY Interviewed by James Colvert   59

Notice, I'm Still Smiling
REYNOLDS PRICE Interviewed by Wallace Kaufman   70

Down Home
WILLIE MORRIS Interviewed by John Carr   96

Honkies, Editors, & Other Dirty Stories
LARRY L. KING Interviewed by John Carr   120

The Unique Voice
DORIS BETTS Interviewed by George Wolfe   149

Kite-Flying and Other Irrational Acts
GEORGE GARRETT Interviewed by John Carr   174

The Making of Fables
JESSE HILL FORD Interviewed by James Seay   199

Dealing with the Grotesque
FRED CHAPPELL Interviewed by John Sopko and John Carr   216

The Lumbees, the Klan, and . . . Hollywood
GUY OWEN Interviewed by John Carr   236

Waiting for Joiner
JAMES WHITEHEAD Interviewed by John Carr and
John Little   263

Have you ever stopped to think that for the first time, there have been no rational rewards for writing in the way that there were in the past? Much earlier, if you had a patron, that was why you wrote. Obviously, a different type of man is writing books today than was even in the nineteenth century, because when Dickens wrote there was a very definite cause-and-effect relationship. If he wrote the book and it was good and it was published, then he made a lot of money and improved his situation and was highly regarded. And if Shakespeare's plays did well, as they did, and he was a stockholder in his company, it was a rational enterprise. Nowadays, it's about as rational as saying, "What do you do for a living?" "Well, I'm a kite-flyer." I mean, there's not a great demand for kite-flyers around. There may be a few who draw a little money. Therefore, today, writing appeals to a different mentality. A Shakespeare today might be doing something else that's more rational. Now the other thing is that because this is true, fundamentally writing doesn't matter in the world of commerce. It has a certain kind of—I wouldn't say *purity*, but *freedom* that it never had.

George Garrett

The Making of
an Interview Book

When I realized in the spring of 1969 that what had begun as an individual study project under George Garrett at Hollins College could become a book, I decided at least to try to avoid some of the obvious pitfalls of a book of this kind. I had been reading interviews with writers for years and what was noticeable about some of them was the shortness and stiffness (and thus the shallowness) of the interviews. At other times, I had the feeling that the individual interviews were merely rephrasings of the standard public utterances most writers make when they know that the interviewer lacks the energy or resources (because of the format of his newspaper or magazine) to print the complex answers the questions demand. And sometimes I ran across one where the writer had either not been given the opportunity to speak directly to younger writers or had foregone the chance.

There are no doubt errors of structure and approach in this book, since every choice reveals paths that might have been taken with equally rewarding results, but my idea was to interview each writer myself or have the writer interviewed by someone who either knew him or was fascinated by his work, and to give each of the writers both provocation and space. I also wanted each writer to speak to younger writers (and readers) and for each interview to start off "inside" the craft and toil of producing a fiction or a poem—or at least to reach that point as quickly as possible.

I had decided by that time that my main interest was Southern writing, and that it was not only still a force, but the kind of force it was because of social, historical, and economic forces that had not been discussed much by literary scholars. And it was soon evident that few living Southern writers had said much about what *they* thought about the relationship of their writing to the history and socioeconomic make-up of their region. Did, for instance, they write about the South because there was something here that they realized was as good an effigy for their imaginings as, say, Detroit or Costa Rica? Or did they recognize in their culture and history certain qualities that they believed in—but not in the sense that they had become boosters—and had these qualities helped them gain insights they might never have come to in other parts of America? I personally felt (and was encouraged in it by a few entirely unprompted answers by the interviewees) that these writers, who were raised here and still lived here (except for one), were producing works that had more than surface resemblances to each other. That to call writers Southern, in other words, is to say more about them than that they are from the lower right-hand corner of the USA. We didn't get much of a chance, because it was their show, to get into my favorite theory—that the South is an underdeveloped country inside the world's most industrialized empire—but that will be the subject of another, and much longer, essay.

You have noticed by now that all the writers included here are white. When I began this book, I felt that only black interviewers could interview black writers. That only black critics could discuss works of art by black people. I no longer think that is true. In fact, I now recognize it for the silly, if gentle, form of racism it is. And in the three years between the beginning of this book and its publication, there have been no collections of interviews with black writers, Southern or militant or a combination thereof, by interviewers who were any of the above, so I am looking forward to including the ones who are around and some new ones in a future collection of my own. It will probably have to deal with black writers as part of a Southern subculture that has become a national subculture through emigration from the South just before, during, and after the First World War, but that hypothesis is itself a fascinating takeoff point, and worth a book of its own, interview collection or not.

Another problem with the book is that there was only space for twelve writers. That is partly due to the exigencies of publishing in our mini-depression. I had twenty interviews originally, but to have published them all would have required a 700-page book retailing for about $20. Neither I nor my editors believed interest in Southern writing was that overwhelming. There were also some writers who declined to be interviewed, some a little apologetically (I don't think they trusted the tape recorder) and at least one because, I think, he has a horror of his voice on tape surviving him. This book also has a slight bias in favor of writers from the Upper South (as opposed to the Deep South) because I was in the Virginia–North Carolina area for two years, the book was not funded, and anyone who lived more than a two days' drive in a Volkswagen was definitely too far away from me. Another writer was out of the country. And so on. My hope is that I will eventually be able to publish those interviews in another collection.

But this book was also planned, quite apart from being a probe into Southern writing, as an effort to give writers a chance to talk about writing in general, and I think the general reader will be enormously enlightened by being present at conversations that fight hard against being public utterances. Just as one becomes a better reader by trying to write, so—I believe—one becomes a better critic, in the general *and* uncorrupted sense of the word, by learning what the writer wants the story to do.

I also wanted to include some people who had had their ups and downs in the business, as opposed to the art, of writing—ups and downs that have little or no relation to the admiration of other writers and of critics. And since I think the same genius guides all good writing, I wanted some people who had chosen to write nonfiction in an age which devours it in ever-increasing quantities. The two included in this collection are among the best essayists of our time. In addition, I wanted some writers who had written for the movies. In the process of seeking a balanced collection I inadvertently was given at least one interview, with George Garrett, which should knock the fairydust out of the eyes of those who think publishing is still full of fatherly, earnest types like Maxwell Perkins. That and some of the other interviews should help the young writer realize that, although finishing a book is the end of the creative act, it is the beginning in an artist's struggle to find a rational reward for his or her efforts. That although writing is irrational in its impulse and largely in its action, getting published and trying to exist in society as an artist is an exercise in trying to make the rationale of the system reward and encourage you at the same time that it sets limits upon your vision and your work.

This book is also about—and not really because of any planning; it was just sheer luck—what writers are thinking and feeling when they have just finished a book. Every writer in this collection had just finished a book or was seeing it off to the publishers or was in the midst of late drafts when the interviewer came to call. Their responses to the experience of completing a book may be amended in the years to come, but here in front of you is what they thought as they were coming up for air. They were awaiting, and by now most of them have received, the verdict of the critics, of their friends, and of the marketplace.

I should also like to offer a brief explanation of our methodology. The tape recorder has become very popular among reporters, writers, and historians in the past few years, and for good reason: it is absolutely trustworthy. No one need be misquoted, nor will the interviewer lose, through the screen of his memory, or the formal composition of a letter by his subject, the nuances of speech that reflect not only habit and upbringing, but a way of looking at the world.

All of these interviews were recorded except Jim Colvert's with Marion Montgomery (they exchanged memorandums via Marion's mailbox). And in doing the interviews, most of us found that there was yet another reason to use the recorder: most of our interviewees wouldn't have had time to take days off from their current projects and collaborate in a lengthy correspondence. Most were already under a heavy double load—writing and working for a living—but none had any reservations about sitting down and talking for an afternoon.

The principal objection to tape recording is an unfortunate corollary of the respect most of us have for the written word, and it goes like this: "They won't be serious when they talk to a recorder, or they'll exaggerate." Well, I can report that they were all serious, and as for exaggeration, anyone is perfectly capable of doing that with a pen or a typewriter, as any student of history has appreciated by now. And writers are probably more capable of it than most people since they build their lives around crafting things that are not, in the literal sense, true. All things considered, it is the man, not the medium, that is the key.

One last word: one or two of those we interviewed changed the syntax here and there; Larry King later added substantial material to his interview; others will see their interviews here for the first time. Neither we nor they, however, have changed anything else nor censored any response.

Kite-Flying
and Other
Irrational Acts

It's Worth a
Grown Man's Time:
❧ SHELBY FOOTE

Interviewed by JOHN CARR

Shelby Foote was born in 1916 in Greenville, Mississippi (a Delta town; he is not one of the "Piedmont folk," a recent journal article to the contrary), grew up there, attended the University of North Carolina at Chapel Hill, served in World War II in the European theater as a captain of artillery and, later, as a Marine in the Pacific. He has written five novels, Tournament *(1949),* Follow Me Down *(1950),* Love in a Dry Season *(1951),* Shiloh *(1952),* and Jordan County *(1954),* and has finished two volumes of his three-volume* The Civil War: A Narrative History. *Volume I,* Fort Sumter to Perryville *appeared in 1958, and* Volume II, Fredericksburg to Meridian *in 1963. His current project, the narrative history, will be recognized, after the third volume is published, as one of the standard studies, if not the standard study, of that war. He now lives in Memphis with his wife and young son.*

This interview was completed at his home in Memphis in April, 1969, the day after the Martin Luther King Memorial March.

It was only the second time I had ever talked to Shelby Foote, but of course I had heard of him, years before, when I was in high school at Greenwood, Mississippi. Now, one of the things you have to understand about the Delta is its enthusiastic and malicious parochialism. The Greek city-states never simmered in the juices of envy as much as the three large towns of the Delta, and when I was growing up, you knew from your elders and betters that Greenville had sinned and sinned grievously: they had attracted industry, most of it Yankee, once even a whole plant complete with workers, and, worst of all, they tolerated within their precincts Hodding Carter, who

3

had won a Pulitzer Prize after World War II, for, they said, pandering to Northern liberals on the race question. (Years later, when I was a reporter for the Delta Democrat-Times, I read the editorial and the message was that we owed our black citizens some respect. But in the hysteria of the fifties, it was as if Carter had advocated integration and black Republicanism.)

Eventually I went to Greenville to a party with some of my high school buddies. Then, as now, there was the myth (partially true) that it was the intellectual oasis of Mississippi (well, consider the competition). We ended up at somebody's house and as the girl who was our host staggered by me to change the record on the hi-fi, trying to balance her Scotch and Coke (well, some of the reports of degeneracy in Greenville were true, it seemed), she looked at me and said, "You ever heard of Shelby Foote?" Since at the time I was laboring under the delusion that Willie Faulkner was a director who made dirty movies about the South, I naturally hadn't.

"Well," she said in that inimitable Southern accent which unless you've been there you ain't heard, because it don't get too far from home: "Ah hear he writes books—even though he comes from a fine old family, y'unnerstand—and Ah hear they're so dirty you have to ask the librarian for permission to read them." That girl is probably teaching high school English now. In Mississippi. Or Pittsburgh. Or Cleveland.

When I first met Shelby Foote, he told me that he had once been fortunate enough to hear himself discussed in a beauty parlor unbeknownst to the teller of the tale, who had said, "Well, they say one of his novels is about his grandfather, but I knew his grandfather and he was a nice man."

For the past fifteen years he has been working seven days a week, eight hours a day, on his study of the Civil War. It will soon be over and he may begin writing novels again. Foote is a novelist par excellence of the human passions, and they are worked out in a context more metaphysical than we are used to having to deal with in a story about a love murder or the death of a jazz trumpeter or the death of married love. I hope this interview—the first since Harvey Breit's in the April 27, 1952, issue of the New York Times Book Review—will revive interest in Foote the novelist. That interest is long overdue.

INTERVIEWER: Now that you're almost out of the Civil War narrative history, do you plan to go back to Jordan County and pick up on those people again?

FOOTE: That's right.

INTERVIEWER: Is there more, planned out now in your mind?

FOOTE: There's a great deal I've got planned out in my mind. All sorts of minor characters in these books are important characters in later books. If you remember a story called "Pillar of Fire" in *Jordan County*, you remember the Union lieutenant who comes down to help burn houses. Well, this lieutenant, whose name is Lundy, returns to Jordan County after the Civil War as the Yankee who burned all the houses and lives there and is the founder of a very strange dynasty of people, which is what a big novel I plan to write called *Two Gates to the City* is about. He had a son who was a scamp businessman who cleaned out the town and had three daughters, and the book concerns the sons of these three daughters.

INTERVIEWER: This is next in the works after *The Narrative History?*

FOOTE: I'll probably write a short novel to get my hand back in and then I'll go on.

INTERVIEWER: Let's talk about your working habits. Do you generally go very slowly in the average workday, the average workweek?

FOOTE: Five hundred words is a good day.

INTERVIEWER: Is that right?

FOOTE: Yeah, it's a good day. I've done as many as 1,500 [*laughs*] but I've also done as few as 200. Five hundred words is a good day with me, and I manage to do about that.

INTERVIEWER: You're probably the foremost practitioner of history as novel.

FOOTE: Well, the historical novel is about bankrupt, and perhaps it was bankrupt when it started, in spite of *War and Peace* and *Red Badge of Courage*. But a novel should, I think, be rooted in the place where it happened and in the time in which it happened. And I think you owe that place and that time accuracy. I think it's a great sin to put words in the mouth of a person who really lived, unless you know what those words really were. I don't think you have the right to do that. I don't believe it's right to have Billy the Kid come walking into a novel and have him say a few things

and then walk out again—let alone write a novel about Billy the
Kid, which is absurd. You could call him Joey the Fact or something, but not Billy the Kid. Billy has got his validity, and that
you shouldn't fuck with. And so the historical novel as it's been
practiced is a bad form . . . unsatisfactory. I thought that
Styron's novel on Nat Turner was a serious mistake, a very serious
mistake. It's a beautifully written book; it's a hard-thought-out
book; but the sum total is a mistake. It's not Nat Turner, it can't
be Nat Turner. It's a distortion of truth, even though he's trying
for a higher truth. It is not a higher truth, it's a distortion of the
truth. So I think the historical novel is about bankrupt. That is not
to say that I think a novel shouldn't be accurately sited. I think it
should.

INTERVIEWER: Do you think a new horizon would be to write about the
man in the street during the Civil War?

FOOTE: Yes, I think that has validity, but it puts a cramp on you that I
think you shouldn't have. I like to be limited by forces, but that
somehow seems to me to be too great a force. It's best to write
about what you know about, so that you're free to have the truth
available in your head rather than out of documents.

INTERVIEWER: So your approach to the historical novel is not really to
recreate actual people, but to recreate the time and place. Is that
fair?

FOOTE: Yes, that is fair. But keep in mind at the same time that I would
not write a historical novel, but if I did, that is what I would do,
and any novel I wrote I'd hope would do that. I really have no
plans for anything that could be called a historical novel. I'd intended to do Shiloh, which I did, and a big fat book on Vicksburg,
the whole siege, and then another small book on Brice's Crossroads, but I doubt now that I'll do so.

INTERVIEWER: And so the next Jordan County efforts will be more or
less as contemporary as Follow Me Down?

FOOTE: Yeah. Now this doesn't mean I won't write about people in
the 1870's and 80's and 90's, but they won't be historical novels.

INTERVIEWER: Do you think the whole genre has suffered because so
many patently B and C writers dabble in it?

FOOTE: I don't think that cheap writers do good writing any harm.

The novel is right there, ready to come alive again. This doesn't mean it won't die. I presume it will, sometime, just as the verse play died. But I see no signs of it. I don't mean that anybody today is writing novels as good as Hemingway's or Faulkner's or Fitzgerald's. They're not. But I'm very encouraged now and then by a novel like Updike's *Couples*. I think *Couples* is a good job. Because it's concerned with the things a novelist should be concerned about. It appears on its face to be concerned with nothing but sex, but it's not just about sex. It's very much concerned with people.

INTERVIEWER: What kind of corners have novelists been forced into by the movies and other visual things that—

FOOTE: I don't think that any of these influences have hurt novels. I think the novel is as viable, as jumpy, as alive, as it ever was. Hell, any art form that's got room for *Don Quixote* and *Madame Bovary* and *Light in August* is a big form.

INTERVIEWER: Do you really think modern readers want to mess around with novels anymore? We sell a lot, but I don't know to whom.

FOOTE: I've always known that something like 75 percent of the fiction-buying public are women. But they buy mostly bad books. I mean, most of the bad books are sold to women. I've always had an idea it was men who bought Hemingway, Fitzgerald and Faulkner and Dos Passos, those authors. And that women went way up on the percentage thing on Faith Baldwin.

INTERVIEWER: Do you see any overriding theme in novels in this decade?

FOOTE: No, the novelist's theme has always been the same. It's to tell the truth—to distill the truth out of a story. And no, I don't . . . I see things like Kerouac and all that, but I don't think it has much to do with the novel. It's always a delight to come across a novel that *is* a novel. It can be as experimental as *Ulysses*. *Ulysses* is a novel; it is a real *novel*. It gets to the heart of the situation the way a good George Eliot novel does. All good novels are kin to each other because they're concerned about the relationships between people. I've often thought and straightened it out in my mind that a good writer's conception of a story is: "How about a man *who*, in a situation, does so-and-so?" A bad writer starts: "How about a *situation* in which a man does so-and-so?" The people come first, as they do with George Eliot, as they do with James Joyce, as they do with Ernest Hemingway . . . the people. Not the trick situation that put *these* people into that situation, but the people made the problem. See, the Greeks knew that better than anybody. A man's own character is his demon. Not what society is trying to do to him. Not this, not the other. His own character, his inner workings are what made his tragedy. And all the good novels I know, the writers knew that. And that was what made the novel.

INTERVIEWER: That's what makes Proust fascinating.

FOOTE: Proust I put right with Shakespeare; right with him. Proust is the greatest writer of modern times because of this thing that I'm talking about . . . a superb craftsman who had all the talents. He had 'em all. They all came his way.

INTERVIEWER: A tormented life though.

FOOTE: That doesn't make any difference at all. And it didn't make any difference what Proust wrote about. He was tremendously concerned with homosexuality, being a homosexual. But Proust could have written about labor trouble if he'd been a working man, and it would have had the same validity. He was a very, very great writer. One of the giants.

INTERVIEWER: You know, a lot of people nowadays are getting off into what's branded as the topical novel—you know, the novel about integration troubles and . . . .

FOOTE: It's okay. It's not my bag, but it's okay. Dostoevski's *Possessed* is such a novel. So is *Crime and Punishment*. So is *The Brothers Karamazov*. Great, great, great, monumental works. So I have no objection to topical stuff . . . . It's the writer. It's the man pushing the pen across the page. He's got to have a combination of talent, knowledge, intelligence, and luck. He's got to have those things.

INTERVIEWER: Luck is the cherry on top of the pie.

FOOTE: Yeah. Luck is nice to have. I'm not talking about the kind of luck that gets his book published and sold. I'm talking about the kind of luck that makes it possible for him to *understand*.

INTERVIEWER: How much do you owe to the remote Southern background, such as Stribling and Joel Chandler Harris?

FOOTE: Some, no doubt. I remember reading T. S. Stribling with great pleasure, coming out . . . I remember Stribling with affection. I wouldn't try to read him again, but I remember reading him with great pleasure.

INTERVIEWER: Do you think that the present American concern with . . . ? I don't know, I think that America's trying to become a nation instead of sections and races, even though all the surface proof points somewhere else. Do you think there will continue to be a Southern novel, a Jewish novel, a Midwestern novel?

FOOTE: It appears so, and it's somewhat regrettable, because I think the Southern novel has run its string. Maybe Faulkner used it up. Certainly Carson McCullers is the last little kick left in it . . . and it often read to me like parody when she worked it. But I think there'll always be regional fiction, and I think that's good. I found out a thing: that you never have to worry about people not understanding conversations your characters have because they use phrases and things that would be unfamiliar in another part of the country. They understand perfectly well and in some ways even get more from it than the people who understand it best, because it has a strangeness to them that's very attractive. I never worry about whether somebody from out of my region will understand a regional thing as I write about it. I think it will help the book far more than it would hurt it. So I never worry about being regional or provincial.

INTERVIEWER: What problems exist for someone writing a narrative history of the Civil War?

FOOTE: They're all technical, and therefore enjoyable. I'm fascinated with doing it because everything I learned in writing those five novels has been of enormous use to me in this. It has sharpened my talent. It has made me more aware of certain technical problems that I didn't even know existed. It's been very good for me. A historian just wants to know what happened. That's what a historian ought to be doing, he ought to be able to tell you how it was, what it was like. What was Lincoln like when he walked across a room? So, you read a lot of descriptions of Lincoln crossing a room until you know how Lincoln crossed a room. And you write it. And there he is, crossing a room. And it's *very* important . . . how he sat down, what his knees looked like when he sat down. They were very strange. They rose much higher than his waist. Lincoln's height was all in his legs. When he sat down to talk with you, he was no taller than you. When he stood up, he went six feet four, and it was all these legs of his. He was split high. It's important to know those things. If he were in a novel I was writing, I would want to know all about him. He was a vivid character. And so when I'm writing history, I want to know all about him.

INTERVIEWER: There's been a lot of discussion of what is history. Can we know? Do you think we can know what went on in the minds and hearts . . . ?

FOOTE: No, but that doesn't keep us from trying to find out, and it doesn't keep us from being responsible *to* find out. History at its best is an approximation. But that's no reason for not trying. And I think we can approach the truth even if we can't present it. And of course, my truth would be different from yours. And mine would be read as mine, and yours would be read as yours. And it would be absorbed by someone who would—absorb both of them and put them together and come up with a third truth.

INTERVIEWER: So that you get third, fourth, fifth distances away.

FOOTE: The best historical reading is the source material . . . the writing by people who saw it.

INTERVIEWER: Do you allow for their particular intellectual and social hangups?

FOOTE: You allow in a tremendous way. You find out that some men lie, for example, and others tell the truth. David Dixon Porter—he's not capable of telling the truth, so I have to take everything he says with tons of salt. But he's very useful to me now that I know he's a liar. And another thing about history; I don't make judgments against men, or at least I don't let those judgments determine how I handle them. Edwin Stanton, Lincoln's secretary of war, was a scoundrel. The word really describes him. But I delight in him. I'm crazy about him. I don't approve of him, but my approval should be no factor in this thing. I delight in the life Stanton lends a page. When he heard the *Merrimac* was coming up the Potomac (and of course it wasn't) his legs shook under him. And I think it's marvelous, that his legs shook under him. And I don't have any contempt for Stanton being a coward.

That's all right. He was a bully and a coward, and that's good
. . . for my purposes, anyway.

INTERVIEWER: There was an extraordinary set of characters in that war.

FOOTE: Oh yeah, sure. But the war would have made any set of characters extraordinary. It would have made any President extraordinary.

INTERVIEWER: Do you think that's the reason Lincoln is revered?

FOOTE: No. Lincoln put something in there. Lincoln was a genius. I
once told Bedford Forrest's granddaughter, who died a couple of
years ago, that I had given the matter considerable thought, and
I considered that the war produced two authentic geniuses, Abraham Lincoln and Bedford Forrest. She paused and said, "Well,
we never thought much of Mr. Lincoln." It was not a compliment
at all, coupling her grandfather with that scamp.

INTERVIEWER: What are some of the blank spots that you've found in
your research?

FOOTE: It's very hard to get straight in your mind how different
people in the South felt about the war. It's hard to get hold
of, balancing their pride against the strain, balancing their losses
against their hopes, balancing their early hopes against their later
realizations, the bitterness of the thing. They had a terrible ad-
justment to make. They thought they were going to be successful
at the start. There was no doubt about it. They thought there
wouldn't be anything or if there was any fighting, it would all
be over real quick because Southerners could whip Yankees. They
had to adjust to it. And then when it was over, they had the
hardest time of all. They had to admit that they had been
whipped, and that was hard. They explained away being whipped
by saying the other side had all the money and men. Then
they had to say that they would have been whipped no matter
what happened, because the North won the war fighting with
one hand, and if it had had to use both hands, it would have
done it.

INTERVIEWER: I hate to draw parallels, but I think the Normans were
able to completely subjugate the Anglo-Saxons because the *culture*
just wasn't able to carry on.

FOOTE: Yeah. I think the Southern culture was not able to support
the strain that was put on it. People were not able to unite

and lay aside differences. They were not able to give up things. Southerners have a curious way—they would send their sons, but they wouldn't lend their slaves. They would make all kinds of sacrifices, but they would not make *certain* sacrifices. I was talking about Alec Stephens earlier. Their conservative principles were more important to them than their new country was. They would pass resolutions saying, "Better that we be tumped off the end of the continent into the Gulf of Mexico than that we should compromise our principles."

INTERVIEWER: Sounds like two bunches of very limited people fighting a tremendously bloody war.

FOOTE: You don't want to overlook something that they did have, though, and that was tremendous courage. I've studied and studied hard the charge at Gettysburg, the charge at Franklin, the charge at Gaines Mill, or the Northern side charging at Fredericksburg in wave after wave, and I do not know of any force on God's earth that would have gotten me in any one of those charges. It absolutely called for you to go out there and face certain death, practically. Now I will do any kind of thing like that under the influence of elation and the adrenalin popping, but it's just inconceivable to us nowadays that men would try tactics that were fifty years behind the weapons. They thought that to mass your fire, you had to mass your men, so they suffered casualties. Some battles ran as high as 30 percent. Now that's just unbelievable, because 4 or 5 percent is very heavy casualties nowadays. At Pickett's charge, they suffered 60 percent, and it's inconceivable to us—the stupidity of it, again. The stupid courage is inconceivable. Originally, the South had a big advantage. They were used to the castes of society and did not take it as an affront that a man had certain privileges. They didn't think that it made him any better than they were. Those privileges came his way, and they were perfectly willing for him to have them so long as he didn't think he was any better than they were. But the Northern soldiers, they weren't putting up with any privileges. A Massachusetts outfit spent its first night in the field and damn near had a revolution because the officers wanted to put their bedrolls out of the line. Well, Southerners never had that problem. It seemed to them sensible that the officers should be over here, and the men there.

INTERVIEWER: Are there any campaigns that are not as clearly documented as you would like?

FOOTE: Plenty of them. All the Western fighting is underdocumented. When I have to do the Virginia thing, the research is quite simple, and I get in five or six good authorities, and there it is. But when I start writing about the battle of Smyrna Gap, I got to dig.

INTERVIEWER: What are your sources for this front?

FOOTE: Well, sources come in different categories. There are the memoirs by the men who were there. There are the reports in the *Official Records of the War of the Rebellion*, which were written at the time. That's my main source. Then there are good studies. The work of Bruce Catton has been of great help to me. Douglas Southall Freeman's books, Stanley Horn's books, Robert S. Henry, Kenneth C. Williams, a lot of good treatments, and they serve as a guide through the labyrinth of this material, to keep you from missing any of it and really show you the salient features of the source material.

INTERVIEWER: Is there any state whose soldiers did not keep enough memoirs? Do you run across that, not enough regimental history and so forth?

FOOTE: Well, regimental histories are not much count. They're always interesting to read. You pick up good little features out of them. But they were written after the war, and the war took on a sheen when it was over.

INTERVIEWER: What impresses you most about the accounts written during the heat of the conflict?—letters home, I mean.

FOOTE: One simple thing impresses me, and it's very interesting: the good hand they wrote, as compared to now. It's funny—they wrote a lot better hand than we do. Penmanship was much better. Their spelling wasn't as good, but the penmanship was superb. That seems like a simple little thing, but it tells you a good deal about the soldiers. Soldiers' letters are mostly concerned with food and clothes. They're begging their folks to "send me that pair of blue jeans I had. I need 'em. Send 'em on."

INTERVIEWER: Northerners as well as Southerners?

FOOTE: Well, Southerners did it more because they had a harder time getting ahold of clothes . . . . And I find a great deal of similarity between soldiers of that time and soldiers of our day. They felt the same way about the rain. They felt the same way about "hurry up and wait." They felt the same way about the stupidity oppressing them from above, and it was the same kind —it never changes, not really. Of course 99.9 percent of that war was fought by home folks. The fighting men were of very high quality, too. You see, those units were together for four years, some of them, and they became superb machines. You take an outfit like the 23rd Virginia: after four years and large numbers of casualties in great battles, it becomes a very skillful military instrument. You tangle with the 23rd Virginia and you've got a problem. They can melt into the ground, and they can hit you with the damnedest blast of lead that ever came your way. They were superbly skillful in handling their weapons. And after all this experience, they really knew how to kill. They didn't shoot their guns up into the air and everything else. They were superb machines, and everybody knew it.

INTERVIEWER: A citizen army must be a fearful thing to behold.

FOOTE: It is after it's been in existence a while. They never went home. Very few furloughs were given—some during the winter months to a few people . . . . The Civil War was an interesting time. It was very important to make what was called "a good death." When you are dying, the doctor says you're dying, he tells you you'll die about 9 o'clock tonight, you assemble your family around you and sing hymns and you are brave and stalwart and tell the little woman that she has been good to you and not to cry. And you tell the children to be good and mind their mother, Daddy's fixing to go away. That was called making a good death, and it was very important. It was of tremendous importance.

INTERVIEWER: I don't see how we could get that far into the acceptance of our role, which is to die.

FOOTE: The doctor now won't even tell you you're going to die. It would be too cruel. The best thing to do is to let you think you're going to be all right instead of leaving you to suffer in anguish. But back then, it was thought very important to give a man a chance to make a good death.

INTERVIEWER: Let's veer away a little bit. What is the advantage of a narrative history over a monograph or a considered work about one campaign?

FOOTE: The authors are after different things. I want to know how it was, and the writer of a monograph is generally concentrating on explaining some action, the consequences of it, how it began, what it did, and what came of it. You could say that what I'm writing compares to a monograph the way that, say, Flaubert compares to Victor Hugo. That's not right, really, but I'm talking about the way Flaubert realized perfectly well that how Bovary ate the arsenic, the motions of her hand while she ate it, are enough explanation. He doesn't have to say, "Poor sinful woman, there you are, getting your due." He just describes her eating the arsenic. The monograph man would want to say that she had gotten her due. And I'm not concerned with that. Now what the superiority of Flaubert's novel is over the other novel, I'm not prepared to say. I'm not even prepared to say it *is* superior. It just *seems* so to me.

INTERVIEWER: Are you at Brice's Crossroads now?

FOOTE: Right at it. I've finished the Virginia campaign of the spring of '64 up to Grant's crossing of the James. Now I'm going back to deal with Joe Johnson in Georgia and Brice's Crossroads was adjunctive to that. All the time Johnson is fighting Sherman, Forrest is being kept out of it by these various victories he won, none of which was of any value whatsoever except that they were victories.

INTERVIEWER: What do you think about Brice's Crossroads? [also called Tishomingo Creek; the battle took place between Ripley, Mississippi, and Baldwin, Mississippi, in June, 1864, and was a complete victory for the Confederates under Forrest, who routed the much larger forces of General Sturgis. The battle was so badly handled by the Union forces that a full-scale investigation was made. The reports, which are voluminous, make that section of the *Official Records of the War of the Rebellion* an adventure in humor. Ed.]

FOOTE: It's beautiful. Just absolutely magnificent. I intended—if I hadn't gotten into the Civil War the way I have now—I intended to do a short novel on Shiloh—which I did—and a big novel on Vicksburg, and I intended toward the end of my life, whenever that was, to do another short novel like *Shiloh*, and it was to be about Brice's Crossroads, but I probably won't do it now.

INTERVIEWER: When I was investigating the war in the West, I found out that there were some white Mississippi outfits fighting in the Union armies, for instance, the Tippah Rangers and Tishomingo Rifles, who were attached to Union Tennessee units. What did you find out about dissident Southerners?

FOOTE: I found a whole belt of dissident Southerners right along the lower reaches of the Appalachians. It comes down through the end of Tennessee down into northern Alabama and peters out in north Mississippi. There were a lot of Union-loyal Alabamians, for instance, along that range of hills, and they rode with Streight on his raid through there. They were mountain people who did not have any use for slavery or slave-owners. They were not abolitionists, they just didn't *like* them.

INTERVIEWER: There was a social chasm between them and those who were Confederates, wasn't there?

FOOTE: Yeah, there has always been a chasm between those Piedmont or mountain people and the plains people, and the sea coast people. The Red Strings, those were the Southern Copperheads, were more active in North Carolina than anywhere else. The Red Strings wore little red strings in their buttonholes, just like the Copperheads wore a penny in theirs.

INTERVIEWER: Have you ever read Tatum's study of—well, she calls them disloyal Confederates, still laboring under the delusion that they were disloyal to the Confederacy instead of loyal to the Union? It was a wonder to me that the South was able to carry on with all the people down here who, for one reason or another, didn't much like the war and didn't much like the ruling class.

FOOTE: What the Union-loyal Southerners had, more than anything else, was not a love of the Union as much as it was a fierce independence. They were not going to let the state of Mississippi carry them into something that they had no interest in.

INTERVIEWER: Do you think that the political descendants of the Populists and before them the Union-loyal Southerners are behind the third-party movement in the South?

FOOTE: No, I don't, but I think certain advantages have been taken of these movements. For instance, there is a vestige of the Populist movement left, and people are cashing in on it, like George Wallace. George Wallace is no Populist by a long shot, nor is Wallace anything faintly resembling a Confederate. Wallace and his followers are about as different from the whole conception of the Confederacy as can be. I have told Mississippians that anytime that I have spoken in Mississippi. There was an artist at Ole Miss, Kerciu, who was kicked off the faculty and threatened with prosecution for painting a picture in which the Confederate flag was prominently displayed and obscenities were written across it. I said they couldn't have been wronger. The man simply painted what he saw, and the ones who should have been prosecuted were those who carried the Confederate flag in any kind of illegal operation, because the Confederacy was legal above all things. [George Kerciu painted this after the Ole Miss riots in 1962, if memory serves. *Ed.*] The Confederates asked for nothing more than to get their case before the Supreme Court, and their tragedy was that they couldn't get it there. Davis, after the secession of Mississippi, stayed in Washington, hoping to get arrested as a secessionist, because then he could get to the Supreme Court, and the Supreme Court would almost certainly have declared secession legal. Almost certainly . . . The Civil War was fought in the wrong decade, so far as the South was concerned. It was fought at a time when no one in Europe could interfere. If it had been in the 1850's, England would probably have come in. If it had been in the 1870's, France would probably have come in. It was fought at the wrong time. Don't misunderstand me, though. I don't really regret having lost the war, but from the South's view it was fought at the wrong time.

INTERVIEWER: The thing that always interested me about the Confederacy was that as a nation, it was stillborn. There was Joe Brown of Georgia, for instance, who never could understand that he was hampering the Confederacy with his constant refusals to let troops fight outside Georgia, and the other things he did to trip up Davis and his cabinet.

FOOTE: You see, they were trying to do an extremely difficult thing;

they were trying to mount a conservative revolution, and it is an extremely difficult thing to do if your people are not radicals and won't hang together. Anytime you ask one of them to give up something for the sake of the whole, he says, "Not me, that's not why *I* got into this thing, to give up *anything.*" Alexander Stephens said if he had to have a despot ruling him, he would prefer it to be a Northern despot. He said about the suspension of the writ of habeas corpus in certain areas, the use of conscription, various other things—all utterly necessary if they were going to survive—that he would rather go down in defeat than enact any of those things.

The Confederacy's position got idealized because it was never put to the test. The Northern position got run down something awful because it was put to the test and failed. They won the war and had their way, and led us through one of the worst eras in this country's history. The South never had a chance to do anything, so it can't be blamed—practically. The monument at home says: "To the memory of the Confederacy, the only nation which lived and died without a sin on its record."

INTERVIEWER: Do you think the administration inserted the moral issue of slavery into the war as a kind of public relations gesture?

FOOTE: The question was handled by Lincoln in a political and, above all, a diplomatic way. It was Lincoln's Emancipation Proclamation which absolutely insured that the one thing the North had most to fear was not going to happen: that England might come into the war. The British people, once the war was defined for them by Lincoln as a war against slavery, were not going to let their leaders get in it on the slave side of that war. And if England couldn't move, neither could France. And Russia was already pro-Union; they had freed their serfs in '61. So Lincoln used the slavery issue as a tarbrush against the South, and used it with complete success. This is *not* to say that Lincoln didn't believe in freedom and emancipation, but it was, frankly, a wartime measure.

INTERVIEWER: I was thinking, for some reason, just now, of the lawyer Nowell in *Follow Me Down.* He is thinking about what is happening, what has happened, and just before he makes his final plea to the jury he says, "It is all a failure of love, and maybe we failed back in '65."

FOOTE: He is a highly romantic person, and he's looking back at a situation in which, specifically, the two people off on the island fall out of love. Love did not sustain them in that island retreat, nor had it sustained Eustis in his relationship with his wife, with the idiot daughter, and everything else, and Nowell saw the tragedy as a failure of love, that love was not enough to sustain a relationship between two people. That certainly is an oversimplification of what is happening, and Eustis' explanation is too: when he thought God told him to do this and the devil told him to do that. These are all simplifications which you just have to shake together and come up with something. Any reader is as capable of knowing the true answers as I am.

Jordan County, if it is a novel, is a novel which has place for its hero and time for its plot. *It* is the main character in the novel—the land itself. And you go backwards through time to find out what made it what it is.

INTERVIEWER: I remember the man who kills himself after a very unsuccessful marriage. Is he punished because of what the whole plantation system has done to the land and the people?

FOOTE: Yes, I think that it was his mother's pseudoplanter outlook on life that forced him into the negation he arrived at. That story was also an attempt to write a modern Gothic novel, which has always interested me, with ghosts and spooks, creaking doors . . .

INTERVIEWER: There are an awful lot of what people would call "white trash" women in your novels. Are they fascinating to you?

FOOTE: Yes, I like them. I like simple women; I always have. And I don't like complex women. Of course, some people would probably say that I'm afraid of complex women. Could be, too.

INTERVIEWER: Many modern novels deal with woman as destroyer. Would that have been the next phase in your consideration of the women in Jordan County?

FOOTE: Not really, that I know of. I agree that woman is a destroyer. If she's allowed to destroy, I think she will.

INTERVIEWER: Jordan County is actually Washington County, Mississippi, isn't it? And Ithaca is the town of Greenville?

FOOTE: Yeah. The geography is exactly the same.

INTERVIEWER: Greenville has influenced a lot of people. Well, Jessie Rosenberg, David Cohn, William Alexander Percy—you can see this is not in any order—Hodding Carter and Hodding Carter III, the woman who writes under the pen name of Ellen Douglas, Charles Bell, Walker Percy, and you, all of you who lived or are still living in Greenville. You know them. Now, Faulkner was brought up in the hills. Would one get a different interpretation of the South if he was raised in the Delta?

FOOTE: Yes. And of course, we in the Delta have been strongly influenced by Faulkner and so we were raised where we were and also reading Faulkner, which is a tremendously persuasive thing to encounter. It had an influence on us similar to the influence of the Delta itself. So that you got both of them. So that writers since Faulkner have tended to make Delta people sort of like hill people, under the Faulkner influence, but they are very different people.

INTERVIEWER: What about this whole black-belt mentality?

FOOTE: Well, the first thing you have to understand about the Delta is that all this business about moonlight, magnolias, and Anglo-Saxon bloodlines has to go out the window. The Delta is a great melting pot. It is totally different from the hills, where the bloodlines are clean. The Delta is a . . . conglomeration. When I was a boy, the population of Greenville was fifteen to eighteen thousand. There were in those days fifty Chinese stores in the town. The Assyrians were a big part of the population. It was a great melting pot. The people came down the river and stopped in the Delta because of the richness of the soil and ease with which you could make a living. The Chinese influence is considerable. When I was a boy, the Chinese had their own schools in Greenville.

INTERVIEWER: I think it was in 1948 that they were finally admitted to the white schools.

FOOTE: That's right. And four years later, my old high school had a Chinese valedictorian.

INTERVIEWER: Do you think this has made the Delta more liberal than the hills?

FOOTE: The Delta has been more liberal than the hills because of this: this commingling, at least for one thing, so they are more sophisticated or whatever you want to call it. At least they are aware of an outside world and ties with the Old World. My grandfather, for instance, came from Vienna. My mother's father. I was perfectly aware that there was a world outside because my grandfather came from that world.

INTERVIEWER: I have been kind of wondering what you would have to say about the Snopes family. Are they typical rednecks, do you think, or something larger? Many readers think they have no value in the myth except as rednecks.

FOOTE: They have typical characteristics, but the Snopeses are very private monsters all their own. They are not representative of anything, I mean the Snopeses.

INTERVIEWER: You don't think Faulkner meant this to be a slam against the peasantry of north Mississippi?

FOOTE: He did, especially when he first started out. He was trying to draw a cunning poor white, but they very quickly developed their own characteristics, which were so special as to take away their representative qualities.

INTERVIEWER: How about the poor whites in your work? Do you try to get closer to the bone of what it is to be poor? You handle the Eustis family very well.

FOOTE: You see, the Delta is not only a melting pot where different races assemble, but the Delta is a place where the credit is easy and the crashes are hard. I do not know personally of anybody in Greenville, Mississippi, who didn't have a grandfather or a great-grandfather who amounted to something considerable. Things are so up-and-down in the Delta. Both of my grandfathers were approximate millionaires at one time in their lives. And both of them had scarcely the money to dig the hole to bury them in when the time came. And that is normal for the Delta, so that's why most of the very poor families could look back to a time of affluence. That is, if they had been there, and when I was a boy, they *all* had been there. They were not newcomers.

Now they have put in things like rug factories or whatever, and some people have come in, but the people who were there when I was young had lived there always. They might have come from Belzoni at the farthest. But they were all native Mississippians.

INTERVIEWER: Do you think this takes people's minds off materialism? If you know, for instance, that you are likely to go down as far as your grandfather went down, does this put your emphasis on something else?

FOOTE: No, because it is a very acquisitive society in the Delta. The opportunity to make money breeds a great desire for money. No, you see, the villain of the Delta, and maybe of the whole South, is the planter. He's the son of a bitch who fed false information into the society. He's the one who said, "Do as I say do, because someday you will be in my position and you will be allowed to do as I do. So don't rock the boat. I have your best interest at heart. And you must understand that." And they used to pretend to subscribe to the whole *noblesse oblige* notion. Well, that was pretty quickly shown not to be true. The planter is less conscious of that. What he is likely to say nowadays is "I got mine," not "I owe society something which it has made possible for me to get. I owe it to society and must put back into it." He doesn't say this at all. He has no respect for art in any form. He leaves that up to his women, and they have no respect for it either.

INTERVIEWER: Right on. A thousand times right on.

FOOTE: The planter is the real villain of the piece and he should have been brought down by the Populist movement, but the Populist movement got all caught up in the anti-Negro thing, which was started by the bourbons, not by the Populists. So the Populist movement never got anywhere in the Delta. Bilbo was the tail end of the Populist movement. And everybody in the Delta hated Bilbo. When I was a boy, you perfectly understood that Bilbo had a pair of horns under his hat. And that the man on the white horse was Leroy Percy, a decent, honorable man —which indeed he was. But later study has shown me that Bilbo, who would steal, literally steal, money, really did have the people's concern in his mind at all times, if no other reason than to get their vote. Whereas, Leroy Percy, that honorable man, had his own concerns to look after. I don't mean that in an ugly way; I mean that he would do what he thought was best for the people whether they wanted it or not.

INTERVIEWER: Right.

FOOTE: Well, Bilbo would do what the people wanted. And I incline, after looking back over the whole thing, to think that Bilbo, in spite of his thievery, is a better man to run a region than Leroy Percy, who was completely honest . . . . It's a spooky business.

INTERVIEWER: Did you hold out any hope for a black-white movement when, for a time, nonviolent tactics and integration seemed to be winning?

FOOTE: I think it still is, you see. I don't think that has gone by the board. I don't think the Black Panthers, the Negro radicals, are in control of anything, really. I think they have already served their purpose. I think that violence is going to decrease, not increase now. I think integration is the answer and I think everybody thinks so—white and black—except a few nuts.

INTERVIEWER: What did it mean to you to be raised in Mississippi? Now you were educated in the Upper South at a fine institution, at the Chapel Hill campus of the University of North Carolina (it was the *only* UNC at that time) and it has a tradition of liberalism. What did it mean to you to go from Mississippi to the Upper South to be educated—if you can remember what it felt like back then?

FOOTE: It did not appear greatly different. It was different enough for me to be thoroughly conscious that I was in a different atmosphere, but it was not like going to New York City. Chapel Hill was still a country town.

INTERVIEWER: What does it mean to you as a novelist to be from Mississippi?

FOOTE: It means a great deal to me. It means that I have been in touch with the grass roots of American life. I really know what they feel like. And that is very important to me.

INTERVIEWER: Why is it so many good writers come from Mississippi?

FOOTE: There are a lot of jokes about it. One being that there's nothing else to do down here. But I *know* why there are so many writers from Greenville, instead of from Greenwood or Clarksdale. It was the presence of Will Percy. There was no literary coterie, no exchange of manuscripts, no deep discussions about novel plots or anything like that, but he was an example of a man who had written and published books, and you not only believed it could be done, you *saw* that it could be done. And I think if Will Percy had been from Greenwood, it's entirely possible that Greenwood would have been the place the writers came from. There is more to it than that. Will Percy also had a fine library, so that good books were available in Greenville, which perhaps they were not in some other places.

INTERVIEWER: When you were growing up, you were around the Percy family. Did Will Percy influence you personally?

FOOTE: He influenced me by example, but his writing did not influence my writing. But, yes, he was a big influence on me because Will Percy had a culture that was alien to me and to that country, and it was a good thing to come into contact with.

INTERVIEWER: Then you don't think Greenville has any special sociological makeup that makes it produce these people?

FOOTE: It has that, too, but there again, it was done by Will Percy and by other men around there. Greenville never had but one lynching, for instance, and that was a horrible mistake. They lynched the wrong man . . . . It's a crazy story. There was a telephone operator raped in the alley next to the telephone building and she raised the outcry somehow and some men came running and there was a Negro standing there and he said, "I seen him runnin' that way." So they followed, running, and went into a Negro house in Lickskillet and found a young Negro man in bed with his shoes and clothes on, the covers pulled up to his chin, pretending to be sick. So they dragged him out and took him back downtown and hung him from a telephone pole in front of the telephone office. And it was, oh, some years later when the man standing outside the alley, who had told them he had seen the man running, confessed that he had raped the woman and told this young Negro that was passing, "Boy, you better run, there is going to be trouble around here." That was the only lynching Greenville ever had and that is enough to cure anybody of lynching anything.

INTERVIEWER: Let's get back to the Civil War narrative a minute.

What are your working methods for this? Is there a steady regimen
that you follow?

FOOTE: It is a steady regimen of work from a fairly complete outline
and much taking of notes. I can show you over here how I do
it. I organize it into blocks of time and geography. For instance,
I am going to be 80 or 120 pages in Virginia. And I have a
calendar showing everything that happened in the area at that
time and I am going over to Georgia and cover the same amount
of time that was happening over there. And my calendar is drawn
up so that I can see that these things were happening simultane-
ously. And I tie the two together. What I try to do in that, except
for the obvious breaks, which are made on purpose too, is to
lead from one to the other. For instance, if Lee and Burnside
are fighting up in Fredericksburg, I draw back and go to Davis
and get his opinion on the battle and what he has in mind to
do next and then it is a very simple step to get from Davis to
Lincoln and then back down to Burnside. It's a question of
plotting, and it's a fascinating business.

INTERVIEWER: Do you think Lee really wanted to win?

FOOTE: Oh, yes. The trouble with trying to deal with Lee is his
amazing simplicity. It is almost impossible that anyone could be
as simple as Lee is. "Simple" I say as a high compliment. That
is the unbelievable thing about him. Freeman discusses that at
some length. He says there are not any problems, there are no
questions.

INTERVIEWER: It is almost like a put-on.

FOOTE: It is, it is. Now Lee *is* a very complex man, but he had
achieved simplicity. He had trained himself to resist all kinds of
urges that were in him. So by the time the war comes along and
he is past fifty years old, he is not even having to resist them
any more.

INTERVIEWER: Wasn't there something in his family that is partially
brought out in biographies, about his father being—

FOOTE: Many scandals. His father was involved in money scandals
and his half-brother was involved in an incestuous scandal. All
those forces were in Lee. And you only see little glimpses of
them occasionally. Such as when he said of one of his daughters:
"She is like her father, always wanting something." And when

after the war—wherever he went after the war—crowds would always gather around and hold up babies for him to kiss and everything. Some woman handed him a baby to hold and he held it. And as he handed it back to the woman, she said, "Is there anything you can tell me that I can repeat to the boy?" And Lee said, "Yes, teach him to deny himself." Lee had done that all his life, so he had more or less burnt this wildness out of himself. He is a gentle man, and that is a paradox, because he would literally rip the living guts out of a man. He is a great killer, but a very gentle man. Capable of enormous anger, but always in control of himself.

INTERVIEWER: What about Forrest, to look at another leader, even if he's thought of as a lesser light? Don't you think that the people in the eastern theater were under some kind of delusion that he was this ole boy who was an illiterate, if somewhat lucky, tactician?

FOOTE: Sure. Someone once said to Mrs. Davis, after the war, that it was most regrettable that Forrest had not been given a higher position sooner and she said, in not as snobbish a way as it sounds, but said, "Well, I admire General Forrest enormously, but if we were really going to have people like that in charge of our revolution, we would have lost the revolution while we were winning the war." Davis was here in Memphis for Forrest's funeral, in 1877. Riding to the funeral in a carriage, someone with him regretted that Forrest had not played a bigger part earlier in the war, and Davis said he absolutely agreed, but, he said, "We in Richmond did not appreciate him. We thought he was a partisan and ranger type, and it was not until late that we saw his qualities."

INTERVIEWER: Do you think that is the sort of thing that would have torn the Confederacy up eventually—the class difference?

FOOTE: No, I don't. The thing you have to understand about the Confederacy and the people who made it up is the fierce independence of the Confederate yeoman. He was not only convinced he was good as you were, but if you questioned it, he would shoot you off your horse. Literally. If he had to hide in the bush to do it he would—which is not unfair. After all, you have got many advantages over him, so if he shoots you from ambush, that's all right because God knows what you could do to him without ambush. You own the big house and he's got nothing but an old shotgun or something.

INTERVIEWER: People who write about the South say that the white Southern yeoman was willing to go along with the whole bag as long as there was a model of white supremacy around, i.e., the Southern planter. But how long do you think the system would have held up? The economics of it would have destroyed slavery eventually, don't you think?

FOOTE: I never have been really sure how long it would have taken economics to destroy slavery. It seems economically feasible to me today. Economically. Slavery was perfect for cotton farming. It was a marvelous thing to have a couple of hundred slaves working the plantation, and you could make a lot of money doing it. How long it would have taken slavery to die—and, of course, it would have done so sooner or later and probably sooner—I don't know. The condition of the Negro when I was a boy was not very much above slavery. He couldn't move. It certainly amounted to peonage.

My grandfather, that is, my mother's father, was involved in serious peonage charges. He and two other men, Leroy Percy and a man named O. B. Crittenden, brought southern Italians and Sicilians over to a plantation they owned just across the river in Arkansas, named Sunnyside. And they brought them over by the boatloads and they were marvelous workers. They'd get down on their hands and knees and pull the grass. It was truly beautiful. But my grandfather and the others were wide open to the charge of peonage. These people were working out their passage on the boat.

INTERVIEWER: Like indentured servants.

FOOTE: That is right. It was very much like that. And the priest who was ministering to them in that parish or that section said that it was peonage, and encouraged the workers to enter suit in court, and they didn't have any trouble proving the charge at all. It was fortunate that my grandfather, O. B. Crittenden, and Leroy Percy had known Theodore Roosevelt, because my other grandfather, Huger Foote, had Theodore Roosevelt down here on a bear hunt and asked Leroy Percy along, so he (Percy) was able through his friendship with Theodore Roosevelt to get the indictment quashed. But to get it quashed, they had to turn these people loose, and these Italians and Sicilians, most of them were from a region in Sicily called Cefalu, sent out a delegation to Arkansas resembling the Cefalu region, and they finally settled in the northwestern corner of Arkansas and they are still there.

INTERVIEWER: I know there is a family called Cefalu around Leland. Are there any other remnants of the crew, people who didn't leave?

FOOTE: Yeah, plenty of them. Some left, some didn't. Greenville has the Muffulettos, the Mascagnis, the Signas. I can name you twenty more names.

INTERVIEWER: I knew they brought in Chinese labor at one time, but—

FOOTE: They worked on the levees and railroads and so did the Irish. You see, at one time, you could get a good hard-working Irishman for fifteen cents building those levees. It was very dangerous work, and you weren't going to waste any seven- or eight-hundred-dollar Negro doing such work.

INTERVIEWER: They were buried right in the levees sometimes, weren't they?

FOOTE: Yeah. If he had an accident, throw him in the hole.

INTERVIEWER: No wonder they knew they had to disenfranchise both blacks *and* whites in the 1890 constitution.

FOOTE: They sat down and wrote, as Bilbo said, a state constitution that "damn few white people and no niggers at all" would understand. They made damn sure of it. And so the Mississippi Constitution is the wildest reading you ever saw. Paragraphs in there scarcely make any sense at all. If you want to eliminate somebody from voting, you ask him to read and explain that paragraph. It can't be done.

I believe things are pretty squared away now, though. I think that what is going to happen can be seen clearly enough. I believe integration is at hand, and that everybody believes in it, as I say, except a few nuts. And it just depends on the *will* in which people enact it—it is the only answer.

What you can do, for instance . . . Women, and the majority of voters are women—you can just tell women, "Suppose you have a child and when he gets to be three and a half years old, you have to tell him, 'NO, you don't go drinking in that fountain, that's for white people, you do not drink that.' Put yourself in that position, telling your child that he is not good enough to do things that he sees other children doing. Would you do that?" And they say "No."

Most of the fear of Negroes, which is a very real thing, is based on what you would do if you were in his place, and that will scare you to death. You think you would kill people all over the horizon. Well, you wouldn't. But you think you would. So you're afraid of him. I've seen people just frozen with fear when some Negro who had too much to drink got out of line. They think he's fixing to blow them up, because they're thinking that if they were in his place, they would blow everybody up . . . .

INTERVIEWER: Let's talk about your work. Who influenced your writing?

FOOTE: I was influenced, like most people, most strongly by people in two categories. One, I was influenced by the writers I liked most. That's a simple kind of thing to say, but it's true. For instance, Robert Browning had a great influence on me because I liked his work. And William Faulkner influenced me for that reason, plus another one, and that was his proximity. He was writing about people that I knew, and I took it that that was how you wrote about people you knew. So that his influence was greater on me. But Faulkner and I were very different writers. I'm not talking about Faulkner as a *greater* writer, which of course he is; but we have a totally different approach to the work. I am more interested in sociology than Faulkner was; Faulkner was more interested in the human heart than perhaps I am—or he certainly liked to think he was.

INTERVIEWER: Your work is very lyrical, while at the same time it is very terse.

FOOTE: Well, I am crazy about words and I am crazy about compression. You talk about the writer that influenced me more than any other writer, and that is William Shakespeare, because he is the greatest writer; it is just that simple. And the lyricism, such as I have, is an outgrowth of my awe of Shakespeare—

tremendous admiration. It's a miracle that anybody was able to do the things he did.

INTERVIEWER: Who do you think is a good writer now?

FOOTE: I think John Updike is a good writer, and this boy Cormac McCarthy.

INTERVIEWER: Are they among those who have proven themselves, or are they still in the company of those who are struggling?

FOOTE: Well, it is very difficult to talk about writers because of vogues which have nothing to do with who is a good and who is not a good writer. I think there is something utterly ridiculous about the fact that John O'Hara is living and writing and that none of these coteries seem to know that he is alive. It doesn't make any sense.

INTERVIEWER: I agree.

FOOTE: O'Hara is a good writer. Now he may not satisfy their desires in various directions, such as symbolism and so on, but O'Hara is a very real American writer. I don't mean he is of Hemingway's caliber, let alone Faulkner's, but how they can pretend O'Hara is not there? I don't know.

INTERVIEWER: Killing him off.

FOOTE: Well, a lot of people have been killing him off all this time, but he is not dead. It's absurd. It's like ignoring Thackeray, who is not a very great writer either, but it's silly to ignore him. So I don't know what to make of it. I do know that a lot of people who are being taken as good writers are very, very bad writers by any standards that I know.

INTERVIEWER: Aren't you rather alarmed by fads in the literary world?

FOOTE: No, not at all. I think that those fads have always been with us and that they will be with us. You see, I remember a time when all criticism was Marxist. ALL of it. I am never inclined to take very seriously the judgments of literary coteries. I think they can be depended upon to miss the point.

INTERVIEWER: Right.

FOOTE: They will discover O'Hara safely after he is dead. They are not going to discover him while he is living. They are not going to have anything to do with him because he wrote for the *Saturday Evening Post*. Now you get him good and dead and they will look at him. And I think it is entirely possible that O'Hara will be considered a serious writer after he is dead.[1]

INTERVIEWER: He's influenced me, I know that.

FOOTE: He is a superb technician.

INTERVIEWER: Do you prize felicity of expression?

FOOTE: Very highly. Yes. I don't want it to be precious, I want it to be felicitous, just as you say. My favorite of my books, sometimes, is *Love in a Dry Season.*

INTERVIEWER: Why?

FOOTE: Not because it's any better than any of the rest of them, but because I had a very happy time writing it. I had a felicity of work that I remember with great affection.

INTERVIEWER: Are some of your novels hard work, and some, like *Love in a Dry Season*—

FOOTE: They are all hard work, but it was work I enjoyed. You know, "labor we delight in physics pain" and so on. They were *all* hard work. I have always worked very hard, very long hours, I write eight or ten hours a day, seven days a week, because I never believed writing was something you could do in your spare time. It had to be everything with me. First thing I ever sold was to the *Saturday Evening Post* and I got $750 for it, and the day the check came, I quit my job, went downtown and bought a shotgun, a leather jacket, and a desk light. And I have not worked for anybody since then and I am not thinking about doing it, ever.

INTERVIEWER: What would be your advice to a young man or woman who wanted to be a writer, yet had to live at the same time?

FOOTE: Go get a hard job, like driving a taxi or digging ditches, or anything else, and write when you are not working, and work when you are working, don't even think about writing.

INTERVIEWER: You wouldn't advise the life of the academy?

FOOTE: I would advise against it as strongly as I could.

INTERVIEWER: Some of us have this problem.

---

[1] Poignantly enough, John O'Hara kept his own appointment in Samarra a year after Foote praised him in this interview and commented that the critics would discover him after he was "safely dead." We had no way of knowing it would happen so soon, and ask that our comments not be thought disrespectful.—JC

FOOTE: Well, it is a problem now that I didn't have then. You get
a good life, an enjoyable life, good money—decent money, anyhow—and complete protection from the shocks and throes and
convulsions of the world. Well, that is very tempting indeed.
But when I was coming along, I don't know whether I would
have succumbed to temptation or not, but there wasn't any
temptation. Nobody wanted me to come to a college campus.
They had no use for me, thank God. But that was not one
of the things I might have done. No college campus would
have me on it as anything but a student.

INTERVIEWER: You more or less have to forget about making a great
deal of money?

FOOTE: The only way to make a lot of money is to forget it. Work
at your craft, and if you are lucky, you will make a lot of
money. There *is* a lot of money to be made, so that your expecta-
tions are not unreasonable.

INTERVIEWER: What do you think about this thing—and I think it's
just the foundations and the government trying to appease people
in a pitiful little way—I mean the whole thing about writers
getting grants and living from grant to grant? Of course, you
have it pretty good right now.

FOOTE: Well, it is my craft, and anything which makes it easier for
the people who practice it I should be for, but I am not.
I think grants are a bad thing for young, beginning writers.
I think after a writer has established himself, and begun to get
soft in the belly, and perhaps in the head, a little money is good
to have and it is not going to hurt him. I think it is very
important that you make your living, pitifully poor and small
though it may be, with your pen. It gives you a sense of ac-
complishment which you can't get from a grant, and which
a grant will interfere with. That is one trouble with this boy
Cormac McCarthy. He is a writer, and god damn, he has had
two or three grants, Rockefeller and this, that, and the other,
and I am sure it has slowed him down. It is a bad business. You
see, when my first novel came out, I had just finished my second
one. When my second one came out, I had just finished my
third, and when my third one came out, I was hard at work
on my fourth. And that's the way it should be. Now I don't

mean for everybody. There were writers like Flaubert and Joyce who turned a book out every six or eight years. And I guess that's all right. But I think a young writer should be a very hard-working person and learn how to write by writing. . . . I don't believe that you should be in a hurry to get into print. I think the best thing to do is to sit down and do your very best writing for two novels, and then, no matter how good they are, put them away. Then write your third one and let it be your first novel. Go back later and get them, if you want. I didn't say burn them. Because anything that's in the closet, you'll make more money off of later than you will now, anyway. There are a hell of a lot of writers who wish they *had* put those first two away.

INTERVIEWER: Writing is very hard on people who are married, isn't it?

FOOTE: Oh, you see, what you have to give up is *enormous*, but it always has been. Some guy was telling me, "What do you expect me to do? I have a wife and two kids." And I said, "You ought not to have two kids." You shouldn't. And if *you* are willing to go hungry, you ought to be willing to let *them* go a little hungry. You will wind up a lot better in the end. What you are going to wind up with now is a busted-up marriage and everything else, probably. It is tough. I am not denying that for an instant. But it is supposed to be tough. It is a tough and a sad metier, as Hemingway said. It is a *metier triste*. And that's why it's worth a grown man's time.

Rotation and Repetition:
❧ WALKER PERCY

Interviewed by JOHN CARR

Walker Percy was born in 1916 in Birmingham, Alabama, and was raised in Greenville, Mississippi, by his uncle and adoptive father, William Alexander Percy, a poet who is remembered now for Lanterns on the Levee, *one of the classic American autobiographies. Walker Percy graduated from Greenville High and the University of North Carolina and the Columbia University School of Medicine. After a severe illness, he gave up his career in medicine and started writing. His first novel,* The Moviegoer, *one of the most admired novels of the past decade, won the National Book Award in 1962. The Last* Gentleman (1966) *and* Love in the Ruins (1971) *have continued to build his reputation.*

This interview was conducted in Percy's isolated, quiet home in Covington, Louisiana, in January, 1970. When I drove up, his children were busily filming a movie on the lawn. Other children drifted in and out in costume and make-up. Percy saw nothing unusual about it.

INTERVIEWER: I wanted to ask you about Shelby Foote. We just talked a little about him. He dedicated *Shiloh* to you. Did you grow up together in Greenville, Mississippi?

PERCY: Yes, from the age of about . . . I moved to Greenville when I was, I think, thirteen or fourteen. He was maybe one year younger. I remember we started out in the same study hall at Greenville High School. At the time, I was writing poetry, verse, for a high school class. I got very proficient. The teacher would assign sonnets, and I would crank out a sonnet and sell it for fifty cents. Everybody had to write a sonnet, so . . . Shelby saw me writing poetry, so I really take credit for launching Shelby on his literary career.

INTERVIEWER: Did you sell any sonnets to Shelby?

PERCY: Shelby was not in the same class, but otherwise I might have.

INTERVIEWER: You were graduated from Greenville High School and then went off to North Carolina to school, to Chapel Hill?

PERCY: Right.

INTERVIEWER: And Shelby went, too?

PERCY: Shelby came a year later, right.

INTERVIEWER: In *The Last Gentleman* you say the town was named Ithaca because the man who named it that had a fondness for Pericles and had had enough of Southern Baptists, or words to that effect. Shelby has named Greenville Ithaca in his novels. Is this kind of an in-joke with yall?

PERCY: No. I liked the name. I wanted to use it, and I told Shelby I hoped he didn't mind. He said he didn't mind. It wasn't a joke.

INTERVIEWER: You characterized Greenville in your novel as having a degree of culture that the rest of Mississippi did not. Do you think that was true, then and now?

PERCY: I think it was very much true then. Mainly because of my uncle, who was also my adoptive father. When my parents died, we went to live with him. Of course, he was a remarkable man. He certainly had a powerful influence on me. The whole idea of the Greek-Roman stoic view, the classical view, was exemplified in him more than any other person I ever knew.

INTERVIEWER: Did he reject Christianity, or just not have much use for it?

PERCY: Well, he started life as a Catholic, a Roman Catholic. He said in his book that he'd lost his faith at Sewanee and I think that what he did throughout much of his life, much of his writings, was take the side of the classic Greco-Roman view as against the Judaeo-Christian view. At the end, I don't know. It's hard to answer that.

INTERVIEWER: In another interview, you described the ambience pretty well, with Faulkner coming to play tennis and showing up too drunk to play and so on. Did Mr. Percy, that is, your uncle, influence you in the direction of writing?

PERCY: I think he did. Most certainly he did because he had an extraordinary quality which only a few really good teachers, as you know, have, and that's the quality of making you see a poem or a painting the way he sees it. And he could read poetry aloud, which very few people do well, and he could make you see the beauty of a passage in Shakespeare. Shakespeare and Keats were his two favorites, and I could see it exactly the way he read it. He could turn you on. And music, too. He owned a Capehart, a huge monstrous thing. It was one of the first automatic record changers. And it was the first time I had seen anybody play classical music. And so we were exposed to all these good things—literature and music—for ten years. Not only that, but he had a great influence in the town itself. He was quite influential, affecting other people like David Cohn and Hodding Carter. David Cohn came to the house for a weekend to talk about a book he was going to write and stayed a year.

INTERVIEWER: Stayed a *year?*

PERCY: He had just retired from being manager of Sears Roebuck in New Orleans. He worked there for twenty years and made enough money to quit when he was fairly young. He was forty-five or so. And he quit and said he was going to write and he did.

INTERVIEWER: You started writing late, and you have said elsewhere that you were a scientist until you were in your thirties, when you were at Bellevue and caught TB. There's a question in my mind about whether you're a philosopher who exemplifies his philosophy in his writing, or a writer who perfected his craft writing philosophic essays. How do you feel about that?

PERCY: All I can say is that I was interested first in philosophy, in writing essays, although I never took a course in philosophy at Chapel Hill. I spent most of the four years in the chemistry lab, biology lab, and so on. But later I began to read philosophy and got interested and developed violent agreements and disagreements.

INTERVIEWER: I noticed that.

PERCY: I've always found . . . my main motivation, the wellspring of my writing—I hate to say it—is usually antagonism, disagreeing with somebody and wanting to set it right. Sombody provokes you and that's good, you like something, you don't like something else. I remember I read Suzanne Langer's book *Philosophy in a New Key*, which was for me a very, very exciting book. But I thought it went wrong at the end. And so I just thought I would write and say how it went wrong and I wrote a long review and sent it to *Thought Quarterly*, and lo and behold, it was published.

INTERVIEWER: Was that the first thing?

PERCY: It was the first thing I had ever had published.

INTERVIEWER: You were saying in another interview that as a teenager or perhaps when you were even younger, you wrote short shorts for *Liberty* magazine.

PERCY: I was about eight years old.

INTERVIEWER: Eight years old? Any success?

PERCY: No. God, I'd forgotten. Then *Liberty* folded up. That was back in the twenties, I think. It seemed like a good idea. They were short short stories. One page, and it had a little thing like *Reader's Digest*: any short story accepted will be paid $200.

INTERVIEWER: Let's go back for a moment. Not in time, though. How do you react now, now that you're about the age he was when he was publishing, to Will Percy's *Lanterns on the Levee?*

PERCY: Well, I think it's a minor classic in its way. That and the W. J. Cash book that came out at the same time, expressing two very different points of view. I was greatly influenced by it, of course, and sympathetic to much of it. In the end, there's an ideological division between the way he saw it and the way I see it. A lot of it may have to do with time. The times are different now. In those days, believe it or not, he was considered a liberal. But now it seems that *Lanterns on the Levee* really professes a paternalism, a *noblesse oblige*, and a rather dark view which is based on stoicism, Greco-Roman stoicism, in which a man doesn't expect much in the world and does the best he can and tries to make one place a little better and knows in the end . . . knows that he'll probably be defeated in the end. I ended with a different view. I became a Catholic and accordingly I have a different view of how things should . . . of attitudes of whites towards blacks and blacks towards whites. I have probably, I think, more hope.

INTERVIEWER: There have been a number of books about the South. Mr. Percy's book and W. J. Cash's we have mentioned. But I've never completely found my way inside of them, or thought they proved or told a lot about the South. And both men were professional writers. What is it about writers that they can't write a non-fiction book about the South that catches it completely?

PERCY: The South is a very complicated place to write about. Faulkner had Quentin Thompson telling his roommate "I don't hate the South." And any writer, any Southern writer, is stuck with this ambivalence, I think, by hate and love. I don't know. A couple of people suggested I write a book about the South. What does that mean? Look at the difference between Atlanta and Birmingham, between this place here and New Orleans, or between North Louisiana and South Louisiana. I sometimes think that some parts of the New South are more like the North than the North itself. There are more Cleveland suburbs in the South than there are in Cleveland.

INTERVIEWER: If you don't mind my asking, when did you become a Catholic?

PERCY: I think it was 1946, twenty-four years ago.

INTERVIEWER: Was that after you'd gone through the Bellevue thing?

PERCY: Yeah, right.

INTERVIEWER: Did that have anything to do with it, or is that unfair?

PERCY: Well, it came as a result of being . . . I was ill and I quit medicine, and I was laid up for a couple of years, and I was doing a lot of reading. I could get into a long thing there. I don't know whether you want to go into it.

INTERVIEWER: Yeah, I'm interested.

PERCY: Well, just in general terms, what I got interested in was anthropology, in the European sense of the word, in a view of man as such, man as man. My orientation up until that time had been strictly scientific, in the then-prevailing naturalistic scientific mode, which very much attracted me at North Carolina and also at Columbia. Later it troubled me, because it amounted almost to mechanism.

INTERVIEWER: Behaviorism?

PERCY: I remember at North Carolina that classical behaviorism in the psychology department was running very strong. And at Columbia, it was the idea of the mechanism of disease, which is very valuable, the idea that disease is a mechanism of response in the body to the disease agent. So I began to be interested in a view of man as such, man as man. And I saw one day—maybe it was something of a breakthrough, something of a turning of a corner—that science can say so much about things, objects, or people, but by its very method, by its own definition, by its own self-imposed limitation, the scientific method can only utter a statement about a single object, a glass or a frog or a dogfish—or a man—only insofar as it resembles other things of its kind. If you want to make general statements—which scientists recognize; that's the nature of science, insofar as one dogfish resembles another dogfish —that is what science is interested in—making general statements about certain kinds of things and certain kinds of responses and reactions and changes. Well, I suddenly realized that when you apply this to man, you stop short at the very point where it matters to man. Science can say everything about a man except what he is in himself.

INTERVIEWER: You quoted Kierkegaard's reaction to Hegel, which was that Hegel and taught him everything, except how to live as a man. And you have a violent reaction in your psychological and philosophical articles against the objective-empirical view of man in current psychoanalysis and psychology. Did you become interested in existentialism through Kierkegaard and Heidegger?

PERCY: I'm trying to remember. I think it was probably through Sartre first, probably through reading *Nausea*. And then later going back to Kierkegaard and then coming forward to Heidegger and Marcel.

INTERVIEWER: In almost every article you've written, there's a reference to Marcel.

PERCY: I read quite a bit of him some time ago, but Kierkegaard is probably the one who deserves the most credit. He saw it most clearly. Although he was speaking of Hegel, you could say the same thing of the scientific method: that it's a quantitative thing, that science cannot utter one single sentence about what a man is himself as an individual. Of course, it doesn't even attempt to do so. And therefore, if a man embraces this particular view of the world, he is left with a very peculiar view of things in which he sees the world ordered in scientific constructions with himself as a great lacuna, a great vacuum. There's all this business about identity crisis nowadays, and I think it has a lot to do with this cultural attitude. What I was protesting about so much of the time you are talking about was the view of so many, not merely scientists, but also writers and artists, that only scientists and only science is interested in telling the truth. Provable, demonstrable truth, whereas art and writing have to do with play, feeling and emotions, entertainment. I've always held that art and even novels are just as valid as science, just as cognitive. In fact, I see my own writing as not really a great departure from my original career, science and medicine, because—to get back to what we were talking about—where science will bring you to a certain point and then no further, it can say nothing about what a man is or what he must do. And then the question is, how do you deal with man? And if you are an anthropologist in the larger sense, interested in man, how do you study him? And it seemed to me that the novel itself was a perfectly valid way to deal with man's behavior.

INTERVIEWER: I object to philosophical superstructures which expose their joints in a man's writing.

PERCY: I don't believe in writing in enigmas and acrostics. I've read novels that you have to have read some sort of handbook in order to understand. In fact, I think if this sort of novel—the philosophical novel or whatever it is, the sort of thing that the French pioneered—is any good, then the philosophy is part and parcel of the novel, and there's no illustrating of theses. You don't have a thesis and then illustrate it. What you do is put a man down in a certain situation and see what happens.

INTERVIEWER: Were you ever interested in Albert Camus?

PERCY: Oh, *yeah.*

INTERVIEWER: Nothing of his is ever really mentioned in any of your writings. He's only . . .

PERCY: Well, he himself didn't want to be called an existentialist. He made that very clear.

INTERVIEWER: But I wondered if his view of man had come through to you.

PERCY: Not so much that as his style. His style in *The Stranger,* particularly the opening section of it, was dead, flat, declarative sentences, which suited the environment so well.

INTERVIEWER: Have you ever read Robbe-Grillet? What do you think of him?

PERCY: I think his stuff is interesting simply as a change, something to get away from the traditional novel, with a set of characters and plot and action which has certainly been overworked, and everybody's gotten tired of it. Robbe-Grillet throws all that out and talks about things. And it's interesting as a reaction. But I can't see that it has much future, because, the way I see it, what you're really writing about is the way a man is in the world, and after you describe the still life on a table, the teacups and the coffeecups and the geometry of the wall, that will say something about the way a man is, but not very much.

INTERVIEWER: There's some suspicion that *The Moviegoer* was written about your nephew Billy and his good compadre, Ugg McGee, who go to about four movies a week in Greenville.

PERCY: Billy's in bad shape. He goes to the afternoon movies. It's very bad to go to an afternoon movie and come out in the daylight. That's like withdrawal after a heroin trip.

INTERVIEWER: Do you see many French movies, which, it seems to me, have gotten more and more intellectual lately?

PERCY: No, I haven't. I don't see many foreign movies. In fact, I haven't seen any recent ones. The last one I can remember is *Last Year at Marienbad*, which was five or six years ago.

INTERVIEWER: Robbe-Grillet wrote the script for that. That was a totally nonrepresentational kind of movie. Do you think that's where movies are going?

PERCY: I had a kind of strange experience going to a movie the other night. I went to see *Easy Rider*. My wife and I went and we were the only people not just over forty, but over twenty-five. The house was full and everybody was under twenty—seventeen, eighteen, nineteen. I suddenly realized that the new films are really aimed at these kids. I was astonished at their absolutely rapt attention. Whatever was going on in the movie, it was on their wavelength. They knew exactly what was being said and they were understanding.

INTERVIEWER: Well, I'm out of that particular age group and never had the money or time for the heavy drug scene, so maybe I ought not to comment, but I think the secret of that movie is not what's in it, but what the kids *think* is in it.

PERCY: I think there's nothing particularly new about it. I think they very much sympathize with the rebellion, with the cutting out and coming to New Orleans. I've talked with some kids about *Easy Rider* and they don't see that there's a double-edged morality there. They see it as a morality play, you see, and therefore I think it's fair to speak of it as a morality play, a morality film. The morality, of course, is the toleration of different people. If you're different and have long hair, you shouldn't be killed by North Louisiana rednecks. Okay, that's all right. But there's also the morality of the drug culture, the drug morality there, saying that getting killed by the hicks is a bad thing, but smuggling heroin from Mexico is a good thing. I can't see any good in the heroin scene. *Easy Rider* is a queer mixture of a lovely rotation plus the morality of a schizophrenic twelve-year-old.

INTERVIEWER: Speaking of that, you wrote a great essay, "The Man on the Train," which appeared in *Partisan Review.* You talked about the three ways of attempting to escape from alienation, the misery-loves-company approach, repetition, and rotation. The people in *Easy Rider*, it seems to me, are attempting to escape via rotation, and yet when they come to New Orleans, the bottom falls out and they only undergo a repetition of themselves.

PERCY: *Easy Rider*, as I say, was a perfect rotation all the way, a beautiful trip through the desert. Until they got to New Orleans. Then it blew up. It was curious about . . . it had something to do with Mardi Gras, because Mardi Gras is a good thing to be heading towards. But I've never seen Mardi Gras done in any way, in a book or movie, which wasn't almost a catastrophe. Mardi Gras in *Easy Rider* ended up as a very dreary stereotype of masks and throwing doubloons and so forth. It looked like bad television. The psychedelic freakout was just as bad. And that was a strange dialogue in that movie. Every sentence begins with "Man."

INTERVIEWER: Why weren't you influenced by American writers? I've never seen a reference to an American writer in your essays.

PERCY: That's true. It had to do with the original reason why I began to write. As I say, I fell out with philosophy and started to . . . and the philosophy I was interested in was what was called then existential philosophy. Of course, the word no longer means much. It still means a concrete view of man, man in a situation, man in a predicament, man's anxiety, and so on. And I believed that this view of man could be handled very well in a novel, and I was interested in phenomenology, which is very strongly existentialist: the idea of describing accurately how a man feels in a given situation. And that's certainly novelistic.

INTERVIEWER: Does existentialism aim for the salvation of man, or propose the salvation of man, in your opinion? I'm thinking now about your and Marcel's peculiarly Catholic existentialism.

PERCY: I think it would be the idea of transcending the everydayness, of transcending being so caught up in the everyday world that even religious reality, especially religion, becomes a sort of stereotype and something you go through every day. And Marcel speaks of something he calls "recollection." That is, a man recollects himself, so he can recover things anew and afresh. And, of course, here is where the great divergence comes. Both Marcel and the theistic existentialists like Sartre will agree that there's a certain absurdity and ugliness in the world and a certain alienation of man in the world. Of course, Marcel would say this reality can be transcended by an I-to-you relationship, which is ultimately theistic, a belief in God. Sartre would say that this is impossible, that there's no authentic I-to-you relationship, that it can only be transcended by authentic political action and so forth. I think Sartre already undercuts himself because, although his philosophy disallows any real communication between people, still he spends most of his time writing books.

INTERVIEWER: You wrote in your article "Symbol as Hermeneutic in Existentialism" that "Sartre is surely mistaken in analyzing the sources of my shame at being caught out in an unworthy performance by the look of another. It is the other's objectifying me, he says, that makes me ashamed." Then you say, further on in the article, "No. I am exposed—as what? not as a something—as *nothing*, as that which unlike everything else in the world cannot be rendered as *darstellbar*." And, further on, "When Matthiew stops in the middle of Pont Neuf and discovers his freedom in his nothingness—'Within me there is nothing. I am free.'—he is after all only hypostasizing the unformulability of self. The tell-tale sign is his elation, his sense of having at last discovered his identity. He is something after all—Nothing! And in so doing, is he not committing the same impersonation which Sartre so severely condemns in others? If the structure of consciousness is intentional, to be of its essence directed toward the other, a being-towards, then the ontologizing of this self-unformulability as Nought is as perverse as any other impersonation—really a kind of inferior totemism."[1] Are you here referring to Marcel's "Existence and Human Freedom,"[2] which Marcel dates from February, 1946?

PERCY: It might well be, because as I remember, Marcel wrote a long piece on Sartre, and I remember I read it, but I've forgotten what it was.

INTERVIEWER: I just wanted to ask you if you were indebted to Marcel for that view of Sartre, because in "Existence and Human Freedom," Marcel says, "There is perhaps nothing more remarkable in the whole of Sartre's work than his phenomenological study of the 'other' as looking and of himself as exposed, pierced, bared, petrified by his Medusa-like stare. My subjective reactions to this form of aggression are, in the first place, fear (the sense of being endangered by the liberty of another) and, secondly, pride or shame (the sense of being at last what I am, but a distance from myself, for another who is over there)."[3]

PERCY: I'm sure that I am indebted to him. That reminds me that I remember at the time that one of my objections to Sartre was that, although as I say, I felt a very strong attraction, his character in *Nausea* was always being revolted by some aspect of reality which was usually described in terms of being viscid or wet or organic. And he was revolted by anything organic, particularly the idea of a home being a nest or . . . a nest where the children are, the babies are, the birds are, and mother. These things provoked a kind of horror in Sartre. Which is all very well, but I think he confuses the aesthetic with the philosophical there. He has an aesthetic revolt, but I think he allows that to become a premise for philosophical conclusions from it.

INTERVIEWER: In your article "Symbol as Hermeneutic in Existentialism," you say, "Yet even Sartrean existentialism can only be

---

[1] Walker Percy, "Symbol as Hermeneutic in Existentialism," *Philosophy and Phenomenological Research*, XVI (June, 1956), 529.

[2] The article referred to is "Existence and Human Freedom" in Gabriel Marcel, *The Philosophy of Existentialism*, trans. Manya Harari (New York: Citadel Press, 1968).

[3] *Ibid.*, 71.

edifying to the empirical mind. For whatever the sins of bad faith of an existentialism which *postulates* atheism, it has been able to recover that which the empiricist in his obsessive quest for reducibility and quantification has lost—the uniqueness of human being."[4]

PERCY: Well, presumably I meant a philosopher has no business postulating theism or atheism. It's arriving at one or the other, not setting out from atheism or theism. I think Sartre begins with atheism and erects his system on that. Not even Aquinas postulated theism. But, of course, Sartre changed completely. He has, in so many words, repudiated this whole period we're talking about. He's rejected that as being bourgeois and individualistic now.

INTERVIEWER: He's a Marxist now.

PERCY: He's a Marxist, yeah. He says at least he's seen the right of things. In a way I think he's right, in the sense that he does at last see the social dimension. It's not just one man wandering around the streets and sitting in the cafés and being revolted by the roots of a chestnut tree. At least he is aware of a social dimension, even though it's Marxist. Of course, Marx was the first one I think who adumbrated alienation, but he put it strictly on the basis of production, of a man making something . . .

INTERVIEWER: Which he had no control over. Do you continue to keep up with Sartre, or have you pretty much left that behind?

PERCY: As a matter of fact, *Nausea* was the only novel that excited me. He wrote a series of novels, about three or four novels about a character named Matthew, mostly involved in the Underground and in politics with his girlfriend in Paris, a girl like Simone de Beauvoir. I found those pretty boring. *Nausea* to me was a very exciting book, an important book, even though Sartre has repudiated it.

INTERVIEWER: I detect in your work a certain will toward theism which was there before you started building a philosophic outlook. Do you have any feeling about it?

PERCY: Well, I guess we're all what we are. If you're a Marxist, you can't help but be affected by that orientation in your writing. And I'm a Roman Catholic, although many Roman Catholics

---

[4] Percy, "Symbol as Hermeneutic in Existentialism," 529–30.

don't understand how I could write the novels I do and be a
Roman Catholic. Of course, that's an interesting subject in itself.
What is a Catholic novelist? Is he a novelist who happens to be a
Catholic, or is he a novelist who is first a Catholic before he's a
novelist? All I can say is, as a writer you have a certain view of
man, a certain view of the way it is, and even if you don't
recognize it or even if you disavow such a view, you can't escape
that view or lack of view. I think your writing is going to reflect
this. I think my writings reflect a certain basic orientation toward,
although not really controlled by, Catholic dogma. As I say, it's
a view of man, that man is neither an organism controlled by his
environment, not a creature controlled by the forces of history
as the Marxists would say, nor is he a detached, wholly objective,
angelic being who views the world in a godlike way and makes
pronouncements only to himself or to an elite group of people.
No, he's somewhere between the angels and the beasts. He's a
strange creature whom both Thomas Aquinas and Marcel called
homo viator, man the wayfarer, man the wanderer. So, to me,
the Catholic view of man as pilgrim, in transit, in journey, is very
compatible with the vocation of a novelist because a novelist
is writing about man in transit, man as pilgrim. I think it would be
a disadvantage, for example, to be a Freudian and a novelist. I
think a great many novels have been spoiled by Freudian preconceptions. Or behaviorist preconceptions. And I think most
Marxist novels are bad.

INTERVIEWER: I think novels that have a basis in radical thought are
good, it's just that the novels which try to take the latest "correct
line" are bad.

PERCY: And by the same token, nothing is worse than a bad Catholic
novel. Nothing is worse than a novel which seeks to edify the
reader. As Binx Bolling said, "It's not my business to edify
anybody."

INTERVIEWER: There's a consistent refusal to edify anyone in any of
your novels . . .

PERCY: This is Kierkegaard. Kierkegaard was always saying . . . . He
wrote a wonderful, a very important essay called "The Difference
Between a Genius and an Apostle." It's very, very important. He

said a genius could see the world *sub specie eternitatis*, the way things are in general, and he can tell people this—the way things are in general—but he did not have the authority to come to anybody and tell them any news. Or if he told them the news, he didn't have the authority to make everyone believe the news. Whereas an apostle is precisely a man who has the authority to come and tell somebody the news.

Kierkegaard . . . well, of course, Kierkegaard had much more claim to having authority than I do. He was a preacher. But he was still not an apostle. A novelist least of all has the authority to edify anyone or tell them good news, to pronounce Christ King.

INTERVIEWER: The ending of *The Moviegoer* has always disturbed me. They go back to New Orleans. She's going to take a streetcar somewhere, and he tells her that he's going to look after her. I don't know. That seems like a complete cop-out at that point.

PERCY: Well of course, Kate was the sort of person who was on the point of blowing up in a thousand pieces all the time, suffering acute anxiety and, in fact, being so shaky that she wanted somebody to tell her what to do, and I think she complained about her psychiatrist not telling her what to do. And so, at the end, Binx decided to marry her and she said, "Well if you tell me what to do, I'll believe you." So Binx said, "Okay." He was above all accommodating. And in a way, it's almost a hypnotic-suggestion relationship. She said, "If you tell me that I'll be all right on that streetcar, I'll be all right on the streetcar." So he said, "Okay, you're going to be all right on the streetcar." And she said, "All right, I will be."

INTERVIEWER: Isn't that just a temporary victory over alienation?

PERCY: Yeah, I'm not . . . . This is not set forth as any life plan. Kate in fact is a cripple and remains a cripple.

INTERVIEWER: As a matter of fact, you reject that thing all the way through. You keep coming back to a funny line, you must have read it somewhere, that Socrates, Jesus, and Buddha were all *mature* personalities. Is that from some ridiculous pamphlet or something?

PERCY: Well, in a way, I suppose it's a reaction against my Uncle Will, whom I loved and admired, but he was always telling us about the great ones of the earth. He would always list them: Buddha, Jesus, Socrates, he'd always include Richard Coeur de Lion, Philip Sidney . . . . So, it's sort of the pantheon of the sexless saints.

INTERVIEWER: Shelby Foote mentioned that he thought that Aunt Emily in *The Moviegoer*, who gives the speech about the broadsword virtues, is your uncle in disguise.

PERCY: It's very close. In that particular scene, when she tells off Binx —and she tells him off in good style, too—that's the way Uncle Will would have told him off. And of course he'd be partly right. A great many people think . . . People in the South think that's the best part of the book, where Aunt Emily tells off Binx, and they think that Aunt Emily's point of view represents my point of view! She was setting him straight, you see. And they give me the credit of coinciding with Aunt Emily.

INTERVIEWER: That must be kind of wild . . . . You said at one point that Binx was on Kierkegaard's plane of the aesthetic, and that's why he lived in Gentilly.

PERCY: Yeah, that's true, although not at the end. Binx lives in Gentilly as a kind of . . . as a conscious cultivation of a certain kind of experience, whereas anybody else who comes to New Orleans or wants to live the free life in New Orleans would naturally go to the French Quarter and get an apartment in the proper dilapidated style with a balcony and so on, but just as a reaction he does the opposite. But Binx goes to Gentilly . . . This appeals to him simply because it's not like the French Quarter. He doesn't want to be down in the French Quarter with a lot of guys who are artists and writers.

INTERVIEWER: The hip young set.

PERCY: They're exactly the kind of people he's trying to avoid. There's also a rather conscious parallel between Binx going to Gentilly and Philip going to the Gaza Desert. A man goes to a desert to seek something. Gentilly is a desert if ever there was one. The same thing happened in *The Last Gentleman*. They end up in the Western desert.

INTERVIEWER: I knew there was something I wanted to ask you. In your essay "The Man on the Train," you mentioned three ways of trying to deal with alienation, one of which is to write a book about the experience of being alienated, which is to say, "This is the way it is and we can all be together, after all, because you and I have the same experience of being alienated." Then the other method is rotation, which seems to work best. And then there is repetition, which is, unfortunately, conversion back to the way you were. It occurred to me that *The Moviegoer*'s two main characters escaped alienation by confirming each other's alienation, and *The Last Gentleman* showed a man escaping alienation by rotation.

PERCY: Well, they overlap and interweave, but they are different. Binx lived almost entirely in what Kierkegaard calls the aesthetic mode of consciously cultivating certain experiences, of living in a certain place with a certain feeling to it and having sensations about being there . . . . You walk across the street to the parochial school, and sit there in the evening looking in the papers for the movie schedules, very much aware of how it feels, and very much aware of getting on the bus and going ten miles to Algiers, across the river, to see a movie. This is to oversimplify what Kierkegaard calls the aesthetic mode of existence. But in the end—we're using Kierkegaardian terminology—in the end Binx jumps from the aesthetic clear across the ethical to the religious. He has no ethical sphere at all. That's what Aunt Emily can't understand about him. He just doesn't believe in being the honorable man, doing the right thing, for its own sake.

But at the end, a couple of hints are dropped; for instance, the end is also a commentary, or gloss, on the end of *The Brothers Karamazov*. He goes out to the car. Lonnie's brothers and sisters are in the car, and they ask him about Lonnie and Binx says, "Well, he's dying" or "He's dead," I've forgotten. One little boy jumps up and says, "Is it true, Binx, that Lonnie will rise up on the last day, and there will be a resurrection and Lonnie will be well in the resurrection, not crippled?" And Binx says, "Yeah."

INTERVIEWER: And Kate's mad at him because he's so cold-blooded.

PERCY: Well, Kate missed it, missed the whole thing. No, I think Kate said, "You were very sweet with him," and Binx just looks at her. She's missed it, you see. But Binx doesn't joke. Like Alyosha, he tells the truth. He wouldn't have said, "Yeah" if he didn't mean it. The implication is that . . . You see, in *The Brothers Karamazov*, Alyosha does the same thing with those kids. One of the kids says, "Is it true we're all going to rise up on the last day and be together?" A little boy named Kolya had just died. And so Alyosha said, "Yeah, that's true. We're really going to be there." And the kids say, "Hurrah for Karamazov!" And so this was a salute to Dostoevski.

INTERVIEWER: Binx always kind of disturbed me. Even knowing about the Kierkegaardian aesthetic mode, I always felt that Binx was holding himself in abeyance, that he was acting in a very self-centered way.

PERCY: It's what Kierkegaard called aesthetic damnation. You mentioned *The Last Gentleman*. That was different. This young man, Will Barrett, was both a great deal worse off than Binx and better off. He was worse off because he was sick; he was really sick. He didn't know where he was. Half the time he was in a fugue or amnesia, and he'd go into a fugue and come out of a fugue, and he'd wake up somewhere, not knowing where he was yet. He really existed in what Kierkegaard would call the religious mode. He was a real searcher. He was after something. He was clinging to a piece of wood, a floating spar; he's a drowning man, clutching at straws, really on the ragged edge. The abyss was always yawning at his feet. The book is nothing but a journey. The question, you see, is whether it is better to be a drowning man or alive and well in East Orange.

INTERVIEWER: The journey is rotation.

PERCY: Well first, rotation—he's wandering around through the South —but then repetition. He goes back home. He goes back to a place like Greenville, and there he stands in front of his father's house, he recovers his . . . I think Kierkegaard says, "Every man has to stand in front of the house of his childhood in order to recover himself." So Barrett is obsessed with this thing that had happened, his father's suicide. And the whole first two-thirds of the book is going back to this thing that happened, which actually had shocked him so much he'd almost become a hysteric. He was deaf in one ear.

At first, there's a repetition back to Ithaca and then he gets hold

of Sutter's diary and he follows Sutter to the desert. There's an
encounter there where he meets Sutter in the desert which is
something like the encounter of Philip with the eunuch in the
Gaza Desert. But at the end, this is different. He knows that Sutter's
on to something. Sutter's got something he wants to know, and
Barrett has this radar. He knows that people know something he
doesn't know. So he fastens on Sutter, but he has to find out what
it is. He leaves him this diary which has all kinds of clues and
such, but he still doesn't know exactly what Sutter's getting at. So
he finally catches up with Sutter, and in the death scene, a baptism
takes place, with a very ordinary sort of priest, a mediocre priest.
And here again, Barrett has eliminated Christianity. That is gone.
That is no longer even to be considered. It's not even to be spoken
of, taken seriously, or anything else. But he still has this acute
radar. He knows what people are feeling. And he is aware of
something going on between the dying boy Jamie and Sutter there
across the room and the priest. And he is aware that Sutter is
taking this seriously. So after the boy dies they leave and Barrett
catches up with Sutter and he asks Sutter, "What happened there?
Something happened. What happened?" And Sutter brushes him
off as usual. "What do you think happened? You were there."
Well, it ends, unlike *The Moviegoer*, with Barrett missing it, like
Kate missed it. He *misses* it! He says something to Sutter like
"Why don't you come back to a town in the South and make a
contribution, however small?" So presumably, you see, Barrett,
who existed in a religious mode of search, repetition, and going
into the desert, which are all in Kierkegaard's religious mode, at
the end, misses it. Whereas Binx, who exists in the aesthetic mode
of damnation, as Kierkegaard would call it, in the end becomes
a believer in his own rather laconic style.

INTERVIEWER: A real flip-out. You never look for that. I look and what
has he done? This guy is now a Christian! I didn't see this coming.

PERCY: Well, most people didn't see it at all. In fact, most people will
deny that it's in there. They stand me down. "That's not true.
You don't baptize Binx in that book." They accuse me of copping
out.

INTERVIEWER: There's something really strange about the way you handled the death of young boys and their conversion, or at least a giving of religious significance to their death. Does this bother you that this occurs in both novels?

PERCY: Well, somebody told me—who was it? it was Susan Sontag— "You've written two novels, both of which end with a philosopher bending over a dying youth." My wife said, "Enough of that."

INTERVIEWER: There's also a strange kind of matching up of Binx and Kate and Billy and Kitty.

PERCY: Except that Kate is very different from Kitty. Kitty's an Ole Miss cheerleader.

INTERVIEWER: Yeah, lovely girl.

PERCY: You know how nice Ole Miss girls are. They're nice girls.

INTERVIEWER: Real nice.

PERCY: Kate is one jump ahead of Kitty all the time.

INTERVIEWER: Kate may have more feeling because of that. Kitty . . . Of course, there have been some pretty dense comments about why you wrote Kitty in in the first place. You must have read some of them.

PERCY: Well, I guess so. Yeah. I forgot what they said.

INTERVIEWER: Goodman, who reviewed *The Last Gentleman* in *Life*, said that you stood back from sex all the way through the novel.

PERCY: Well, he probably means from that that I don't actually describe the physiology of sexual intercourse, which everybody does now in novels. And which I have no particular objection to, except that I don't think it's necessary. I already had physiology in med school.

INTERVIEWER: You don't think anything can be learned about the way people approach sex?

PERCY: Well, it's gotten to be such a formality now. The description of sexual encounters is now almost as obligatory as their avoidance in the Victorian novels. I'll be damned if I'm going to be dictated to by either style. I do it my own way.

INTERVIEWER: I guess they objected to the whole thing about impotence in both novels, well not so much—yeah, impotence. In *The Last Gentleman*, when they're in Central Park, he can't do anything until much later and by the time he wants to, she is running off.

PERCY: Yeah, they misfire. He's ready and she's not and so on.

INTERVIEWER: In *The Moviegoer*, when they're on the train it's never
. . . I never could say one way or the other what happened. When
Binx refuses to say anything to Kate's aunt, I thought Binx was
just refusing to be on the ethical plane, but I still didn't know
what had happened.

PERCY: It didn't come off. That's what happened.

INTERVIEWER: But then I read some stupid magazine review that said,
yeah, they did have sexual intercourse.

PERCY: "Flesh, poor flesh," it says. "Quailed and failed."

INTERVIEWER: Maybe the reviewer just assumed something happened
because there has always been an obligation to have sex scenes,
and he assumed that you had merely understated it.

PERCY: I take pleasure in turning Freud upside down. Instead of
something being a symbol for sex in the Freudian style, I use sex
as a symbol of something else. Sex here is a symbol of failure on
the existential level.

INTERVIEWER: In the May 11, 1962, *Commonweal* you reviewed *A
Dream of Mansions* by Norris Lloyd, *The Wanderings of Desire*
by Marion Montgomery, and *Judgment Day* by Thomas Chastain.
And in that review you said, "A sense of place can decay to the
merely bizarre. A sense of person can be pushed to caricature and
a whole region populated with eccentrics. An ear for language is
ever in danger of being beguiled by the names of trains and
states—O Lackawanna, O Alabama, O ye wide Missouri—or of
doing duty as the background virtuosity of Jeeter Lester." And of
course you've taken the opposite tack. Binx is not really average,
although he does enjoy a comfortable life, but he's not unusual
either. He's certainly not a dwarf or a gnome. Do you purposely
stay away from the Southern kind of thing of peopling your novels
with physical eccentrics and mental eccentrics?

PERCY: I stay away from the Southern novel in several ways. There's
a certain thing everybody always says about the Southern novel.
In almost any interview with a Southern writer, the writer always
says something about "Well, the reason Southerners can write
good novels is that they were raised sitting on front porches listening to people tell stories, and Faulkner sat on a bench in the
courthouse in Oxford and heard the people tell all these stories.
And we're exposed to family sagas and all sorts of bizarre and

eccentric characters, also interrelationships." This may be true. Yeah, sure it was true, but hell, it's gone, it's all over.

INTERVIEWER: Do you think so, really?

PERCY: As far as I'm concerned. Whatever impetus I had towards writing owes nothing to sitting on a porch listening to anybody tell stories about the South, believe me. I think that the day of regional Southern writing is all gone. I think that people who try to write in that style are usually repeating a phased-out genre— or doing Faulkner badly. I don't think that's the way it is. I think the South is sufficiently corrupted, or at least amalgamated with the rest of the U. S., so that a young man coming back to the South is not so different from a young man coming back to Denver or San Francisco. Except the South has certain advantages. I make use of the Southern scenery, the Southern backdrop, but just as that, as a place where a young man can react. But I think it's just fifty years later than that time of family stories and sagas and histories and so on.

INTERVIEWER: Well, I think probably you could find instances of that, but why do it anymore. Maybe that is what the attitude should be. I've read a couple of interviews with you and you don't consider yourself a Southern writer.

PERCY: I'm not sure of that. I do. If I were in Colorado or New York, I'd be writing something different.

INTERVIEWER: Really?

PERCY: I think what we're stuck with in the South and what's of value are two things: one is religion and the other is the Negro. And Flannery O'Connor says there's no way you can be raised in the South without being affected by the very strong fundamentalist Christianity, usually in rebellion against it, but certainly you bear some kind of relationship to it. Compare yourself or myself with somebody growing up in Shaker Heights in Cleveland. The subject never even arises. You and I have seen Jesus Saves signs. We were brought up seeing Jesus Saves and Garrett Snuff signs. And then there is the black thing. Of course, this is a hideously complicated business, very ambivalent, a very rich source for relationships because no matter what you say, or how bad the South is, there's still a long history of viable relationship here, a long history of people getting along with each other.

INTERVIEWER: For one reason or another.

PERCY: Yes, and a certain civility still exists here. And so you find yourself attacking the South, and at the same time falling back on ways of communication which still exist. I can't help but think it's an advantage. I mean, if you're in New York writing about . . . Well, there's no way to write about it now. In New York, you're either a revolutionary, you have either joined the Movement, or you have . . . I notice many Jewish novelists simply ignore the Negroes. The question doesn't even arise.

INTERVIEWER: You said in that same review in the May 11, 1962, issue of *Commonweal* that ". . . faults or no, a great deal of very good writing is being done in the South, and much of it by young women. Anyone speculating about Southern writing had better know something about Southern girls—and small towns in the Deep South. For that is who is doing it and that is where it is coming from: there are at least a dozen women writers of the first rank from Georgia, Alabama, Mississippi, and Louisiana." What about Southern women writers? Do you read many of them, and how do you feel about them?

PERCY: Well, I think there are quite a few dozen competent, or *more* than competent, women writers in the South. In fact, the South seems to produce them more than any other part of the country. I don't know exactly what it is. Some of them are very good indeed. Two of them that come to mind are Flannery O'Connor, whom I have a high opinion of, and Eudora Welty, the best fiction writer in the South. But below that rank, there are probably two dozen competent female novelists scattered around in towns in Georgia and Mississippi. Somebody's always doing a novel about a Southern girl. They're usually pretty good. Dave Cohn used to say every woman in Greenville was writing a novel and had a thesaurus under her bed.

INTERVIEWER: Do you think there is "a feminine perspective" in the writings of these women?

PERCY: Well, yeah, in a sense. Eudora Welty, the best, certainly sets the style in her interest in weddings and families and family doings. You think of Carson McCullers talking about what the cook says to the little boy in the kitchen, and Ellen Douglas writing about the family, the whole set of kinfolks in a Mississippi town. That's what they know about. Marriage, families, husbands and wives falling out. I didn't have many kinfolks. But Flannery O'Connor's a horse of a different color, now. She's something else. I think the reason they're good, better than most American female writers, is probably the same reason nineteenth-century British lady novelists were good. They led the same kind of life. Think of living in a small place possessed of a strong tradition and combine that with a pair of sharp eyes, leisure, and the ability to observe, and you've got the makings of a good novelist, just as you did in a parsonage in a British shire.

INTERVIEWER: Charleen Whisnant says, "With Southern women writers, you could not possibly tell they were women unless they signed their names." Do you agree with that?

PERCY: No, I don't. Now, I have in mind a certain category of a white-lady Southern novelist and a certain type of book that they write, and I can read the first paragraph and tell it's written by a woman novelist.

INTERVIEWER: Well, what are the trademarks?

PERCY: Certain views of a family or of a kitchen, or a man and wife seen the way a woman would see it, descriptions of a house or a garden or clothes. But written in a very decent, competent style. There have been dozens of them in the past twenty-five years which were interchangeable. I do know they usually turn me off because I know what it's going to be about. I know what's going to happen and what's not going to happen. This is not true of Eudora Welty, who is a great writer, as you know, or of Flannery O'Connor who, like the novelists I'm interested in, had ultimate concerns in her writing. Like the French writers, she was interested in ultimate things.

INTERVIEWER: I detect an affinity for Catholic writers here.

PERCY: No, an affinity for Flannery. Actually, most so-called Catholic novels are pretty bad. I usually prefer . . . I suppose my great favorites are the Russians, Russian nineteenth-century writers. Certainly they didn't have much use for Catholics.

INTERVIEWER: Why do you suppose we have never produced a major female poet in the South?

PERCY: I never thought of it before, I think it's true. I can't think of a single one. That's a good question.

INTERVIEWER: Do you think women have been oppressed in the South?

PERCY: I suppose they've been oppressed as the word is used by the liberation movement, but enshrined at the same time they are oppressed, elevated. There are so many ramifications of that. I can think of all kinds of things. Women in the South have been expected to be the Ole Miss, the lady of the house, and they were very happy to take the role and become very strong people, almost matriarchal in some parts of the South. So you can hardly say oppression. I'm thinking of all the old ladies I used to know. The word *oppression* doesn't fit them at all. If anybody was oppressed, it was the menfolk by them. But I suppose there would be oppression in the modern sense. They have been required to fit into a feminine, a female role, and had done it very well.

I can't see that it's a Southern question. As a matter of fact, I see very little difference between the Southern college girls now and any other college girls. They seem very much of a piece to me. You would know more about that than I would. You see them. But the ones I've seen have a lot more in common with their own generations in other parts of the country than they do with their parents here.

INTERVIEWER: There aren't any very strong women in your fiction except Rita, who is by turns strong and not so strong. Kitty is just pitiful and Kate is not much better.

PERCY: I write about women in fiction from the exclusive point of view of the hero or anti-hero. As such, the view of women or anyone else may be limited by the narrowness of the vision. The nature of the narrowing, however, I would hope to be significant. If Binx Bolling tends to see people oddly, then perhaps the times are such that people get seen oddly. Accordingly there is no attempt to flesh out female characters—or any other characters—in the style of the nineteenth-century novel. It was said that Tolstoy knew exactly how it felt to be a horse five minutes after his first acquaintance with a horse. Presumably this held true of women too. Certainly I am no Tolstoy and cannot do this. But I wouldn't if I could. What interests me is not how it feels to be that particular horse or that particular woman but how it feels to be a particular consciousness, male or female, set down in the world the way it is now.

INTERVIEWER: Did you read Ellen Douglas' pamphlet about you which she wrote for the Religious Dimensions in Literature published by the Seabury Press?[5]

PERCY: Yes.

INTERVIEWER: What did you think about it?

PERCY: I thought it was quite good in most ways. Very sharp. I thought she handled my . . . She asked me if I was still a Catholic. I told her I still was, and she sounded as if she didn't believe me. She wrote something about the Percys having a tendency to toy with Catholicism. This does a bit of injustice to both the Percys and the Catholic Church. I may not be a good Catholic, but I hope I am not a dilettante.

[5] Ellen Douglas, *Walker Percy's The Last Gentleman*, Religious Dimensions in Literature Series, Seabury Press Reading Program (New York: Seabury Press, 1969). This is an excellent twenty-seven-page pamphlet by a Mississippi novelist who is an old friend of both Walker Percy and his family. Although it has not been listed in any bibliographies of Percy I have seen, it is very valuable. Mrs. Douglas (a pen name) makes use of personal letters from Percy.—JC

Makar:
🍂 MARION MONTGOMERY

Interviewed by JAMES COLVERT

Since 1960, when his first book of poems, Dry Lightning, *appeared, Marion Montgomery has published two novels,* The Wandering of Desire *(1962) and* Darrell *(1964); a novelette,* Ye Olde Bluebird *(1967); two other volumes of poems,* Stones from the Rubble *(1965) and* The Gull and Other Georgia Scenes *(1970); and a critical study,* T. S. Eliot: The American Magus *(1969). His fiction, poetry, and literary criticism have appeared in numerous literary magazines and in various anthologies of Southern writing. In 1967 he received the first Award in Poetry from the* Carleton Miscellany. *He also received, earlier, the Eugene Saxton Memorial Award from Harper and Brothers, the M. G. Michael Award from the University of Georgia, and the Georgia Writers Award for fiction.*

Marion Montgomery was born in Thomaston, Georgia, in 1925, received his A.B. and M.A. degrees at the University of Georgia, and attended graduate school at the University of Iowa, where he was also assistant editor and later managing editor of the Western Review. *He now teaches English at the University of Georgia and lives in nearby Crawford.*

The interview was conducted in September, 1970, at the University of Georgia.

INTERVIEWER: Flannery O'Connor, referring to your novel *The Wandering of Desire* as a "solid achievement," argues that "the Southern writer can outwrite anybody in the country because he has the Bible and a little history" and "that you have more than most" Does this advantage count as much in our day and time as it did for Southern writers of Faulkner's and Tate's generation?

MONTGOMERY: "Our day and time" has implicit in it an acknowledgment that the past day and time *was*. Even when we aren't aware of it, as we increasingly fail to be, we are "in addition to"—extensions of—the past. Part of what we are is what we were as individuals and as particular human points in that line of descent from our fathers. I notice the new poet or novelist always supplies biographical material, in the work as well as for use on dust jackets. He tends to advertise difference. From what? Usually from his fathers or from what he was in his last book. We ignore our history at risk, because to ignore—to avoid acknowledgment of it—is to blind ourselves to its inevitable influences upon us, an old chestnut but far from rancid.

INTERVIEWER: Hemingway ignored it, by and large.

MONTGOMERY: We don't have to, shouldn't. And we mustn't allow ourselves the error of substituting for Hemingway's narrow pursuit of a personal, recent moment, "the way it was," our own decade's error, "the way it is," striving to deny "was." Faulkner's work is present tense in *Go Down Moses*, in the sense I mean the term. It starts with "was" as the best way of talking about the abiding "is" we're affected by.

INTERVIEWER: You seem to see this progressive loss of historical perspective as a phenomenon of contemporary civilization. Does this mean that the Southern novelist, as you and O'Connor define him, is steadily losing his audience? What, for example, could a reader who can't see in history the radical causes of the present make of *The Wandering of Desire*, except that there is a lot of interesting local color in it?

MONTGOMERY: So far as I can tell *The Wandering* hasn't been much read, even as local color. I live in the innocent expectation of its being discovered, "revisited." Perhaps one of the side effects of such revisiting will be to point some reader back toward the importance of history to art.

INTERVIEWER: But this reader doesn't know any history. It's a blank, an absence, and so how can he be shown its importance to art?

MONTGOMERY: It's possible to know an absence without knowing the absent, or the almost absent, thing. The pleasure of metaphor seems to me to point that way. I read or hear a striking metaphor and my response, if I could say it in words, is "Why, I was about to say that." That feeling about a way of seeing the world depends on history—you've got to know already at least one term of a metaphor (or go learn it and then come back to the metaphor). And we add discovery to that knowledge: we have known something all along that we didn't know we knew. That's what Darrell means when an innocent asks him whether he knows a particular community song. "I might have wrote it," he says.

INTERVIEWER: This is Darrel Lemons, the hero of your novel *Darrell*. Yes, he "could have wrote it" as he says, and I take this to mean that he has retained something of the gift of identity through community, though he's well on his way to throwing it up for something else. *Darrell* is a funny book, but I didn't laugh too much when I read it. It's about people who are throwing all their gifts away. Some sinister quirk drives them out of their community, and thus out of themselves. *Darrell* celebrates the gift of identity and the grace of community negatively, by showing their irretrievable loss. Are you really as pessimistic as your metaphor suggests?

MONTGOMERY: I don't admit that they're irretrievable. What I hope I've done in *Darrell* is dramatize a dissatisfaction with the emptiness, that hunger that I'm having such difficulty talking about here. I see it in people in the world about me, and I'm encouraged. And I won't admit to being pessimistic. I'm reassured by the endless possibilities of man's foolishness.

INTERVIEWER: You claim foolishness as a saving virtue?

MONTGOMERY: I think maybe it makes virtue possible, or at least it makes courage and love possible. I see it in Darrell's Granny. And in Darrell, too, for that matter. With the hunger and the foolishness—the desire and the inclination to action—going for us, we might make it.

INTERVIEWER: Well, you're no pessimist, you say, but you're also saying that Darrell shows that we *might* make it?

MONTGOMERY: Well, he is, as you say, throwing all his gifts away. But they're the gifts he is looking for. It's sort of hard, when you're born in a wreck, as Darrell is, to know where you came from, and so it's harder to know where you're going. It just occurs to me that Darrell is a secularized, dehistoried everyman. Atlanta can be too easily a delusion in that circumstance. But maybe in one way Darrell makes it. He doesn't stop looking for what he is throwing away. So you see I'm really a secret optimist, which I don't suppose it hurts to admit in an "interview."

INTERVIEWER: Well, I'm just trying to get you to admit that there's an awful lot of foolishness in this secularized dehistorical everyman, that maybe we can't survive it.

MONTGOMERY: We have to bear human foolishness, human absurdity, without resorting to making despair a virtue. Momentary despair—we can't escape that. It's as likely as indigestion, when a new absurdity is being absorbed. I think I mean that the existentialists' absurd—which has frightened too many of our writers out of wit and humor—is a prospect of the world we come to again and again. We can't escape coming to it. But it can't be enough just to come *to* it: one has to go *through*. The ticket to it is the tragic eye, which I suspect is innate. The passport that allows us to come back from it we have to be given or earn—the humorous eye. Humor is a necessary complement to the tragic, if one is to preserve what our age insists on calling "sanity." (I call it soul.) There are advantages of place and community and family to one's earning or being given that eye, I think. That is one of the gifts to the Southern writer that we haven't quite outgrown with our new arrogance. It was a gift to Homer, too, and Shakespeare, wasn't it? That's why Shakespeare is so much greater than Euripides, I think. There's a strain of Darrell in Euripides, a poverty of vision. Euripides made it to the country of the absurd, in *The Bacchae* for instance, but didn't escape to tell it.

INTERVIEWER: You go a long way back. My impression is that existentialists solemnly claim the original discovery of the absurd.

MONTGOMERY: The absurd is older than Euripides. Or Homer or Job. It has to be. But it is also as new at the waking up of any particular mind. Some minds wake up to the absurd and believe they have discovered the sunlight on a broken column never before beheld by man. They may say, as Eliot finally does, "If the temple is to be destroyed, we must be forever rebuilding it that it may be destroyed." That is, they may go *through* their discovery. Eliot had to learn that. Faulkner was luckier—he was born knowing it, and "War" or "Spotted Horses" is one of the ways he says it.

INTERVIEWER: Homer to Faulkner—a pretty long view. What seems likely in the short view is that Crawford will become a suburb of

Atlanta, planted in concrete and ribboned in freeways. As a
Southern writer, you may be under great pressure after all to retreat to existentialism and black humor. What is this new arrogance you mention? It sounds sinister.

MONTGOMERY: I see Crawford as already a suburb of Atlanta, and I
don't like it. I resist it. But then, a few weeks ago I was in Atlanta
and noticed, as I have before, grass and weeds growing in cracks
on the sidewalks. Literally. Just a step away from bull nettle and
dog fennel in the country cow lot—given the long view. Doc, in
The Wandering, doesn't notice the wilderness at the lot fence,
though he fights it. The new arrogance? Sinister? Yes. But not decisive to mankind. Just to the individual man.

INTERVIEWER: I still don't understand "new arrogance." Just what is
this "new arrogance" you keep speaking of?

MONTGOMERY: This sinister new arrogance? I really shouldn't call it
new. It's rather that we "make it new" in each generation. It's
perhaps more spectacular in ours—new in that sense, but not essentially so. It's given the dignity of pageantry by television, or
Life magazine specials. Sort of our age's version—or rather per-
version—of Dante's final cantos in the Purgatorio. The spectacle
is confusing, cut off from history as it is. When Hawthorne used
the black mass in "Young Goodman Brown," we were close
enough to the mass for it to be more than a literary gimmick in
the story—it certainly was more than a gimmick to Hawthorne
anyway. Spectacle is confusing, signs are taken for wonders themselves, rather than as signs of wonders. Let me try to disengage
my "arrogance" from our age's collective spectacle of it—the young
versus those over thirty, for instance. Let me say it something
like this, thinking of a man rather than men, the individual rather
than community: My wakening awareness of myself tempts me
to engage my moment as if it, and the world, existed not only for
the sake of my engaging it, but even because I engage it. That
arrogance is the energy—the necessary energy—that makes col-
lision in the world of the absurd inevitable. I would call it original
sin manifest. But, as Milton argued, man's first, and continuing,
disobedience—self-elevation or presumption—makes reconciliation
both necessary and possible. It's a perverse blessing: it makes
possible one's action in the affairs of men, but it is a spiritual

action in the individual. And in varying degrees it is always ignorant action, whether Agamemnon's or Allen Ginsberg's. Another name for it is youth, though thirty years is no point of demarcation from its favors or errors. It occurs whenever, in the immediacy of one's engagement in the world, there is an absence of perspective, that historical awareness we were speaking of, which the details of local history and family and community remind us of as we live with them. The decisive problem is to reconcile the necessity of the private act—the movement of individual spirit—to public act, to one's relation to his fellows in family and community.

INTERVIEWER: This is a moral and ethical problem, a religious problem. Are you directly concerned with it, though, as a literary man—as novelist and poet?

MONTGOMERY: I wonder whether the problem isn't at the very heart of drama, whether embodied in play or novel or even lyric. It's the point in individual awareness where, to borrow from Aristotle, *recognition* makes *reversal* tolerable. Where one can get along with the absurd world with a new, even humorous, vision of it. (The Southern writer's "tragic-comic" mode blends the satyr play, figuratively, rather than saving it till last.) The point of arrival that I'm talking about is where one escapes the dangers of self without abandoning identity. Where one in fact stops worrying about identity, the problem which our age stokes the fires of its self-terror and self-pity with. So Oedipus moves us on beyond pity and terror. On the other hand, there's Macbeth. The most terrible, the most terrifying thing about Macbeth isn't the murder of Duncan or of Banquo or of Macduff's children. Not even the death of Macbeth himself. It's what Macbeth learns about himself that he can't go beyond. There is the real country where action is decisive—not in the signs of spectacles, trees as men walking in *Macbeth*. That's why, when I'm looking with the long view, I don't despair. It doesn't mean that I don't resist the Atlantization of Crawford, or advertise the dangers of DDT or water pollution. As you know, I don't minimize that sort of danger to mankind. It's just that, in the long view, those are dangers of a secondary order.

INTERVIEWER: You said a while ago that the decisive problem is to reconcile the private act and the public act, and that this concern is at the very heart of literature, of the novel, drama, or lyric. What you've said about *The Wandering* and *Darrell* holds true also for your books of poems?

MONTGOMERY: I believe it holds true for my poems. I notice about them, in retrospect, that they tend to be gestures in that direction, an action that attempts the ceremonial. One description of ceremony is that it is formal, public gesture of feeling that, by its formality, prevents feeling from destroying the person on the one hand or the family or community on the other. In the poem feeling finds an appropriate order. It becomes a center from which possibilities are defined—whether the technical aspects of verse or of the prospect of ideas that enlighten verse but goes beyond verse also. I don't know whether I'm making myself clear: poetry, like fiction, makes a concrete gesture—it's both being and motion of being.

INTERVIEWER: We're instructed by advanced theorists and artists that traditionalists like you, regionalists and ceremonialists, are hopelessly outmoded. The virtue of the new "concretism" in poetry, says Eugene Wildman, is that it is "genuinely international in character." It is, he goes on to say, "a radical approach to poetry and it tends to worry the person who really loves, say *War and Peace.* I would say he has reason to be worried. . . . It leads the mind to contemplate a future art in a future world that is as remote from our sensibilities (however much we have always tried to deceive ourselves) as the poetry of the bards or of a Greek tragedy is."

MONTGOMERY: Well, the new theorists such as Wildman who argues significance—international significance—of concrete poetry disproves himself by the argument. All that's left to him is to produce concrete poetry, the closest he can come to a nonsignifying act. He's really practicing a kind of perverted Platonism, trying to hit us over the head with a black abstractionism, with such a violence of gesture that we have the illusion that the thing we're being struck with is concrete. I'm not worried by Mr. Wildman. Earlier I was amused by his ilk. But his argument has become so traditional that now I only feel bored. Mr. Wildman is just the latest character in the old morality play called the Hollow Men. One point about the quotation you've given me is, on second thought, amusing. He assumes the prophetic voice in talking about a future art beyond the possibility of our sensibilities. His is the rhetoric of the radical evangelist. The hellfire preacher. He's Jonathan Edwards, and the traditionalist is the sinner in the hands of an angry abstract, nonsignifying world. At best he is another footnote of an historical interest, saying the kind of nonsense about poetry that led to *Ubi Roi*. But he is *saying*. His best argument would be to produce the thing he's talking about. This is *ad hominem*, but words are an extension of the man in some wise; to attack the silly (in the old sense of that word) requires pointing to hay in a speaker's hair. Who is he, anyway?

INTERVIEWER: I don't know, but a biographical note in the *Chicago Review* says he is "sometimes known as 'Eugein' Wildman." He would be astonished, doubtless, at your charge of provincialism. He's an internationalist, as his comments on concretist poetry in an article in the *Northwest Review* prove. He says, for example: "The most important preliminary fact about concretism, what makes it a significant aesthetic approach, is its genuinely international character. It has taken root virtually everywhere."

MONTGOMERY: One might say the same thing for hunger, the Hong Kong flu, and fascism, none of which are without a certain aesthetic dimension.

INTERVIEWER: He has an aesthetic rationale, though. Consider this: "Process is its most important subject matter, the permutations of the constituent elements, general letters of the alphabet. (The idea put through its changes is it. As: rose-ease, reve-ever.)"

MONTGOMERY: The child in the first grade who gets dog and god confused in his flash cards isn't exactly putting idea through its changes. Such con artists as Chaucer's *reve* are, like the poor, with us *ever*. Crossword puzzles are ancient, universal, but of a very low order in the aesthetic experience, considerably below the pun. Did Grandpa Mallarmé start this? Or maybe Laurence Sterne in *Tristram Shandy*? With his chapter that is so good that it is better not printed—thus blank pages? Or is that really concrete fiction as opposed to concrete poetry? They're trying for the best of two impossible worlds.

INTERVIEWER: You're pretty severe on concretism. Perhaps too severe?

MONTGOMERY: It's possible. Still when the fool rejects mind and looks in his heart and writes—or almost writes—what you get is foolish writing, and it ought to be called so.

INTERVIEWER: Well, one more major premise from this new aesthetic: "The perfect linguistic vehicle is ideogrammic, for with the ideogram the gulf between the sign and the thing signified is all but eliminated."

MONTGOMERY: This is perverted Pound. By extension then the most perfect linguistic vehicle, the most nearly universal, the perfect mirror of mind, would be the blank page. Or—to raise it to an additional aesthetic power—one might do what Aram Saroyan announces as his third collection of poems: "an untitled wrapped ream of typing paper stamped © Aram Saroyan 1968." But that's marred, isn't it? It has to be rewrapped, else there's the union stamp on the company wrapper. But even when that's taken care of, there's Aram's stamp, and we are back to the *sign* and the *thing* signified again. There we are back to what the concretist would be forced by his logic to characterize as the spontaneous undertow of irrelevant feeling. Next Saroyan will be telling us that he's the son of the writer William Saroyan. Which, in fact, he does in a note accompanying a selection of his concrete poetry in a recent anthology. (And there is even a full-page picture with the top of his head cut off, one of the possible effects when printing meets concrete poetry.) Talk about traditionalism.

INTERVIEWER: Am I wrong in reading the last poem in *Stones from the Rubble* as a parable of the artist? It seems to say something about the exertion of the artist's will against random disorder, something about an original relation to nature, some fearful trial of the imagination, or rather the powers, of the artist. I'm guessing that this title poem of the book is a kind of signature of commitment, a celebration of certain aims and hopes and perhaps fears.

MONTGOMERY: Doesn't the title poem of *Stones* dramatize the argument I've just made about the decisive struggle's lying in the attempt to reconcile private history to public history in this moment of community? It talks about the problem of tradition and the individual talent, I think. About the temptations to the individual talent to be too concerned for itself. Eliot talks about how a work finds its proper place in a hierarchy of existing masterpieces—

very much as Croce does. The works exist, the new work exists. "The Stone" talks about the private attempt to make the work publicly exist. How one tries, with mind, to throw up something solid, lodge it above sea level, rescued from the grinding back to the elemental through the agencies of sea and wind. It's about, say, the poet's relation to civilization—the ordered community. In that sense private. Public as it is a parable for carpenter or lawyer. It's about finding one's limits without being overwhelmed by them. About the necessity of acknowledging limitations without using that acknowledgment for cowardly refusals. For the poet, about accepting the fact that, willy-nilly, to write a poem is to enter competition with Homer and Shakespeare. That realization can put one off the mark. Because that is a private struggle, where ambition and fear might make one forget that somehow up there on the cliff or beyond it—tomorrow maybe—some mind is heaving the stones further. And maybe, out of our sight—my sight—even building something with them.

INTERVIEWER: My guess is that this is a position you've worked through to. I'm thinking of an early poem in *Dry Lightning*, your first book of poems, called "Application," in which you seem to exorcise Yeats, Eliot, Dylan Thomas, Pound, Lawrence, and E. E. Cummings, as models to be imitated—along with the New Criticism and little magazines. You're looking quizzically at the required "curriculum," of course, but aren't you also exorcising these omnipresent influences?

MONTGOMERY: I think so. I hope so. But not quite "exorcise." Rather coming to an accommodation. That's the start of a poem early in *Stones from the Rubble*, "On Fishing Creek." It begins, "The men I have chosen for fathers release me . . ." But I must say, of "Application," that the target was misusers of Yeats, Cummings, and the others. Those content with imitation rather than emulation or accommodation. And those committees who judge by imitation, that is by what they recognize—dead history or rather history seen with dead eyes. I sent that poem as a part of my application for a Guggenheim, by the way. And guess what?

INTERVIEWER: Well, yes. Would you rather be known as a poet, novelist, or literary critic?

MONTGOMERY: I don't know. That is to begin worrying about identity all over again. I keep working toward a point where it won't make any difference to me. And I have every confidence of achieving that position—one way or another. Right now I write what I can when I must.

INTERVIEWER: You have, among several other things, another book of poems coming out this spring. Will it confirm your position as a traditionalist?

MONTGOMERY: I think whatever I write will confirm a traditionalist position. As Sweeney says, "I've gotta use words when I talk to you." Or letters of the alphabet, as Wiseman says. Or lines and colors that echo nature. There is no escape of the traditional; only a naïve illusion of having escaped it. Besides which, I'm too curious about now and the future to wish an escape. I can use all the help I can get in satisfying that curiosity.

INTERVIEWER: Well, Sweeney would have to admit that you are much enabled. Thanks for patiently attending all these questions.

MONTGOMERY: And I'm grateful to you for your kind role as innocent straight man. Your questions belie innocence, and I appreciate very much your asking about things that seem to me worth talking about. Good questions are, after all, rarer than passable answers.

Notice, I'm Still Smiling:
❧ REYNOLDS PRICE

Interviewed by WALLACE KAUFMAN

Reynolds Price was born in 1933 and educated at Duke University and Merton College, Oxford, where he was a Rhodes Scholar. He now lives in Durham, North Carolina, and teaches at Duke.

His novels have attracted high praise and have been widely reprinted and translated into several languages. His first novel, A Long and Happy Life, *appeared in 1962. The next year* The Names and Faces of Heroes *appeared. A* Generous Man *was published in 1966 and* Love and Work *in 1968.* Late Warning *(poems) came out in 1968 also.* Permanent Errors *(stories) appeared in 1970 and* Things Themselves *(essays) in 1972. His short stories have been published in* Shenandoah, Red Clay Reader, *the* Southern Review, Esquire, *and other magazines.*

The best interview is a conversation, and the best conversation is one that does not end but lives on as its participants live on, finding new ideas and changing old ones. This is also the kind of conversation that cannot be fully recorded. What follows, therefore, is not so much a thing in itself but evidence of something—evidence of the nature of one writer's mind.

The first part of this conversation was recorded in May, 1966. I begin it by looking back to even earlier conversations. The second part is from January, 1970. These pages added up are samples of eleven years of conversation.

I

From a grove of gray beech trees Reynolds Price's house looks over a small pond. In mid-January five years ago when Reynolds lived in a trailer on the other side of the pond, I was out on the new ice, skating figures. Reynolds sat on the hard-crusted snow, watching because he had never in his life lived outside North Carolina (except for three years as a Rhodes Scholar in England) and had a Southerner's fear of ice. But when coming down from a miscalculated leap I fell and struck my head so hard the ice cracked, he jumped up to rescue me. He slipped on the snow crust, went down on his back and threw his shoulder out of joint. So when I came to and looked through the blood from my forehead, he was lying on the snow, his arm bent behind him as if no longer attached. I pulled his arm back in place, he cleaned and bound my wound and for five minutes we laughed like lunatics.

Literally and figuratively we have been doing that for seven years, kind of a Laurel and Hardy friendship. Price was born in 1933 in Macon, North Carolina, brought up in Asheboro, rural Warren County, and Raleigh—a lonely kid who was never an athlete but whose earliest hero was Tarzan. I met him at Duke his second year of teaching, my second as a student. Brought up in New York City and on Long Island, I had come down to Duke to get nearer a girl in Alabama, for a good scholarship, to play soccer and wrestle. And to write poetry, which had been my hidden work since sixth grade.

So now, in May, 1966, I am pulling up his driveway with a tape recorder on the engine box of the van, coming with a batch of questions I am going to ask and thinking I know what kind of answers I'll get. I began getting the answers when Reynolds, advising student writers, said he thought I should work more on my visualized writing, images which were hard and clear and blunt. He was not far from his own real beginnings as a writer. It was just the year before, 1958, that the English magazine Encounter *gave him his first publication by printing the long story, "A Chain of Love." The advising session was seven years ago, Reynolds was talking about poetry, and I was a stranger.*

I have to shift into first to get up the first slope of the drive. The rain has washed away much of the bluestone dumped last month. The drive crosses a small brook, turns in front of the low dark brick house and turns again to pass under the side carport into a gravel parking area. I park beside the Mercedes sedan which is disguised by a coating of red dust and oil from the dirt roads near the house. I haul out the recorder and go to the back door.

*"You almost hit my car," Reynolds yells coming out. (He **has had***

two wrecks in the past year, both in his own yard.) He is standing on a brick patio I engineered for him last summer. Behind him are the big plate-glass windows which make one wall of the living room and look out on the beech grove behind the house and the pasture beyond that.

Inside, the first thing I do is see what is new. I was here last week but there has to be a new picture, a Noh mask, a fossil, book, or lamp. Today it is a sun-bleached cow vertebra hung on the brick chimney wall. So before I even plug in the recorder I'm asking, "Where did the cow come from?"

"Let me finish the coffee before you start the interview, Buster," Reynolds says from the kitchen.

I go to the birch-paneled wall opposite the windows. There are twenty or thirty nicely framed pictures on this wall—the "new" things Reynolds has been collecting item by item since he was a student at Oxford in the mid-fifties. He spends almost everything he makes, even in today's relative affluence, buying what he likes. These pictures I'm looking at are mostly etchings—a series of three from Blake's Job, two of Rembrandt's Abraham and Isaac etchings, two Malliol nudes; then a drawing by Graham Sutherland, two Sidney Nolan illustrations from Price's story "Uncle Grant," a small oil by Philip Sutton, a large Picasso aquatint of a satyr unblanketing a sleeping nymph. I suppose it is a conservative collection—no pop art, no abstract expressionism. But it is not for the sake of prestige, for there are also the unknowns—an English girl's pencil drawing of an apple sprig, a small rather conventional eighteenth-century English landscape in oil, a watercolor of a sick child in bed (by Arthur Severn, son of Keats's Severn). There is nothing you could call topical or timely, only the television in one corner of the room, and this, I know, is well used—every night for news, often for documentaries and sometimes for the latest serial.

Reynolds comes in with the coffee tray and unloads the cups, sugar, cream, and a coffee cake while I get the recorder wired up.

When we sit down and I start the reels, we are laughing so hard I have to turn the machine off and drink some coffee. Then we start.

INTERVIEWER: When we first met in 1959 I was writing poetry and you were working on a short story that became your first novel. But you started in high school and college by writing poems, didn't you?

PRICE: To be accurate, the first things I wrote were plays. When I was in the eighth grade, I wrote a Christmas play about the Magi; and at some point I wrote a play called *The Jewels of Isabella* about Columbus and Queen Isabella of Spain and then a screenplay for an eight millimeter neighborhood version of the life of Bernadette Soubirous (never produced; funds unavailable). But yes, the first things that I wrote, thinking of myself as a writer, were poems, in the third year of high school in Raleigh, in the class of Phyllis Peacock. Looking back on those poems now—which I don't do nightly—the interesting thing about them—bad as they were—is that they were, almost all, poems about *people*; poems proceeding from my relations with people who held large places in my life—a girl named Jane Savage, another girl dying of leukemia, my parents, Marian Anderson, who first excited my interest in music. A great many novelists have tried to begin as poets; but if one looks back at those early poems, one generally finds tired Swinburnean lyrics.

INTERVIEWER: What made you give up writing poetry? Can you see some basic difference between the way you think and see now that makes you write prose instead of poetry?

PRICE: The chief reason was that I knew the poems weren't any good, as poems. I wrote poems on into the middle of my college career; but by that time I had read enough good poetry in classes in Elizabethan and seventeenth-century poetry, in Milton, Shakespeare, and in a most important class in modern poetry taught by Helen Bevington—Yeats and Eliot and Hopkins—to see very clearly that my own verses were pale and loose. Only when I began to write narrative prose—to order, on class assignment—and had written a quantity of prose, did I begin to feel that this was my *intended* work, this *was* my vocation; that verse could not be for me a means of examining my experience and controlling my experience, of understanding and controlling my life in the way that prose has become. I don't know why verse failed me—or I failed it. I often wonder; still try an occasional poem for a friend's birthday, say; and I've done a good deal of translation—Michelangelo, Hölderlin, Rimbaud. Perhaps because a novelist's gift is for structural and visual stamina, not verbal intensity.

INTERVIEWER: And there was that poem we wrote together one evening while you were doing A *Long and Happy Life*, the poem for Rosacoke's unborn child.

PRICE: That's right. It's on the shelf here.

INTERVIEWER: Read it. We might as well give it a first publication in this interview.

PRICE:

Reborn to light this day in late July
When blinded fields send up their cries for rain
As silent waves which break against the sky
Bleached blank of hope but what hope you may bring
(Who shuddered from your father's lonely joy
That autumn night when like a funeral ship
He shed you nameless to your mother's sea,
Which, opening, gave you passage through the dark
To where you were encrusted with her life
And stole the print and purpose of her years,
The beauty of her surface and, beneath,
The strength and movement of her secret tides).
We are the waves that break against your life,
In hope against the terror that we know.
The hope is that your living will be rain;
The terror, that your life is only blood
To dry like thousands under blinded fields.
But hope is like the love that caused your birth
And harbors in its heart the seed of death.
No life has yet achieved our general aim,
The circular continuance of rain.

INTERVIEWER: It's not as good as the book; but going back to your change from poetry to prose, did you deliberately turn to prose when poetry failed or was prose something that *came* and then you discovered you were good at it?

PRICE: I don't think there was any deliberate turning. The first story I wrote was in my freshman year of college at Duke University in the class of the late Philip Williams. It was an advanced class of freshman composition, and we were allowed to write anything we wanted for our weekly themes. Almost all my themes were narratives—little episodes (mostly invented) from the lives of people my own age at the time, eighteen or so, or of children—

which obviously was that time of life I knew best. The first piece of any consequence that I wrote was written in that class, a story which eventually was revised and became "Michael Egerton." At the same time I was writing those early prose pieces, I was continuing to write inadequate verses. But I didn't look upon the prose as an escape route from the bad verse. I don't think at that time I'd realized quite how bad the verse was because intelligent people were still telling me that the verse was good. I suppose on looking back at it now, one sees—hopes—that they weren't totally misled, that there was a certain fascination with language visible through all the echoes, archaisms, and general metaphoric fatigue. Auden said once that if a young man came to him and said he wished to be a poet and that if Auden read his verses and felt they were empty of thought but brilliant in language, he would feel that the man stood a chance of becoming a poet but that if the verse were tired and unimaginative in language but interesting in thought, there would be little chance of that man's maturing as a poet.

INTERVIEWER: So you began writing stories. Most reviewers now consider you as a Southern writer. What do you think your relationship is to the first generation of modern Southern novelists? People like Faulkner, Carson McCullers, Robert Penn Warren, Katherine Anne Porter, and Eudora Welty?

PRICE: I would say that my relation to all those names, except Eudora Welty, is a relationship of varied admiration and respect. But a distant relation. Those were not the people I was reading when I was young and formable. Those were not, and have not become, the people I have returned to and read continually at moments of curiosity and leisure in my life. Faulkner, of course, is a special and enormous case. All Southern writers who have written in the last twenty years have had to bear the burden of being called Faulknerian. But the truth, if anyone is interested, is this, certainly and simply: they write about the South, which is their home as well as Faulkner's. Reviewers who lament the "influence" of Faulkner are really only asking that all other Southern writers arrange to be born outside the South. It is a curse, of a sort, to be born a writer in the same region and at the same time as a great regional novelist. Imagine being born in southwest England in the lifetime of Thomas Hardy and trying to write your own novels about Wessex, the world that you also knew. You would have been cursed with being "influenced by Hardy" for the rest of your life, called that at least. I am serious in speaking of "a curse" only to the extent that the cry of Faulknerian influence has become a conditioned reflex among literary journalists, even serious critics; the application of influence labels being—as any college English major knows—the easiest way to (a) write your 3,000 words and (b) avoid at all costs *facing* a work of art, its new vision, its new and necessarily terrible way of stating the injunction of Rilke's Apollo: "You must change your life!" I can say, quite accurately, that Faulkner has been no influence, technical or otherwise, on my work. I admire the work of Faulkner that I know—by no means all—but with a cold, distant admiration for a genius whom I know to be grand but who has proved irrelevant to my own obsessions, my own ambitions. The writer in your list who did affect me greatly, and continues to do so, is Eudora Welty. I had read a few of her stories in high school. I remember especially that "A Worn Path" was in one of our high school anthologies, but it was in my senior year in college that I read her stories in quantity. They were an instantaneous revelation and a revelation about my life, not about literature nor the methods and techniques of fiction. They revealed to me what is most essential for any beginning novelist—which is that his world, the world he has known from birth, the world that has not seemed to him in any way extraordinary is, in fact, a perfectly possible world, base, subject for serious fiction. I recognized in those stories of Eudora Welty's which I read as a senior in college a great many of the features of the world I had known as a child in rural eastern North Carolina, and so I felt confirmed by her example in the validity of my own experience as a source of art. That was her great service to me, and I shall always be grateful to her for that service she rendered me unknowingly, but most deeply grateful for the fact that she came to Duke to give a lecture—"Place in Fiction"—in the second semester of my senior year and kindly asked to see some student writing. One of my stories (the only serious story that I had written, "Michael Egerton") was given to her by William Blackburn. She read it, encouraged me, offered to send the story to her agent, Diarmuid Russell, who has since been my agent, and championed my work in the early years when no one in America was interested in publishing it. What she offered me was what any young writer demands in varying ways at various times in his career—adequate judgment. I knew that she was a sound judge; and I knew it because she was judging my work as *art*, not as the product of a favorite student or a friend. Her mind was filled with the example of her own work and all the work she had seen and read in her life, and she was still able to say to me what was utterly valuable, utterly meaningful at that time—that my story was a good story. Not "This is the best story by a college senior which I have read in the past five years," but "This is an excellent *story*. Let me see the rest of your stories." I said truthfully that there were no other stories because to that time I had only written eight pages of fiction; but at her request I very rapidly went to work and began writing another story—"A Chain of Love." And in the next three years, the years of my study at Oxford, I produced about a hundred pages of short stories, all of which were later published in a volume called *The Names and Faces of Heroes*.

INTERVIEWER: What about the new Southern writers, your contemporaries like William Styron and Walker Percy, Fred Chappell and Shirley Ann Grau? Do you read these people conscientiously? Are you conscious of them as Southern writers?

PRICE: I read them because I think they are serious writers but very different writers. I feel no duty to read them because they are in any sense "fellow Southern novelists." I have never felt myself a "Southern novelist." I am a novelist—who was reared and has lived most of his life in the South. Insofar as the South is a unique world, my work reflects that uniqueness; but my work is not, has never been *about* the South. Some of the agrarians in the 20's, early 30's may have thought of themselves briefly as "Southern"; but I don't think it's been the feeling of anyone in the last twenty years, not any serious writer certainly. No, I read the writers you mentioned and two or three of them are friends of mine; but I don't feel that their work has any special relationship with my work. I don't feel any dialogue between my work and theirs, except that dialogue which exists between all honest artistry—a relationship not of imitation but of emulation. One reads good work and that good work invites not imitation but a parallel effort of quality.

INTERVIEWER: Why do you still live in the South? You often make trips away from it. What does the South offer you as a writer? Does it offer you something culturally or something more intangible?

PRICE: Because the South is my home. It is where I was born. It is where I spent the first twenty-two years of my life and where I've spent the rest of my life with the exception of four years in Europe. The South is a place; and that place has been the scene of most of the crucial events of my life, both external and internal. Therefore I remain in that part of the world which has been—and seems likely to be—the site of my life.

INTERVIEWER: Both your novels and the stories take place in the South, mainly in the area where you grew up. How close does the material in your fiction come to real people and real events? I guess what I'm asking is—to what degree are you a chronicler?

PRICE: Every character in the novels is invented; and even the stories which appear to be autobiographical are really a kind of historical fiction, a drastic arrangement, reinvention of memory. No, I have no sense of being a conscious chronicler—either of Southern life or of human life as I've known it in my lifetime, which has after all been an enormous time in human history (I was born in 1933). What I've chronicled is my own world, that world which has seemed to me (since I began to see at all) to exist *beneath* the world perceived by other people, that world which seems to me to impinge upon, to color, to shape, the daily world we inhabit.

INTERVIEWER: Are the events and people in A *Generous Man* the events and people of a real world? A lot of reviewers have called it a myth and some of them suggest that many of the characters, especially Milo, are more in the nature of symbol than people.

PRICE: A *Generous Man* is about a very real world, yes; but it is not a realistic novel. If I must catalogue it, perhaps I'd call it a romance. If A *Generous Man* has literary ancestors, those ancestors are not really to be found in the novel but in other forms. I was not conscious of this when I began *A Generous Man* nor, in fact, until I had completed the novel; but in all the literature known to me, *A Generous Man* resembles only—in kind, understand—the late plays of Shakespeare (*The Tempest, The Winter's Tale, Cymbeline*), certain operas (say, *The Magic Flute* of Mozart) in that it does negotiate with the "real world" which all human beings perceive, however dull, however bored, however fogged by routine, but a real world which is capable of swelling at moments of intensity to a mysterious, transfigured world, a world in which all manner of "unrealistic" events can and will occur —the return of the dead, outrageous coincidence, great rushes of communication between people, great avowals of love or hate— events of a sort that do not occur in any world which I've experienced with my own eyes and ears which I suspect, almost *know* to lie only slightly beneath the surface of the world of most men.

INTERVIEWER: I'm not trying to push this symbol business; but I can see why a lot of people find them, especially in *A Generous Man*. Because it's not a realistic novel, people feel free to translate its images and events as they wish. The other night a man told me it was difficult to talk to women about the book because of "the all-pervasive phallic symbol of the snake." Of course symbols do exist, in writing and nature. To what extent, if any, are you ever conscious of symbols in your work?

PRICE: I am never conscious of symbols when I am planning a story nor when I am writing it. Any sense that certain objects have become symbolic—such as the python in *A Generous Man*, or, say, the deer in *A Long and Happy Life*—comes to me, if at all, only after the story is done and the whole can be seen. Python and deer were, for me, first—and indeed finally—python and deer, *things* grander in their own mysterious life than I or my characters could ever make them by meditation. More nonsense—criminal nonsense because it is generally inflicted by teachers on their innocent trusting students—is talked about symbols now than about any other single aspect of fiction, even "influence." And most of the nonsense can be attributed to two causes: first, as with "influence," it is far easier to take a little greased-rail sidetrack round the edges of a work, felling a harmless symbol or two, than to plunge through rock to its terrible core—that small clearing in the jungle which may be empty of all but a polished mirror; and second, that there is now a great deal of confusion about what a symbol is, how a thing becomes a symbol and—perhaps most important—*when* a thing becomes a symbol, so much confusion that I almost never use the word myself, least of all when I teach, and would be much happier if it could be retired for ten years, say, and replaced by "emblem." It seems to me that this many true things should be said—and distributed to every college freshman upon arrival: a symbol is a thing (though occasionally an intangible thing—fire, air) which one or more men make imminent with emotional, even spiritual significance. There are two kinds of symbols, private and public. Public symbols have traditional agreed significance for large numbers of people—the cross, the sword, blind justice. A private symbol is a thing containing significance for one person, at most two or three—my father's gold watch there (on the desk) with the blackened dents which are in fact my own toothprints (he allowed me to use it for teething, thirty years ago). Public symbols have variant private meanings for most of us—the dove means more to me now than to you because my brother is in Vietnam. But anyone—artist or critic— who attempts to make a private symbol into a public symbol is almost always doomed to a failure of communication, occasionally ludicrous failure as in Wordsworth's famous address to Wilkinson's spade. Wilkinson was a friend of Wordsworth's, and Wilkinson's spade became for Wordsworth imbued with private power to symbolize both Wilkinson's rural virtues and Wordsworth's love of a loyal friend. The failure results from Wordsworth's inability to convey to an unknown reader the processes—visual and chronological—by which the spade (not suddenly but over a long period of time) became symbolic for the poet. Literature is strewn with nobler but equally incommunicative private symbols—Yeats's tower, Virginia Woolf's lighthouse; even Moby Dick for nine-tenths of the novel, until the whale *appears* and we ourselves see him at last as Melville and Ahab have seen him from the first. All the failures of symbolism—artistic and critical —spring from one great sin: failure to take the world seriously, to respect and revere the singular dignity of each created thing.

INTERVIEWER: It's this then that transfigures your characters, that makes them something more than the surface people we see on the street, in a bus queue, or in a supermarket?

PRICE: Yes. The characters of *A Generous Man*—of all my work—are men and women transfigured by possibility, by the intensity of their own passion, the intensity of their own need for destruction, for communication, order, for contact with the past and with the future.

INTERVIEWER: Does this transfiguration take place in your mind or is it external? That is to say, do you, the novelist, make it happen— transfiguring the characters for a purpose—or are you looking at the character and seeing him transfigured?

PRICE: I look at the character and see him become transfigured—as I look at you now and see you transfigured by our seven years' friendship, by all that I know of your gifts and needs and chances. This is always a difficult thing for a novelist to discuss—the degree to which characters create themselves—but in *A Generous Man* especially, I did feel the characters very much creating themselves as the story created itself from day to day; the characters demand- ing those actions—however outrageous, incredible, coincidental— which would express their passions, needs, potentials. Just as characters in *The Tempest* or in *The Winter's Tale*, as characters in *The Magic Flute*, as characters in Japanese Noh plays behave quite unrealistically and yet with a hyperrealism, with a truth which is beyond question. If one comes to *A Generous Man* ex- pecting it to be a novel like *A Long and Happy Life*—or *Studs Lonigan* or *A Farewell to Arms*—to be in that basically lyrical, realistic tone, then he's going to be baffled, disappointed, and angered. He's going to feel that I've consciously constructed a very artificial myth and an outrageous deck of inhuman symbols. But if he will consider *A Generous Man* as an independent work (though it does concern the same family as *A Long and Happy Life*), as an unrealistic work, which it in fact announces that it is on every page, then he can approach it as it must be ap- proached before it will yield. That sounds forbidding, doesn't it?

—and ridiculous. The book is first—and finally, perhaps—an entertainment. So is all art—the B-Minor Mass, the Sistine ceiling. No, I'm only hoping that *A Generous Man* can be seen for what I know it to be—a unique vision of certain valid, even urgent kinds of human experience, known till now by no one but me (because no one but me has lived my life).

INTERVIEWER: In *A Generous Man,* you have a ghost, Tommy Ryden. Is he supposed to exist only in Milo's head in the novel or is he an actual ghost?

PRICE: The book says quite clearly that what returns is a ghost, on page 200: "What came after, came in two places—in the room itself (bare of all but prone Milo and the kneeling man) and behind shut eyes in Milo's bloody head, a sleeping vision." So the curious stranger had both physical and spiritual reality, objective and subjective. What has interested me always about ghost stories—respectable, well-authenticated ghost stories—is that ghosts almost always appear in unexceptional corporeal form. That is, they do not appear as filmy, vaporous, emanations of light but have simply—and terribly—the opaque reality of a live person walking through a room or sitting in a chair. That is how Tom Ryden, who's been dead for years, appears to Milo; and like so many ghosts, seems not to know that he is indeed dead, useless, unwanted.

INTERVIEWER: You also introduce the supernatural into *The Names and Faces of Heroes.* Do you believe in the supernatural? And how can you create it if you don't really understand what it is?

PRICE: There are a great many things in the universe which we don't understand but make constant use of—electricity, the energy of the atom. We make use of our bodies every moment of our lives; and we certainly don't understand a tenth that there is to know about our eyes, our hearts, our kidneys. I suppose what you're referring to in *The Names and Faces of Heroes* would be that in the end of the title story, the child has a vision of the twelve years which wait between now and his father's death. And in *A Generous Man* there is the appearance to Milo of someone who has been dead for years, whom Milo had never seen in that person's earthly life. It's obviously difficult to discuss one's own relation to what you call the supernatural without sounding fishy in the extreme. I'd rather say this much and then pass on: that I do strongly suspect, even avow the existence and presence of forms of reality quite beyond those forms which we encounter in our daily routines. And whether or not those forms do manifest themselves—ever, in observable, sensually perceptive ways—certainly there can be no question that the dead linger, most powerfully, in our lives; the meaningful dead, those people who by the time most men have reached the age of twenty-one stand as one's ancestors on the black side of death in relation to our present continuing lives. That's all.

INTERVIEWER: Where do you think all this strange stuff belongs in the larger context of literature? You mentioned Shakespeare's *Tempest*, *The Winter's Tale*, and *Cymbeline*; and you mentioned Noh plays. What about your contemporaries and other twentieth-century writers? Where do you think the supernatural or at least the extranatural fits in?

PRICE: There's a long and continuing tradition of the supernatural, not only in the epic, the lyric, and poetic drama but in the novel itself. Very obviously, the novel before the late nineteenth century was not committed to realism. The novels of eighteenth-century England, the great Victorian novels—the Brontës, Dickens—are highly "unrealistic" visions of human existence. Dickens makes as profound and revealing and convincing use of the supernatural as Kafka. His coincidences alone are acts of God. And to mention Kafka is to mention the great modern student of the supernatural. I wouldn't claim that there are many serious novelists who are presently employing ghosts in their novels—there is a credible and necessary ghost in Agee's *A Death in the Family*, and there are the ghosts and demons in Isaac Singer—but I do claim that the supernatural in the form of ghosts is still a possible, occasionally a necessary component of a serious novelist's vision.

INTERVIEWER: Most of your work is quite serious fiction, yet in all of it there's a great deal of comedy. In fact, I believe *A Generous Man* started as an attempt at a comic novel. What role do you see comedy playing in your work?

PRICE: All my work is comic—not by conscious choice but because in attempting to embody the world that I've known, I have portrayed a comic world. Comedy is almost always a function of experience, a function of life. Even in the intensest moments of despair, pain, grief, wild bursts of laughter will insist upon rising and asserting themselves. And any literary form which abolishes or ignores the laughter at the heart of human life—even the laughter on the edges of human life—does so at the expense of its own truthfulness. Certain very large and important kinds of literary art have eliminated comedy, at least so far as we can see. For instance, with the possible exception of two or three scenes, there seem to be no elements of the comic in Greek tragedy. Laughter was simply postponed for plays which were comedies or for the satyr plays which were performed in cycle with the tragedies. But the fullest, therefore truest, most useful picture of human life is a picture which will necessarily and gladly contain much that is hilarious, mocking, and satyric—satyric in the oldest sense: a picture of satyrs, grinning, hairy, ithyphallic dancers, cruel (no indifferent) witnesses of man's only—partially—relevant existence.

INTERVIEWER: What about Pop Art and the Theater of the Absurd? A lot of people say that these forms reflect, more than other present forms, the absurdity of our time, its confusion and the extremes of modern life. Some reviewers seem to have this in mind when they imply that you, in writing about rural life in the South—in your part of the South—are out of touch or at least out of date.

PRICE: I know very little about Pop Art and the Theater of the Absurd. I strongly suspect that as terms they are meaningless. They are mere descriptions of fashions created by journalists, and like all such fashions are irrelevant, not only to the time but to whatever the history of that particular art may be. Pop Art and the Theater of the Absurd seem to me—on slim acquaintance—reflections of a pursuit of, an acceptance of chaos in life. I can think of no art of the past which has made such acceptance, which has collaborated willingly, almost hysterically with the chaos at the center of life; and I cannot imagine any future art, any enduring art which will make such collaboration. I don't think that my art does, my fiction. This perhaps is a reason why some of my work may be unfashionable, seem out of date. I hope though—in fact, I *know*—that there's something more important, more enduring, than fashion and the fads of journalists; and that is the attempt to seize territory from chaos, to clear and tend and fortify a circle in the forest, then to stage games there.

What I really think you're broaching is the matter of rural versus urban art. Rural art is unpopular in America because the centers of book reviewing in this country are urban. Most of the journals of book reviewing are manned by committed urbanites, large numbers of whom have a loudly declared aversion to non-urban life. But this again is simply an irrelevant taste, a peeve, a pet on the part of such reviewers. It has no relation whatever to matters of artistic importance, to the fact that there's a very serious question as to whether or not a totally urban novel is a possible literary form. It's fascinating, for instance, that the novels of Kafka—and at that perhaps only *The Trial*—are the only successful urban novels, novels which occur entirely within the confines of a city. And in many ways Kafka's city is a city of the mind, not a city on the map—not Prague, not Vienna. The great novels of the eighteenth and nineteenth centuries turned on the poles of city and country. One only has to mention Fielding, Dickens, Tolstoi, Turgenev, even Dostoevski, Proust to realize that their novels oscillate between visits to the city, visits to the country, visits which are not mere changes of backdrop for the sake of variety but which reflect profound needs of character and, in turn, shape character profoundly. It's a central dilemma of the novel now—the possibility of an entirely urban novel—and it's going to be fascinating to see what happens to the novel as novelists more and more originate in, live in and write about an entirely urban world, where every tree chokes beneath coats of soot. The possibility of producing anything other than a nightmare—about twentieth-century American cities, at least—is a dim possibility at best.

INTERVIEWER: Aren't you taking the view that rural life is intrinsically better than city life? If human beings are, in fact, social animals, then why can't we have great writing about city life? Especially modern city life in which technology has created ways of living together in great masses?

PRICE: Well, to answer very briefly an enormously complex question, I would say that the danger for the novelist in a forced preoccupation, an obsession, with city life is not that city life isn't a form of social activity which is obviously here for a good while yet but that city life is, by definition in an age of potential nuclear destruction, impermanent. It is literally easier to destroy the city of New York—to vaporize every brick—than to destroy any single human being within that city, for the simple reason that the human being with fair warning can take shelter but the city cannot. Therefore cities have acquired this *added* nightmarish quality of impermanence, of threat—not of threat to destroy but to *be destroyed,* of threat to fail the inhabitants. The countryside, however, has at least the advantage for the artist of permanence. It can provide for him the objects of meditation, in the presence of which the literally human qualities of his life can be understood, calmed, controlled, and shaped. The profoundest examination of this dilemma is Wordsworth's preface to the *Lyrical Ballads,* in which he has already sketched the entire problem and, more than sketched, developed it in great detail (a development which has survived Coleridge's famous but frail objections).

INTERVIEWER: This is going way out on a limb; but would you say that assuming an almost complete urbanization of society in the future, this urbanization could be the death of literature as we know it?

PRICE: It could be the death of the *novel* as we have known it—the urbanization of man combined with the mobility of man, the fact that man is becoming almost infinitely mobile, that even now one can travel from North Carolina to London in seven hours or less (which time will decrease rapidly with each decade). This fact surely means a lessening value in human life of roots, of literal rootedness in place, in land—or in asphalt—in an intimately known and long-experienced atmosphere. What the effect is going to be on the novelist is clearly incalculable. It's conceivable that we might again have a great upsurge of the poem at the expense of the more sustained novel; but this again is to play a fool's game, the game of speculation in matters of art—because art is made, all arts are made, by endlessly devious, resourceful individuals, not by groups of guessers. And it's hard to believe that a time will come when there will not be individual human beings who will need and wish to make from their own visions of their lives—and surrounding life—works of understanding and defense and control.

INTERVIEWER: Let me cover one more objection people have to your work. In reviewing all three books, some reviewers call you a gifted stylist and others say the prose is mannered or contorted. What's your side of it?

PRICE: What critics usually mean in calling a writer's prose "mannered" is that the manner is not their manner. The simplest reply is this: there is no law that forbids to my prose—or anyone else's—the degrees of rhythmic and syntactical complexity which go unchallenged in the verse of Pindar, Shakespeare, Milton, Hopkins. But the fullest reply would be an old one that has gone unbelieved: that the style is the *man*. If *style* means "consciously achieved beauty of diction" or "decoration," then I have never given a moment's attention to style. To be sure, I know that the language of most of my fiction is often complex and occasionally difficult; but the complexity and density are not appliqué, not conscious "effects." They are functions of the vision of one attentive man. They are my literally reflexive responses to a given moment in a story, a character's life. The voice of a story is the vision of a story. I never pause to think, "This is a Price story, therefore must sound like a Price story." I wouldn't want to suggest, though, that I never take conscious care of my language. Of course I do—enormous care but a care which is directed towards fidelity, not "beauty" or "manner"; fidelity to the complexity of experience, to the mystery and dignity of objects. I wouldn't suggest either that some prose (and verse) isn't too complex, too difficult (serious prose, I mean—not rapt purple ranting). There are obviously passages in *Lear* and *Samson Agonistes*, in the late sonnets of Hopkins, in Joyce and Faulkner and Virginia Woolf in which language buckles under the burden it strains to assume. Such failures can be richly instructive—they show us that certain forms of experience have so far not yielded to art; but they certainly do not warn us to shun the attempt. If anything, they urge us on. They affirm and promise that the *whole* truth will at least not yield to copybook sentences, to the clear-water flow of subject-predicate-direct object.

INTERVIEWER: It seems that throughout history, or in terms of our perspective today, when so many people are writing *about* literature, almost every writer can be shown to be intimately connected with his time, perhaps only in the way that you say—that he's making his literature out of his own life—but what about popular culture in your life? By popular culture, I mean things like comic books, hamburgers, automobiles, the fights, advertising, television, movies. How has all this influenced you as a person and as a writer, in a particularly twentieth-century sense?

PRICE: The popular culture that you're talking about is, again, pop culture, isn't it?—a phenomenon of the late 50's and the 60's. I shouldn't have thought that had influenced me at all, either as a human being or as an artist. All the manifestations you mention are simply things I drive past on the way to my work, occasionally stopping for a hamburger. I did, as a child in the 40's, read comic books, play war games, listen to the radio. I was a pretelevision child entirely, never seeing television until I was a college student; but the phenomenon of American culture, American *history* which influenced me most profoundly was all that we mean by the Depression. I was born at the very pit of the Depression, in the winter of 1933, to parents who had suffered great financial deprivation and therefore humiliation at the hands of the economy. I was an only child until I was eight years old, which is tantamount to being an only child; and I was therefore the sharer of my parents' lives, the confidant (whether they liked it or not) of all their fears and shames. So the Depression was for me, as it must have been for most children born in its shadow, the great initial terror, the great vision of possible tragedy and ruin. My fears and fantasies as a child were the fears and fantasies of David Copperfield or Oliver Twist—utter poverty, desolation, separation from one's parents, from one's home, from one's familiar surroundings because of the faceless interference of some quite uncontrollable force. *Destitution.* Not that we ever for a moment went hungry or went without adequate food and shelter but that as a child, reading the whispered worries and concerns of my parents in my own desperately hopeless child's way, I suspected the power of the nonhuman forces in life to deprive one of one's life. Last summer after my mother's death, for example, I was sorting out forty years of family papers and found cold confirmation of my darkest childhood suspicions—checkbooks with balances of eight dollars on payday, letters showing that in 1942 my father lost the only house we ever built because he could not borrow fifty dollars. *Fifty dollars.* Grayest shame, and I saw him wear it most of his life. The Depression was my generation's Civil War, the force which shaped and confirmed my earliest fears, demanded the building of my earliest defenses against the anonymous forces of ruin, humiliation before one's kin, in one's love. These, I suspect, are not the terrors of children born since, those whom I teach year after year in college. Their fears, and therefore their defenses, are quite different, as I suppose their art will be when they come to produce those defenses, statements, celebrations which will be their art.

INTERVIEWER: We've talked about popular culture, about Pop Art, Theater of the Absurd. What about modern music and art, excluding the most recent movements and the most recent fashions? Who moves you in music and art and theater today?

PRICE: Living artists, you mean?

INTERVIEWER: Well, say artists since the 20's or 30's. I suppose what I'm trying to say is, what modernists do you find interesting?

PRICE: I can't say honestly that I'm profoundly moved by any music written since 1920, since *Wozzeck* and the early work of Stravinsky. I'm not a student of contemporary music, however. There might be a great deal which moved me if I only knew of it. The music which I listen to continually—for at least an hour each day, if not longer—is essentially eighteenth and nineteenth century. The operas of Mozart and Verdi and Wagner, the symphonies and quartets of Beethoven, *Fidelio*. In painting, I'm deeply moved by—and I know that my own work has had a continuing, growing, and deepening relationship with—the work of Picasso. I have spent more time looking at Picasso drawings and etchings than in reading Hemingway and Faulkner. But again I feel the profoundest admiration for and communication with older painters—Vermeer, Rembrandt, Michelangelo.

INTERVIEWER: Isn't there part of A *Long and Happy Life* which can be said to be like a Vermeer? I think you compared it to a Vermeer at one time.

PRICE: One of the impetuses to my beginning A *Long and Happy*

Life—or beginning to create the book in my head long before I began to write it—was my first sight of a particular Vermeer in the summer of 1956 in The Hague. The painting permanently resides in the Rijksmuseum, but it was in The Hague that summer for a special Vermeer exhibition. It's a picture of a young woman in her early 20's, in a blue smock before that window of Vermeer's. She's reading a letter against the light. Behind her on the wall is a map, presumably of some distant place; and the woman appears to be, beneath the smock, pregnant. No comment, no explanation, only a picture. But I remember circling that picture in the gallery for long minutes, not at all sure why it held me so, and buying a reproduction of it and propping it on my work table when I returned to Oxford later that summer to work. It was almost two years before I began to think of and plan in great detail the novel which would be about a girl reading letters from a lover at a distant place and that girl pregnant with that lover's child. I'm sure, though, that Vermeer's image had worked in my mind for those two years upon questions and needs and knowledge of my own to produce the story which later became *A Long and Happy Life*. There are other pictures deeply embedded in *A Long and Happy Life*. One of them is the portrait of a young man by Botticelli which hangs in the National Gallery in London, a full embodiment of the sort of man I imagined Wesley to be in *A Long and Happy Life*.

INTERVIEWER: You have a lot of personal pictures around the house; in fact, in almost every room—in bedrooms, in the hallways, even in the bathrooms. Who are the people and why are they so ever-present? What part do they play in your life or in your work even?

PRICE: The pictures or the people?

INTERVIEWER: Both.

PRICE: The pictures are images of household gods, I suppose. Images of what I have loved and love and worship—worship in the sense of offering my life and work to them. The pictures are of members of my family—some of whom I never knew, who died before I was born—and of friends who have caused my life and my work. They are here, and here in such numbers, for the sake of my present and future work, not for the sake of nostalgia, not as souvenirs of a lifeless past. That is an aspect of my own work, as it is of almost every artist's work, which is little understood by people who are not themselves artists—the extent to which any work of art, especially verbal art, is a private communication between the artist and a small audience, often as small as one. If others look on with interest and pleasure—and curiously, artists must almost always make public their most private communications—then one is glad enough, one's ego is stroked, one purrs for a moment; but the others *are* others, not the cause, not the subject, not the object of the labor, the final gift.

And with this last answer as if to imitate a film or a story, the tape pulls loose from the starting reel, wraps itself on the other side. (It actually does!) The last answer has supplied a unifying vision of the relationship between a writer and his surroundings, at least here. You can look around this house at the pictures, the records, the furniture, the views and feel that what is here in the house is there in the work. If you will pardon the kitchen images, Price is like a funnel through which all memory and these material things travel; a funnel which is not only a straight-through narrowing tube but one which is also a blender, which transforms vast quantities of raw material into goblets of clear wine, filled to the brim and a fraction over the brim.

"*Did you ever think of yourself as a wine-making funnel?*" *I ask.*
"*Enamel or tin?*" *he says.*

II

This ought to be a bad time to continue an interview. Of Reynolds' last two books, A Generous Man *is remaindered in first edition at the local store and* Love and Work *got a lot of hostile reviews. Reynolds, however, is satisfied with the work he did on those books, and that ability to survive on his own satisfaction is probably what keeps him working steadily and steering a course that has great integrity. Writers who dry up or who pause to write the formula best seller probably cannot sustain their work on the strength of their own judgments.*

So here we go again: same house and setting, only four more years' collection of pictures and objects. The basement now has a wall full of American Indians. On end tables and coffee tables are new tech-

*nological toys—a kaleidoscope, a magic egg of steel, and moulage for
making life masks (Reynolds calls them death masks).*

INTERVIEWER: *Love and Work* has appeared since the first part of this
conversation. There were no Mustians in it, and some readers said
that this was you launching into an entirely new kind of writing
while some said it was you examining yourself via a main character who is also a writer and a teacher. To what degree is either
of these propositions valid?

PRICE: Both are valid and invalid. *Love and Work* did constitute a
violent break with a number of the procedures of my earlier
work—at least, a number of readers found it a very baffling
change of signal. But the closing down of one's parental family
and home (by death) *is* a violent break with the past: the only
possible death of childhood. That implies autobiography, right?
Well, the novel was begun about a year after my mother's death
and the closing of our family home (in which I hadn't lived for
fifteen years) and it does contain some of the actual materials of
that experience; but I'm being accurate, not coy, in saying that,
though I could confabulate, I couldn't *truthfully* tell you what
"happened" and what didn't. *You* probably know better than I.
But it isn't anyone else's legitimate concern, not while I'm alive
anyhow. I've offered the book as an organism quite independent
of my life, perfectly ambulatory. If anyone wants to deal with the
book, it exists, and seems to me the strongest thing I'd done till
then. One more word though—while *Love and Work* may at first
look radically disconnected from my earlier work, it isn't. It isn't
set in the South, admitted (the places in it are houses, literal
real estate, not towns or counties), and the central figure is a
reasonably well-informed novelist and university teacher; but the
central obsessions of the book *are* continuous with the early
books, thought—I hope—in changed and developed forms. Which
is to say that I hope *I'm* changed and have developed—toward
what? Lucidity, of sight and statement.

INTERVIEWER: How much of all that did you know when you set out
to write *Love and Work?*

PRICE: Impossible to say (in any truthful or usable form), impossible to retrack any impulse to its extremely multiplex—and always mysterious—beginnings. I'm sorry if that sounds oracular. But it's accurate.

INTERVIEWER: I don't mean to try to box you in with a hot new genre, but—returning to *Love and Work*—would you say that it was in any way a nonfiction novel? Or maybe I ought to ask if you think the nonfiction novel exists or maybe if it has always existed?

PRICE: Yes, in a way it is. But so were *A Long and Happy Life* and *A Generous Man* though in all three cases more than 99 percent of the characters were invented from the ground up. So are most good novels surely—*Bovary, c'est moi*. In that sense, surely, serious *fiction* doesn't exist.

INTERVIEWER: You don't like grand schemes and you're not overtly ambitious in any material sense, but you are also the kind of man who makes sure you have insurance and a solid savings account; so have you in any way thought about the direction of your career; have you stored up any kind of literary or creative savings account?

PRICE: Oh I do like grand schemes (the writers I admire most are the grandest available—Tolstoi, Milton). And of course I do think a great deal about the course of my work, because it is to a large extent the course of my life. In another month I should, with any luck, have finished a second volume of short stories—this one called, I think, *Permanent Errors* (because they are all concerned with that—mistakes that cannot be rectified). And these stories again seem to me a break with, or advance on, past work (*Love and Work* included), though there a number of different kinds of pieces in the volume—from what, for want of a satisfactory name, I call personal elegies to recognizable "short stories" to, for me, a new kind of hectic first-person narrative (in no case is the first person "me"). After that, if I live intact and work goes on surfacing in my head, I hope to begin a fourth novel. I have clear ideas for it; I can feel it, in the night, cohering, coalescing—it has been for years now. And it begins to feel—to use your word—"grand"; but nothing would be worse than to talk about it now.

INTERVIEWER: It makes me feel good, thinking you are six years older and grayer than me; so let me put one of the "old man" questions to you. Looking back, do you think now that you would be writing anything you haven't written if you could do it over?

PRICE: Well, works of blinding genius. No, lucid genius. But maybe they are that. Nice to think so, one day a year at least. My birthday's this Sunday, age thirty-seven—I'll try to think it then. No, without meaning to sound sleek and self-adoring, I can't think of anything I've published since 1958 that I wouldn't stand by today (which is not to say that I would *write* it, in that way, today). And there are no great wrecked ambitions back there either, beyond the universal ones—that one wants to be better, as a man, more useful, funnier, wiser, happier. Also as a writer. But mightn't that follow? No—Beethoven, Wagner. Though I think a lot of Milton—old, blind, all but bankrupt, every political hope defeated, his work by no means popular—dependent on a third wife—swinging in his garden and singing in his gout-fits: a better man and a better poet. *Samson Agonistes.* Give me time, though. The Prices have been short-lived enough as it is.

INTERVIEWER: Since the first part of our conversation, I've occasionally thought about your insistence that writers need to see man in the presence of the natural world. Do you think there is going to be any really new sense of relationship between man and nature in the next ten, fifty, or a hundred years? I'm asking this, knowing you've been reading men like Konrad Lorenz and a lot of astronomy and following the astronauts to the moon.

PRICE: Just in the four years since we talked this out before, conservation's hour has struck, hasn't it? Just *this* year, in fact. So maybe "man and nature" will be getting along a little better ten years, twenty years from now—though if man doesn't rapidly stop making other little men, reclamation of nature is going to be literally impossible. When will population's hour strike? I look around at my university colleagues: station wagon–loads of babies. Lovely babies, some of them, but intended essentially as toys, something-to-do for tired couples. Hasn't it ever crossed their minds that the population explosion means *them?* Well, rant, rant—no, to return to your question, I can't imagine any better or closer relations between man and the natural world, the planet, in the next fifty years, say. Only deeper, longer nightmares—

filth, crammed space, *all* waters fouled. There are whole moments when one wonders if some sort of nuclear Armageddon isn't positively desirable—or won't be within the next twenty years. I mean, really, how else do you rectify an error like New York City? And wouldn't it be healthy to have a good poet around saying things like that?—a better Robinson Jeffers; is there one? So far as I understand anything, the two major hopes seem very long-term indeed—first, some sort of genetic reengineering of human folly and secondly, space. The out-there. Both very scary but at least *serious* hopes. It's appalling—isn't it?—that schoolchildren aren't given some basic grounding in elementary astronomy, cosmology. I've taught dozens of university seniors who hadn't the vaguest notion of what a galaxy was or that we belong to one. We should all have the image of Andromeda, say, tattooed on our retinas. For cheer, if not hope—that there's something that lovely. Unreachable, no doubt (or is it?) but *there* and free and eminently usable—for contemplation, calm, exercises in proportion. I'm using it now.

INTERVIEWER: How?

PRICE: Well, I point out that I'm *smiling*. Name three others who are.

Down Home:
❧ WILLIE MORRIS

Interviewed by JOHN CARR

Since Willie Morris' first book, North Toward Home (1967) *is an autobiography, the reader will not only be amply rewarded in a number of ways by the book, but will learn the bare facts (and much, much more) there. Willie Morris was born in 1935 in Yazoo City, Mississippi, graduated from Yazoo City High and the University of Texas, and was a Rhodes Scholar. Later, he was made editor of* Harper's *and then resigned in the early spring of 1971. That conflict of wills has been reported on elsewhere, and Larry L. King, a contributing editor, who also resigned, gives his version elsewhere in this book. Morris maintains a polite but indifferent silence about something that was, however, a painful experience. In 1971 he published a second book,* Yazoo, *about the integration of the schools there. When I met him for an interview in a Chinese restaurant not far from* Harper's *in April, 1970, he had just returned from Yazoo.*

INTERVIEWER: First of all, how did you have the guts to publish an autobiography at the age of thirty-three, thirty-four?

MORRIS: When I started working on *North Toward Home*, I guess I was twenty-nine or thirty years old and I started it as a novel. But when I got pretty much into it, I discovered I was writing an intensely autobiographical book and that I wasn't even changing many of the names and addresses. And after awhile, having gotten into the book, I decided that, at least for this book, I was in the wrong form. I was trying to tell about it as it really was, not attempting to write fiction, finally. I realized that this might seem a rather presumptuous act on the part of a thirty-year-old man, to write the story of his own life, but this ignores the fact that the autobiographical form is a very sturdy form in American letters. I was enormously influenced by a book of Mark Twain's called *Roughing It*. I think it was his second book. It was an autobiographical work. It begins with him going out to the Western territories for the first time right after the Civil War.

So I decided to take a great big gamble and I knew that a lot of people would call me a son of a bitch, thinking that I considered myself so important that I could indulge myself in this form. But I did it, and I'm glad I did it. And I consciously drew on the resources of the novel for this book. I wanted to structure the book as if it were a novel, but to make it true to my own life. When I decided to make this book an autobiography, I didn't do it because I thought I was important, because I didn't, but I did feel quite strongly that I had a story to tell about myself that would be a reflection of many of the realities of my generation, especially, but not exclusively, my generation of Southerners. And in using this nonfiction form, I thought I could tell a lot about this generation, about growing up in the 1940's in a small town in the South, coming to maturity as a member of the so-called Silent Generation of the 1950's, moving around the South a lot, and into Texas and the Southwest, and, as with so many of our contemporaries, eventually coming as a relatively young person to New York City.

INTERVIEWER: The thing about the so-called Silent Generation that interests me—and there has been a lot of criticism of your generation—is how you feel yall have done as opposed to the performance of the Angry Generation, of which I am an aging member?

MORRIS: I think that all labels on generations are largely fashionable, kind of Madison Avenue things. I think they often obscure larger truths about people growing up. It's ironic that in the 1950's . . . I'm now thirty-five years old, I went to the University of Texas from Yazoo City at the age of seventeen—this was in 1952—that whole group of students who were in school during the Eisenhower years was castigated by their elders for allegedly not believing in anything, for being interested only in security and getting married at the age of twenty-one and having a split-level house and a white wife and two kids and a good insurance policy. And now this generation of students in the late 60's and early

70's is being castigated by the fashion mongers for talking too much, so you can't win.

INTERVIEWER: I was really struck by the great bunch of characters in *North Toward Home*. Everybody from Lyndon Johnson to an itinerant female Nazi, but I especially liked—and this is to our point—the Texas baseball players you were around some of the time in college. I was at Ole Miss from 1960 to 1965, and it seemed to me at times that the whole student body was like that. Those baseball players represented to me the spirit of the generation of the 50's. They were outraged that you were going to run for editor, terribly outraged. You were going to do something constructive, and they hated it.

MORRIS: I picked up a lot of my good material from them. A lot of people didn't believe that I was being factual when I described the night before the big baseball game between the Texas Longhorns and Texas A & M, which was being played at that beautiful old baseball field in Austin they tore up and made a part of the mall leading to the Lyndon Johnson Library, called "The Mosque" by everybody in Austin. The night before the game this boy, who was a right-handed pitcher, he was going to pitch against the Aggies the next day, took out this waitress from the Snack Shack restaurant and made love to her on the pitcher's mound while we were all hiding in the Johnson grass under the bleachers. The next day he got clobbered in the fourth inning—I don't know if it was symbolic or not. But there we all were, watching from under the bleachers.

INTERVIEWER: You went to the University of Texas when you were seventeen. From what's in the book, your father picked this out as a great place for you to be and alerted you that that's where you were going.

MORRIS: Well, my daddy was . . . I've thought a lot about that. I went back to Mississippi a couple of weeks ago and I was thinking a lot about that. My father was from Tennessee. He's dead now, been dead for about twelve years, and he never had much of an education and came to Yazoo City, Mississippi, to run the Cities Service station there on Main Street. It's no longer Cities Service, it's now Humble Oil Company. He worked later as a bookkeeper for Goyer Wholesale Grocers. When I was seventeen years old, I was deeply in love with this blonde majorette from a plantation out there in the country, and I wanted to go to Ole Miss. I wanted to play baseball at Ole Miss, and I had visions of coming back and marrying the belle from the plantation and spending the rest of my life lazing around on the banks of the Yazoo River and fighting the NAACP and the rest of it. And all of a sudden one day—it was about three days before I was supposed to graduate from high school—my father was sitting in the front room reading the *Commercial Appeal* and looked up and said "You ought to get the hell out of Mississippi." He'd never talked like this before, and I was a little astonished. Then he told me that there wasn't any economic opportunity for me there in Yazoo City or in Mississippi. Most of the boys in my group who would go to Ole Miss and continue to live in Mississippi had fathers who could pass on businesses or plantations or something to them, and he didn't have anything he could pass on to me, he said, but he wanted to make sure I got a good education. And then he started talking about the University of Texas. Neither one of us knew much about the University of Texas, but my daddy knew it was the biggest state university in the South, and he knew it had the best baseball coach in the country at the time. He said, "I think I'm going out there and look at that place for you and see what I think of it." I said "Fine." He took a Southern Trailways bus out to Austin by himself and spent a week on the campus. I remember I ran into him in the Edwards House in Jackson—I was over in Jackson for a baseball game and I ran into him in the lobby. He'd just gotten back from Austin and he said, "That's the goddamndest thing you ever saw. They have a main building that's over thirty stories high and they have a baseball field that's just cut out of rock, and they have a student newspaper put out by the students that's bigger than the *Yazoo Herald* that comes out only once a week, and the student newspaper in Austin comes out every day." He said, "You've got to go to school out there. There's not a school in this state to compare with it." Well, such is the substance of one's decisions at that age, and I'm glad I did. I was constantly going back and forth between Texas and Mississippi, but always staying within a Southern context. They are both Southern states.

INTERVIEWER: Do you think Texas is Southern?

MORRIS: Texas is flavored by the Western frontier, but a large portion of Texas is quite Southern, and in the South, I don't think there are any two greater extremes than Texas and Mississippi. Texas was wide open. And a lot of us young writers down there, young writers and young journalists, sort of gravitated towards politics. You'll find in these younger Texas writers today a great interest, indeed, sometimes almost an obsession with politics.

INTERVIEWER: You worked at Frank Dobie's *Texas Observer*.

MORRIS: Yeah, I was editor of the *Texas Observer* for about three years.

INTERVIEWER: Although it was essentially a newspaper, it was like a little magazine in that it had a select audience, wasn't it?

MORRIS: Well, the *Observer* never had a circulation of more than 7,500, but it certainly was a select readership. It was read by everybody in Texas interested in politics and literature. When Lyndon Johnson was Vice President, and later as President, he would read the *Texas Observer*, every word, and underline it in red ink. Sam Rayburn read it all the time. I remember the scenes in the Texas Legislature: we'd come out with the *Observer* on Thursday, and when the Texas Legislature was in session, you'd go around on Thursday afternoon and literally everybody in the legislature would be reading the *Texas Observer*. Of course most of them disagreed with it, but they read it religiously anyway. My friend Bob Eckhart, who's now the congressman from Houston, once looked at the state capitol off in the distance on a soft spring evening and he said, "Look at that beautiful state capitol. It was built for giants, and it's inhabited by pygmies."

INTERVIEWER: There's a great scene in your book describing the last day of the legislature, when they're all sitting there with their secretaries and / or girl friends waiting for it to break up. Everybody has a silly hat on and they're having a helluva time.

MORRIS: They had on these leis, and that was the night they had the first fight in the chambers. They were trying to pass a tax bill and they had to adjourn by midnight. And, as often happens in the legislatures, they kept moving the clock back up. It got along to about two o'clock in the morning and violence just completely erupted on the floor. Somebody pulled the cord for the amplification system out of the wall and there were several fist fights. I certainly learned from Texas politics and from the institution of the Texas legislature that the old parliamentary forms are very tenuous indeed.

INTERVIEWER: There's a section in your book where you detail jumping out of the bushes when you were very young and hitting a black kid. Can anybody ever get away from the racist thought pattern that's stamped on you if you grow in Mississippi or other Southern states? The country, I think, is basically racist, but in Mississippi racism has been institutionalized.

MORRIS: I don't think you can. . . . It's in your bones, in your blood, in the whole atmosphere of the place. No matter how "liberated" you might think you have become in later years, those old ingrained patterns will always be with you. And I think, without wishing to sound in the least bit self-righteous, I think it is a mark of civilization in a human being to come out of the sort of place we did and to fight hard within yourself against these almost glandular reactions to other human beings. In the case of that little black boy that I knocked down, I guess I was about ten years old, I was hiding in the bushes, and I saw him walking up the street with his sister. It was something I just had to do. I couldn't control myself. I grew up in a little town in Mississippi circa 1945 and the black people were just . . . You were taught this by your elders and by the whole structure of the town itself. You could do anything to them you wanted to, so I knocked down that little Negro boy. I felt very excited about it. Later I felt quite ashamed. . . . But now I've been back in Yazoo City just this month to see Yazoo City going through what really amounts to a social revolution, that is, the integration of the schools there in the wake of the Supreme Court decision of last October, and it's as close a thing as we've had to a social revolution in this country in a couple of generations. Yazoo City, Mississippi, has integrated its schools—and this is massive integration. And my friend Hodding Carter, Hodding III, was talking to me about all this over some martinis in the Old South Tea Room in Vicksburg. We started off with Rebel on the Rocks and we went to martinis. They also had a drink called a Yazoo Wazoo, made out of rum. A distinctly Southern drink. Hodding said, "It's ironic that Mississippi, which in racial matters has quite obviously been the most recalcitrant of all the states in the Union, is the state that in the wake of the latest Supreme Court decision is bearing the full brunt of the logical extension of the 1954 Brown case." And now the high school is more than 50 percent black. The junior high school for the whole town, in the building that formerly housed the Negro high school, is more than 60 percent black. The grade schools have an even higher proportion of Negroes. And this is a revolution. Sometimes I wish that I could go back to Yacoo City, Mississippi, a hundred years from now, after . . . When I was down there, the Yazoo *Herald* had on its front page a picture of the first child born in 1970, and he got a prize from the merchants. I can't remember the kid's name. Once that kid is dead, say eighty or a hundred years from now, I'd love to go back down there and see how the races are getting along.

INTERVIEWER: Things don't change much, do they? It seems to me that the white people are running away. They're sending their kids to crummy little academies in the basements of Baptist churches, or even to ones with grander physical plants, none of which will ever be accredited.

MORRIS: I would also like to see what the situation would be in a place like Yazoo City or Greenville ten years from now. Will these crummy little private schools collapse? Or will a lot of the white parents decide to send their kids back to the public schools? I think *that* might be a trend that will set in, say, three or four years from now.

INTERVIEWER: When those seniors try to get in Ole Miss, or other places.

MORRIS: Yes.

INTERVIEWER: Unless Ole Miss chickens out and takes graduates of unaccredited schools and loses its accreditation itself. Another thing that has bugged me for a while, and I can't find any real answer to this question, is why have we produced so many writers in Mississippi?

MORRIS: Well, you can say that about the whole South, not just

Mississippi. When I was going to school at Oxford University, I had to pick up Robert Frost once. He was giving a lecture in Rhodes House and I was to take him over to the lecture. We were in a fancy limousine and Frost turned to me and said, "Where are you from, boy?" and I said, "I'm from Mississippi," and he said, "That's the worst state in the Union." And I said, "Well, it might have its drawbacks, but Mississippi has produced a lot of good writers." And he said, "Well, can anybody down there read them?" I once told that story at a cocktail party there in Oxford to Allen Tate. Allen Tate was standing next to David Cecil and—I never will forget this—I told that story about Frost, and Allen's features lit up and he turned to Lord David Cecil and said, "David, I told you. That's why the South has produced such a great literature." I think, to state the obvious, that the whole tradition of telling stories that we all grow up with as Southern boys certainly is a tradition that you don't find anywhere else in this culture. You grow up with words. I took a Northern young lady down to Mississippi for two or three days. She came down when I was looking at the school situation and she came back tremendously impressed by the facility that Southerners have with words. The way the language is used, even in the most casual way. The whole emphasis on the telling of tales. So you grow up with this in a small town in the South, and it's bound to have some effect. And the people who teach you in school, even when they're second-rate, quite often have a facility with words that in the course of things you probably wouldn't find to such a marked degree in, say, a high school in the Bronx.

INTERVIEWER: Right.

MORRIS: And if you want to be really sociological about it—and I suppose this is a quality that is vanishing—I think that the really great Southern writers of the last two or three generations, and we've had some good ones, have been in a position in America that you might compare with the Russians of the nineteenth century, who were a part of Europe, of the European intellectual tradition, and yet living there in Russia, which was kind of a backwater. They were both a part of it and out of it. And you take the case of a man like Faulkner who stayed there in Mississippi, bless his soul, and was able to write about what was happening to our civilization, the rampant industrialization and the rest, as a Southerner, because he never really left. The corpus of his work was largely a map of Yoknapatawpha County but it was also, as we all know, much more than a map of Yoknapatawpha County. What happens, of course, in small towns in America . . . I suppose this is also vanishing, but when you write a book in which you draw on a place that is really identifiable—and this is not just Southern, this is quite American—they hate your guts for about twenty years, and then they name a street after you. I was up in Minnesota about three or four months ago and had to go to a hunting lodge for a business meeting in northern Minnesota. I was driving back to Minneapolis with this executive on the Minneapolis paper and I noticed a sign saying "Sauk Center, 10 miles." That's Sinclair Lewis' home town, and I told my friend I had to see the Main Street of Sauk Center—and of course they had pilloried Sinclair Lewis in Sauk Center. They had pounded him and had hated his guts. Well, you drive into Sauk Center today on that big federal artery and there's a green sign about twenty-five yards long that says "Sinclair Lewis Boulevard, next turn." You get on Sinclair Lewis Boulevard and you drive about another mile and you get to Main Street, and it's not just Main Street, there's another big-assed sign, a green sign that says "The *Original* Main Street."

INTERVIEWER: If he were only alive at this hour . . .

MORRIS: Yes, he would appreciate that.

INTERVIEWER: Speaking of somebody else who should be alive at this hour, didn't you see Richard Wright in Paris?

MORRIS: Yes, I had a number of drinks with Richard Wright in Paris in the fall of 1967. I was a student in England, and I'd been to Spain. . . . I was reading a lot of his work and found out that for a time he had lived in Yazoo County, Mississippi. His father was a sharecropper. And I knew he lived in Paris, so when I got to Paris, I got his number at the *Herald-Tribune* and I just called him up and told him my name and I said, "I'm a student in England and a white boy from Yazoo, Mississippi. I've been reading your works and wondered if I could buy you a drink." Wright said, "You're from Yazoo? Come on over." We went out to this Arab bar and got rather drunk together. I have since met a number of people, a number of writers, who knew Richard Wright during this period. It was only about two years before he died. They said he was extremely bitter personally and that a number of them were trying to get him to come back to America. "Dick, come back to America where you belong. Write about it." And he wouldn't. I didn't detect much of that personal bitterness that evening. He was . . . We sat around and told stories and I said, "Will you ever come back to America?" and he said, "No." And I said, "Why?" and he said, "Because I want my children to grow up as human beings." I wish Richard Wright had come back to America. I think it hurt him as a writer. I don't think one could say that Richard Wright was any towering literary figure. I don't think he compares with Ralph Ellison, just on the basis of Ellison's one novel, *Invisible Man*. I think Richard Wright was kind of a trailblazer for black writers, but I don't think he compared with Ellison as a man of literary sensibility, and I do think that it hurt Richard Wright as a writer to remain away from his sources, this crazy country.

INTERVIEWER: Richard Wright was politically committed, too. Do you think it hurt his writing?

MORRIS: Well, I think too much commitment hurts any writer.

INTERVIEWER: Do you?

MORRIS: Yes.

INTERVIEWER: What about—

MORRIS: Formal political commitment, let's put it that way.

INTERVIEWER: Why is politics the second most popular indoor sport in Mississippi when we don't even have a viable party system?

MORRIS: Because in the South, and I think this is part of our history as a people, politics has always been a great sport and a forum for human entertainment. That's been one of our troubles. But it was a great experience for a young man interested in writing to have the experience I had in Texas. Getting to know politics at a level where it was so visible. In intense personal ways, this kind of experience would, I think, discourage a young writer or a young journalist from the broader generalities. And it was really quite a remarkable experience to see the ways politics really worked in the back rooms and see old reactionary politicians getting drunk with the good liberal politicians, and how the liberals kind of liked the conservatives and how the conservatives kind of liked the liberals. I found also that my best sources, running a paper like the *Texas Observer*, were the old conservative politicians, because they liked to rat on each other.

INTERVIEWER: There was more intramural fighting among them than the liberals?

MORRIS: There is a kind of political myth that a bunch of conservative politicians in the provinces are a monolithic group, but I have found that there is enough intrigue among these people to make the court of the Sun King look like *Our Town*.

INTERVIEWER: When were you in England?

MORRIS: I went to England after I graduated from the University of Texas.

INTERVIEWER: You were a Rhodes scholar.

MORRIS: And then I came back, to the *Observer*.

INTERVIEWER: You've never been able to write about England, though.

MORRIS: I couldn't do it. I tried. A lot of people criticized my book because I didn't tell a lot about my experiences in England, but I really tried and I couldn't do it. I didn't know what it was, but I finally decided I don't think I'll ever really understand that strange four years I spent in England until I'm a little older.

INTERVIEWER: You were there four years?

MORRIS: Four years. Yeah, I broke all records. I was the first Rhodes scholar to be married and still draw my money.

INTERVIEWER: Did they know that?

MORRIS: That took a little politics. Cause they had that old celibacy clause. But England was a strange time for me. Sometimes I think the only contribution I made to English intellectual life in four years was when somebody tried to get me out of bed to go to an 8 A.M. lecture. It had been raining for four solid months, this little sly English drizzle which will drive you crazy. You'd have these beautiful sunsets late in the morning in December. This fellow was trying to get me out of a deep sleep to go to this eight o'clock lecture and I am reputed to have said: "Oh to be in April now that England's here." That was my only contribution to Oxford University.

INTERVIEWER: Then you came to New York from Texas, as we've all read about. How was your progress upwards at *Harper's*? Was it infighting or merit or just good luck or what?

MORRIS: I only sold out about 49 percent. I had a margin of 1 percent. I didn't sell out completely . . . . No, seriously, I had a terrible time getting adjusted to this fantastic city. I hated it for three years, but I got to know some of the best writers and journalists of our day and I tried to get some of them to start writing for this magazine, which is the oldest magazine in America.

INTERVIEWER: You know a good many Southern writers now. What happens to them after they leave the home ground? Faulkner stayed on the home ground. But Styron, for instance, lives in Connecticut.

MORRIS: Styron lives in Roxbury. Robert Penn Warren lives in Connecticut. . . . I'm a little of a mixed mind about this. I think that all writers have this particular problem, but it's more haunting in the Southern boys. They have to carry the burden of memory, which is a very heavy burden to bear. You know, a man's past and his experiences are, if he's a sensitive person, inside him, so that he can never lose them. I think it's very important for a writer—and we're talking about Southern writers, a person who considers himself to be a Southerner and a writer —to keep in very close touch with our home. I believe in going back home as frequently as possible. But I've also found it to be my own experience—and this just might be an expression of this particular period in my life—that I'm not so sure I'd want to live in the South twelve months out of the year. I find there is a certain exhilaration . . . that it is indeed a liberating thing to be obsessed with the South, which you certainly have in your bones. You love it and you hate it. You remember Faulkner writing at the end of *Absalom, Absalom!* that Shreve asked Quentin Compson in the dormitory room at Harvard "Now I want you to tell me just one thing more. Why do you hate the South?" and Quentin saying he didn't and thinking, *"I don't. I don't! I don't hate it! I don't hate it!"* At least, all of that has been my experience, and I think it's been Styron's and Vann Woodward's, and I consider Vann Woodward an artist. He's the greatest of the American historians. These people don't have to live in the South the year around to care for it intensely and write about it.

INTERVIEWER: Isn't it true that we have a myth that is different from the American myth? We have a Southern myth of poverty, defeat, ignorance, and . . .

MORRIS: Well, I think the testament of the Southern intellectual is not Cash's *Mind of the South*, but C. Vann Woodward's *Burden of Southern History*. It's a magnificent book, and I know it's certainly been read by younger Southerners, and I learned a lot from that book.

INTERVIEWER: He mentioned in a talk I heard him deliver at Raleigh in the spring of 1968 that the South is the only country which has a history of defeat, which puts us at a point of sophistication many times removed from, say, the Americans in the Midwest, who have always been taught, "You live in the heartland of a great country which has never been defeated, socially, politically, or militarily."

MORRIS: I think that's true. I think that this is a strong point in Woodward's position. I think it's an easy thing to exaggerate, too. After all, people like you and I—you're twenty-eight and I'm thirty-five—we're several generations removed from that particular defeat even though we were brought up with it. But I agree with Woodward's broader statement about the South's being the only region in America which has experienced defeat, not just military defeat, but the defeat of the very soul. The anguish and the blood guilt have certainly removed us from those Chamber of Commerce, Rotary Club American norms of progress and from the belief that Americans can never experience any kind of defeat, military or spiritual or otherwise. I think that these memories and traditions from our past as a people helped to form us a more distinctive people in this country. Now the black man in the South today does not harbor any connections with defeat in the Civil War, I wouldn't think.

INTERVIEWER: No, just defeat in his life, from cradle to grave.

MORRIS: You remember this marvelous phrase in Vann Woodward, and

I'm paraphrasing it now, but he said the largest, most incorrigible, and (with the exception of the Red Indian) the oldest and most indigenous of the great American minorities are the Southern whites and their contemporaries, the Southern Negroes. And on this trip of mine to Mississippi, I found that things had changed enormously in just a very little while. In recent years, the Southern black man, especially in Mississippi—I saw this—the activist black leaders want to stay in Mississippi. They feel the action is there, that they want to remain there. Of course, you've had a steady exodus out of places like Mississippi ever since World War I to the Chicagos, the Washingtons, the Harlems, and the Detroits. And they have found, as Ralph Ellison describes it, once they get to these rabbit warrens of the North, a mazelike existence where the promise of liberation in the North was not being fulfilled. And I think that for a place like Mississippi, this is a remarkable change. I think it augurs well in the long run for the kind of place that Mississippi could become. After all, Mississippi is 43 percent black. And in some of the areas we know best, it's 80 percent black. As people were telling me in Yazoo City, we've got to live together; we have no choice. And down there now, unlike up here, there can be no race to white suburbia if you want to keep your white kids in public schools. Everywhere you go in Yazoo County, if you live in Yazoo City, the public schools out there are 100 percent black.

INTERVIEWER: You were saying that white kids don't even go to school now; is that right?

MORRIS: I think there are a lot of white kids out in Yazoo County who are not going to school at all.

INTERVIEWER: Thanks to their feeling of . . . oh, Jesus.

MORRIS: The state of Mississippi repealed the compulsory school attendance law a few years ago as the most obvious ploy. A lot of these kids are just not even going to school.

INTERVIEWER: Here we are, almost in the twenty-first century, and a lot of kids in the most backward state in the Union are not even getting what rudiments that state could offer. What in the hell is going to happen to people like that?

MORRIS: I think before it's over, the public school system will survive in Mississippi, and I think there will be white kids coming back to the public schools who are now in those raunchy private schools. In the first place, Mississippi can't afford two school systems. And in the second place, I think they're going to have to live together. Unlike the city where we're sitting right now, there can be no escape. Unless you just leave the state.

INTERVIEWER: It's very poignant. Both sides, black *and* white, love the place and are not going to leave it and yet at the same time can't live there together.

MORRIS: Walker Percy says that he believes the South, and states like Mississippi, may solve the racial impasse in America before any other region.

INTERVIEWER: I believe that myself.

MORRIS: A lot of Southern intellectuals believe this. I think I believe it too. Again, this is something . . . It is a concept that can be overly dramatized and exaggerated, but I think there is a chance that this will happen because it has to, because the South has no other choice.

INTERVIEWER: Let's talk about writing for a minute. Your book joined a long and distinguished list of books about the South by Southerners: Susan Dabney Smede's diary, William Alexander Percy's *Lanterns on the Levee*, and Cash's *Mind of the South*. Personally, I find your book superior to all of them, and I wondered how much you had been influenced by all of them, or were hedging against them, when you wrote yours.

MORRIS: I have not read the first one.

INTERVIEWER: I don't guess anybody outside of a few nutty graduate students has.

MORRIS: You read it when you were at Chapel Hill?

INTERVIEWER: Right.

MORRIS: *The Mind of the South* I certainly have read and I read *Lanterns on the Levee* twice. I had a funny experience with *Lanterns on the Levee*. I read it when I was about twelve years old. I checked it out of the library there in Yazoo City. And I loved it. And then when I was writing my own book and had decided I was going to take a son of a bitch's risk and make it an autobiographical narrative rather than fiction, I went down on Fourth Avenue to one of those old secondhand bookstores down there and got a copy of *Lanterns on the Levee* and reread it and was disappointed.

INTERVIEWER: I was not only disappointed; I was appalled.

MORRIS: Yeah. I loved it when I was a kid. But that didn't really influence me too much. I suppose since I am from Mississippi the writer who has gotten to me most is Faulkner. You can't get away from Faulkner down there. Now when I was growing up, people would say Faulkner was just a drunk who got naked and climbed trees. He was out for the Yankee dollar. I was editor of the Yazoo High School *Flashlight* and when I was a senior in high school, I went up to a convention of high school editors in Oxford, Mississippi. I was just beginning to read Faulkner. I'd been reading *Intruder in the Dust*, which is not a good book by Faulkner. And I was walking along the southern side of the square there in Oxford when I saw a plaque set in the side of a building: "Gavin Stevens, Attorney at Law." They were filming *Intruder in the Dust* that year, in Oxford. What was it Flannery O'Connor said about Faulkner?

INTERVIEWER: I think something like "You better get off the tracks when you hear the Dixie Special coming." Something like that.

MORRIS: And there are other fine writers from Mississippi. Walker Percy is a fine writer. He has only written two novels. People disagree with me on this, but I find *The Last Gentleman*, his second novel, a more effective novel than *The Moviegoer*. He came to fiction relatively late in life, I suppose, when he was in his forties. He brought a lot of impressive equipment to his fiction. He's a tremendously intelligent man. And I have a high regard for Styron's work. *Lie Down in Darkness* is a very impressive novel. It's amazing that a guy could write this at twenty-three, twenty-four and explore the dark side of life as he does. And I'm also a great advocate of *The Confessions of Nat Turner*.

INTERVIEWER: It's come in for a lot of attack by black writers.

MORRIS: And, I think, for the wrong reasons. I think that the extreme black position on *The Confessions of Nat Turner* goes something like this: that a white man as writer can never presume to enter the Negro psyche, ignoring the fact that with the possible exception of Ellison's *Invisible Man*, the one writer who got into the Negro

psyche and character and humanity better than any other writer
was a Southern white man from Oxford, Mississippi.

INTERVIEWER: I disagree with those black writers who attacked it solely
on the basis of their opinion that writing is not imagination, but
testament. I think that if you have the imagination, you can put
yourself inside the mind of an African mercenary in the seventeenth century.

MORRIS: Yes, this is . . . I think this is the toughest thing for a writer,
but also it's his saving grace to have the courage of his imagination. I think *The Confessions of Nat Turner* is a work of imaginative literature, and Lord knows in this day and age, with the
tensions that we have in this country now, blacks and whites and
all the rest, you could have predicted that *The Confessions of
Nat Turner* was going to be suspiciously received by the Negro
activists. Of course, the Negro extremists are, in my opinion, as
Irving Howe said, nothing but pop-art guerrilla fighters.

INTERVIEWER: I wanted to say something on a different subject, and
that is that we are writers in a nation and a decade which prizes
nonfiction more and more. The many pressures this country faces
are making us put a high premium on the kind of nonfiction which
can tell us where it's at. And you're the editor of a magazine which
is, after all, mostly nonfiction. Do you think nonfiction is going
to completely drive out fiction in this particularly troubled quarter
of a century?

MORRIS: No. But there's no doubt, and I'm speaking now as an
editor—I guess as a writer as well, but primarily as an editor—
there is no doubt that certain nonfiction forms are alive and
flourishing in American writing and indeed are probably stronger
now than they've ever been, for a number of reasons. For example,
magazines are better now than they've ever been in America, and
it's ironic that most of them are also in bad shape financially. I
don't know whether there are going to be any magazines left in
America a generation from now. I also think that writers, the
best of our creative writers, occasionally want to indulge themselves in journalistic forms—in the broadest sense, I mean. They
want to write something that will come into print three or four
months after they write it. And it gives them a chance to write
about political subjects in the first person occasionally. I think

indeed the whole stress and tempo of this age has encouraged certain younger writers to be more interested in nonfiction and autobiographical approaches. Now my friend Norman Podhoretz at *Commentary* makes the argument that it's the essay nonfiction form which is the flourishing literary form of our time. I tend to disagree with that. And if it's carried over into an argument that fiction and the novel are dying in America, I don't believe it. I think that all you have to do is look at the corpus of work of eight or ten of our best novelists since World War II to see that the novel is anything but dying in America and that it is alive and flourishing. At the same time, side by side with this, I do think that nonfiction forms are better than ever, and I don't think that the two are mutually exclusive. Quite the contrary. I think they feed on each other. I happened to choose an autobiographical form for my book—I started to say for my novel—because it's what I wanted to write, because I had been encouraged by a few other people who were trying this out, too. I think whatever I write in my future life will not be autobiography. An autobiographical book is for either a very young man or a very old man.

INTERVIEWER: *Harper's* has become, if it already wasn't, but especially under your leadership, one of the three or four leading magazines in America. And you publish the kind of nonfiction which does what fiction should do, which is to make us see our lives in a new way. Do you see the possibility of fiction either going or being driven into the area of fantasy—and books such as Bulgakov's *The Master and Margarita* seem to indicate that it is becoming a trend —while nonfiction takes over the chronicling of our lives as social creatures?

MORRIS: I think it could if the detractors of fiction have their day in the field. I think it could, but I hope it will not, and I do not think it will. I think the importance of great social fiction in American life is still quite real. I live in a city, and I work in a city, where you undergo, you coexist with, these incredible fashions. . . . We're sitting here fifty yards away from Madison Avenue, which I suppose is the paragon of fashion modeling in our country, but the fashions also come from the publishing world and from the magazine world and from the more nonsensical literary critics, so-called, who are always looking for fashions and trying to put labels on things and encouraging and giving awards to certain kinds of writing that don't matter. I suppose this has always been true, but it's more true in this particular time, and the force of fashion is stronger for the very simple reason that the apparatus is more sophisticated than it's ever been. But I think a case can still be made for good writing. Indeed, there are writers sitting out there somewhere now writing in old-fashioned American about questions of real concern to human beings, about, as Faulkner said in his Nobel Prize speech, "the human heart in conflict with itself." Things that make an enduring, imaginative literature. It's still there, and it will always be there. I see people who have read their McLuhan and say that the printed word is going to be dead in another fifty years in our culture, and I say to them, "Nonsense." I want my magazine, *Harper's*, to be the foremost advocate and defender of the written word among all the American magazines. And I think that this is something that we do stand for at *Harper's* that matters to all of us. No, I believe fervently that the old abiding literature of real people confronting whatever it is that we all confront as human beings on this planet will be with us for a long, long time.

INTERVIEWER: Now, to get down to some home truths, why is it so hard now for a writer of fiction to get short stories published in the six or seven quality magazines we have, of which yours is one? Why has the emphasis gone, and I think it really has, from fiction to very well done nonfiction? Is it because the best fiction today is too experimental, or radical, for you to publish and still keep your audience?

MORRIS: I think it's the form itself. I don't think the short story is as strong a form in this country now as it was a generation or two generations ago. I think that young writers, many of whom are our best writers, don't turn to the short story form the way they might have a generation ago. It's also harder for the young writer to be published, to have a short story published, that is, because there are fewer magazines now than there were. We publish one short story an issue. And I think *Harper's* has published one short story a year now for twenty-five years. But we used to have three or four in each issue.

INTERVIEWER: Writing programs and agents and any number of people tell you that if a short story is over 6,000 words, it can't be sold. Your agent may even tell you to go home and write a novel, that he can sell that quicker. Do you think that's having something to do with the death of the short story?

MORRIS: I don't think so.

INTERVIEWER: I had a professor my sophomore year in college who requested that we write a paper. When I asked him how long it should be, he said, "Just whatever it takes, son." And maybe whatever it takes in a short story is beyond an artificial limit which has been set up as a convenience to the publishing industry. What do you think?

MORRIS: Well, the purveyors of short fiction, of course, have always been magazines. And there are fewer magazines now than there were. And I think there is more of an interest in younger writers that want to write about real events, real situations.

INTERVIEWER: Is that because of the journalism of this decade, or does the journalism reflect a very real change in people's imaginations? Maybe this is important, and maybe it's not, but my agent has indicated, as I said, that it will be easier to sell my novel than any short story I might write. One of the implications of the situation being, maybe, that novels do have a reputation for presenting a higher truth than the short stories you read in the big magazines.

MORRIS: I think that's probably true and I think that the publishing apparatus is geared more to the longer fiction than it was a generation ago.

INTERVIEWER: What do you think about the little magazines in the country today? Do you read a lot of them?

MORRIS: I see quite a few, yes.

INTERVIEWER: How do they strike you?

MORRIS: I don't think they have the force in this country they once did. I don't think that you can generalize about the so-called little magazines, but I don't think they're as good now as they once were. There are probably a lot of reasons for this. I think the bigger magazines are better than they've ever been, as I was suggesting earlier. Now you look at, for example, the *Partisan Review*. For a writer living in the East in the thirties and forties, that was a potent place to be published. The magazine was read and talked about, and it had an influence on ideas. You certainly can't say that about the *Partisan Review* now.

INTERVIEWER: No, and you can't say it for a lot of little magazines.

MORRIS: Right, I'm just using the *Partisan Review* as an example. But the people who a generation ago would have written for the little magazines, the real, vital, intelligent younger writers, now are writing for the bigger ones.

INTERVIEWER: Your magazine gives particularly good play, and a lot of play, to very talented younger people who are writing good stuff. Do you think our decade is a good one for the young writer?

MORRIS: Well, I certainly think that the tangible rewards are more obvious, if that means anything, and I suppose it does. The circumstances of the publishing industry are such that bigger and bigger rewards are being given to, sometimes, I think, not so much talent.

INTERVIEWER: You were about to say something about Berry Morgan.

MORRIS: While I was in Mississippi, I drove on down to Port Gibson and went to see Berry Morgan, who lives on this old plantation of about 800 acres now. My great-grandmother had come from Port Gibson. When she was ten years old, she had to testify in a trial. She had seen her father murdered on the main street of Port Gibson, which is a good place to be murdered, I guess. And you know, there's a church down there with the finger pointing to the sky. I asked Berry, "Is anybody in this town named Sims? That was my great-grandmother's maiden name." And she said, "Your great-grandfather owned this land." She was talking about the political situation down there. The county is about 80 percent black, and she said that the black activists now don't like her too much. I think this is happening a lot in Mississippi. She said her only friends in town are the liberal white aristocrats.

INTERVIEWER: Is there such a thing?

MORRIS: And the conservative Negroes.

INTERVIEWER: Two minority groups, if I ever heard of any. . . . You told me once about a friend of yours who had volunteered to go South with you and after she got south of Washington wanted to know where all the Indians were.

MORRIS: That was Larry King's wife. The last time Larry took his wife south—she grew up in Washington—he said they got eighty miles south of Washington and she was asking about Indian raids.

INTERVIEWER: There's always been an air of unreality about the South in the minds of most Americans, I think. Flannery O'Connor wrote about grotesque types, and when people asked her why, she said—I'm doing a free paraphrase—"Because down here we can tell the difference." Now what does that mean in terms of your own writing?

MORRIS: It doesn't mean anything to me as a writer. Flannery O'Connor was a very talented girl and a really fine writer, but she died at the age of thirty-nine and had always been sick and lived there in that house. I didn't know her, but I would suspect that she lived there in that house and devoted practically her whole life to her writing, and it was the workings of a very baroque imagination that produced all that. I think a person who knows the South, who moves around a lot and meets a lot of different people, will not have that particular attitude. Don't you agree?

INTERVIEWER: I think there are *different* circuses in the South now. After all, we have a society which has become industrialized. Now, you've got the same kind of plastic cocktail parties in the South that you've always had in the East. Southern virgins are more dangerous than the local variety, I think, because basically they're mean as snakes and soon slide into a life of alcoholism, but I think the next problem for the novelist is to try to handle what the New South *is*, if we can buy that label for just a minute. I think you handled it pretty well in your autobiography.

MORRIS: Yeah, whatever the New South is. Certainly one of the differences you can see now—and this has come about in just a generation—is the drift towards places like Atlanta, Memphis, Charlotte, Birmingham. All the kids I grew up with in Yazoo City, Mississippi, in the 1950's who didn't have any kind of vested interest in the town through their families in stores and plantations and that sort of thing are almost without exception now living in the bigger cities of the South. Has anybody touched this in literature?

INTERVIEWER: Not yet, not effectively. But it's very important, because the rural population, at just the minute when our citics are writhing in their own coils, are being drawn to places like Atlanta, which can be deadly, deadly. And at this point those cities don't have the cultural opportunities of Boston and New York, or of New Orleans. And if you're going to move to a city, that ought to be the reason: to enrich yourself with the culture available there. But they keep on watching TV and going to the Dairy Queen and to the grade C movies, just like back in Possum Hollow.

MORRIS: This development is having a very important impact on the politics of that whole region in a way that I expect we don't really realize yet. You know we all grew up kind of close to the soil in those small towns in Mississippi. Even if you're a member of what we consider the middle class in a place like Mississippi, you're always conscious of the soil, and some of us were obsessed with it. Lord knows what Southerners moving to the city are going to mean to the economy and what the ramifications will be in race relations. What happens to these rednecks when they leave the soil and go to these split-level suburbias, whether it's Memphis, Birmingham, or Atlanta?

INTERVIEWER: I think they vote Wallace, maybe even get more right wing than they were. Which is not to say they were any bunch of liberals down on the farm, but a bunch of guys who have felt close to the soil and who've lived in small places where there's at least a modicum of civility have *got* to be torn up when they move into these concrete insanities. And I think these people join the groups that express their frustration.

MORRIS: I think there's a lot of truth to that. I've been living in New York City for seven years, and I find that the older I get, the more of a Southerner I become.

INTERVIEWER: Your accent still sounds like what I find when I go home.

MORRIS: I suppose that has a lot to do with the fact I was back in Mississippi two weeks ago.

INTERVIEWER: No, I saw you at Thanksgiving here in the city and was struck by hearing the same kind of accent I'd grown up hearing. Mine's more nasal.

MORRIS: I think the Southerners you find who no longer have their accent are the Southerners who no longer care about the South.

INTERVIEWER: Well, maybe I'm being perverse about it, but you do have to maintain some kind of goddam individuality.

MORRIS: Well now, I've got a little boy ten years old who's coming over here in a minute. David Morris. His great, great-uncle, or whatever, was the first governor of Mississippi. His great, great-uncle was the senior senator from Mississippi in 1840 and defeated Jefferson Davis for governor in 1851, and all his forebears were Southern. And my son is growing up in New York, but I try to take him with me to the South whenever I go, as often as possible. I'm going to go down there with Ralph Ellison in April to speak at Millsaps. I want my son to go with me. I don't want him to lose touch with what his people came out of. I think this is of deep and abiding importance to a kid. He really is a New York boy. He should be. He was brought up in the city, and he is a New York boy. He knows the subway system, and he makes fun of my accent.

INTERVIEWER: Does he really?

MORRIS: Yes. Well, he's not being rude about it. He's just kidding me. But I want that boy to grow up at least having some feeling of the place where his people come from. Because it's quite obvious that a feeling of place is something that is rapidly vanishing as society becomes homogenized.

INTERVIEWER: What kind of literature are we going to produce without a sense of place?

MORRIS: It'll be a placeless literature.

INTERVIEWER: That's a fair answer. Do you think literature can survive without a sense of place?

MORRIS: I think literature will survive as long as the human imagination survives.

Honkies, Editors,
& Other Dirty Stories:
❧ LARRY L. KING

Interviewed by JOHN CARR

Larry L. King was born and raised in Texas and after World War II attended Texas Tech, where he had a "make good" football scholarship. They canceled it, he says, "on the slim grounds that I drank beer at football practice, in addition to which I did not block or tackle very expertly. This so offended me that I left school." After five years as a newspaperman in New Mexico and Texas, King served as administrative assistant to two Texas congressmen from 1954 to 1964. In 1967, he was elected to membership in the Texas Institute of Letters. He was a Nieman Fellow at Harvard in 1969–70.

He has written one novel, The One-Eyed Man *(1966); a nonfiction collection, . . .* And Other Dirty Stories *(originally entitled* My Hero LBJ and Other Dirty Stories, *1968); and the autobiographical* Confessions of a White Racist *(1971). A contributing editor at* Harper's, *he resigned in support of Willie Morris. He speaks at length about the whole affair in an addendum to this interview. He is still a contributing editor to the* Texas Observer. *His work has been published in more than thirty national periodicals, including* Life *and* Esquire *most recently. A former free-lance book critic for* Time, *King periodically reviews for the* New York Times Book Review *and the* Chicago Sun-Times Book Week. *He is currently free-lancing and working on a book about the vanished or vanishing small towns of America.*

The first part of this interview was taped in April, 1970, in Cambridge, Massachusetts. The second part was completed in October, 1971.

I

INTERVIEWER: You were talking about some critics not liking your novel, *The One-Eyed Man*—and, you thought, for the wrong reasons.

KING: Isn't that always the way of it? Much is imperfect in that novel. I can open it to almost any page and wish for the opportunity to write it again. *One-Eyed* was written at a time when civil rights activities were moving so fast, and my own concepts were changing so rapidly, that I felt a stranger to that novel by the time it was published. During the writing, from late 1963 to mid-1965, I foolishly believed that should Congress pass a couple of voting rights bills, then our old "Negro problem" would soon solve itself. Not because people love each other so much, but as a matter of law. In retrospect, I see that the early civil rights bills contained few enforcement provisions. And I have since observed, particularly with respect to the Nixon administration, that the federal government isn't enthusiastic about enforcing civil rights laws. Black people knew, as I am afraid I did not, that it wasn't going to amount to much anyway.

INTERVIEWER: "Integration," you mean?

KING: Yes. Black people knew that their registering to vote in the South would not work immediate miracles. White liberals assumed miracles. Among them was the assumption of willing acceptance of true racial integration by whites: a sense of inevitability about it, and the mistaken notion that a white racist society would reverse its habits and reject its myths overnight. I made these mistaken assumptions in the mid-1960s. And so, very much of the hope expressed in *The One-Eyed Man* for a greater democracy in the South was based on a naïveté I now find embarrassing.

INTERVIEWER: Well, then, where did the critics go wrong?

KING: Not all of them did. Some thought that my governor, Cullie Blanton, was overdrawn, overblown. He may have been. Most first novels are overwritten, and mine was no exception. And perhaps I became so enthralled by my governor that I lost control of him. But some critics complained that several of the governor's political associates sounded and acted too much like him, and here they exposed their ignorance of the political animal. I was on

Capitol Hill for a decade, and much of my life has been spent as a political activist. One thing that struck me early was how quickly and completely the associates of powerful men adapt their mannerisms and colorations. Edwin O'Connor knew what he was doing in *The Last Hurrah* when he named one of Frank Skeffington's loyal aides "Ditto."

INTERVIEWER: Where else did the critics miss?

KING: As prophecy, my novel was very, very bad. By the time of publication that was obvious. Yet, no critic remarked on it. Many critics, especially those with Eastern establishmentarian connections—

INTERVIEWER: New York *Times?*

KING: Well, the New York *Times* critic devoted only twenty-odd lines to *The One-Eyed Man* and I here wish to publicly thank that gentleman for his brevity. Eastern critics in general seemed impatient with the Southern culture. They charged that I said too much of the land and its fruits. The sense of time and place and detail projected by many Southern writers, the slow stirrings that strike the invisible sparks of daily life, are often found irritating by Eastern critics.

INTERVIEWER: Perhaps because of their own insufficiencies?

KING: I don't think they believe the South exists in its fascinating contrasts of thorns and roses, cruelties and nobilities, honey and bullshit. I don't think they know what a powerful force the land is among Southerners: how for generations it has shaped our pocketbooks, our backs, our lives, our moods. Even with Faulkner to guide them they still don't understand. John Kenneth Galbraith has observed that the problem with *The One-Eyed Man's* critical reception was that few Eastern critics know much of (1) the South or (2) the wheeler-dealer backdoor politics indigenous to the South.

INTERVIEWER: Southern politics are more sophisticated than they think? More Machiavellian?

KING: Right on.

INTERVIEWER: You knew Lyndon Johnson when he was back in Texas?

KING: Yes, for a number of years. I had long observed LBJ in the practice of backstage politics. I had seen him do some remarkably Machiavellian and Falstaffian things on the Texas political stump, at state conventions, and behind the private doors of the United States Senate. All this was long before he came to full flower in the national eye. And I took from Lyndon Johnson many of the qualities of my governor, Cullie Blanton, as I took from Earl Long, and a touch from Huey, and bits from dozens of other sly ole flesh-pressing pols I have known.

INTERVIEWER: You've already said how critics sometimes refuse to give books by Southern authors a fair review. For instance, you mentioned one book that was ignored because one of the motifs is Southern music, country music. Don't you think this is unfair and rather shortsighted?

KING: Of course. It may also be natural. Most of us enjoy books with which we can readily identify. We enjoy experiences common to our own. I don't think there's any New York intellectual conspiracy to do Southern writers in, though like Lyndon Johnson I sometimes think they react with too much surprise when they discover that we wear shoes and have at least a rudimentary command of the English language. We don't understand each other very well. There's a sort of undeclared war between Southern writers and the New York intellectuals. It smolders beneath the smiling surface of posh cocktail parties in Manhattan, and after a certain amount of vapors hit the air you can feel it. In short, I think New York intellectuals more willingly and more naturally find merit in new writers from their own stables than they do from ours. Unless a Southern writer has built a reputation over the years—as with Robert Penn Warren, Bill Styron, William Humphrey, Eudora Welty, Faulkner—then he or she may be automatically presumed to bear only minor credentials.

INTERVIEWER: As late as 1950, when Faulkner won the Nobel Prize, there was a terrible editorial in a major Eastern publication saying it was very regrettable that Faulkner had won. They didn't understand him even at that late date. Lately, it's become more fashionable to admire Faulkner.

KING: Death more often than not enhances the reputations of politicians, whores, and Southern writers. Perhaps because it removes them from active competition.

INTERVIEWER: You have privately said that you have difficulty writing fiction right now because you are too much in your times, because events worry you, and because you can't settle down. Is that fair to say?

KING: True. The inner man in the writer must be able to feed off knowledge and convictions he has accrued and gathered to himself over the years. So much is happening in America right now, and has occurred so rapidly within the last seven or eight years, that many of us are discovering new values, discarding old ones, and finding it necessary to reevaluate our feelings. We are, in effect, being forced to learn history as history truly happened and not history as it was taught to us. Or *mis*taught. Our schools, our politicians, our parents, and many of our writers taught that our Constitution meant what it said, that it performed the miracle of perfect freedoms for all. "The Goddess of Justice is blind," they said, meaning that she didn't distinguish between the rich or the poor, the white or the black, the weak or the strong. The Goddess of Justice, it turns out in real life, is often a hag who winks at the word she represents and who would do credit to the more disreputable precincts of hell. Only within recent years have significant numbers of Americans made this startling discovery of a mistaught history, or discovered that our system has not only tolerated, but has encouraged, terrible social ills. I came steadily to this knowledge, though slowly and tardily. And as a result, it's terribly difficult to sit down with any inner serenity and unshakable confidence about what one knows and feels as a human being. The novel, I think, is the highest art form in writing. An artist must know his own values in order to transmit them effectively in fiction. My own values are shaky right now. There's a novel eating on my insides right now. I'm having trouble coughing it up.

INTERVIEWER: What hope is there for somebody who wants to write a novel, yet who is also involved very much in the things of our day? Whether it's conservation or integration or racism or joining the revolution?

KING: I can only speak for myself, and I find it difficult. I think people with static minds—no, make that contented minds—people with *contented* minds write the better novels, the lasting novels. I'm sure you can immediately cite a dozen exceptions to that rule. I note your exceptions, but cling to my gut-feeling. Novelists at their work are digesting what they know, turning their discoveries of life and their certainties into art for the better understanding of others. Those of us who are in inner or mental turmoil, or in political or sociological upheaval, seem to work better in nonfiction. Perhaps we don't have to take so much from within ourselves, or make so many arbitrary judgments on the human condition. We are not responsible for an entire world, as is the novelist who creates one. And then must make some sense of it.

INTERVIEWER: How do you compare the Southern writer's sense of history with that of the non-Southerner?

KING: There's no general rule. I do think that we in the South, and I include here many more than writers, have been particularly reluctant to confront our history and our failings. One of the reasons that Southerners have a reputation for being able to tell stories and talk so well is because much of our talking is done *around* the subject rather than to cut straight through to the heart of the matter. We are great natural bullshitters. We teach ourselves to use the language to conceal as well as to reveal. This has been harmful to our society. Vastly entertaining, perhaps, but harmful. It may have given rise to generations of natural storytellers, but it has also caused the promotion of lies and myths too long regarded as regional gospel. We don't like to face up to the uglier chapters of our history. We couldn't justify treating fellow human beings as slaves, for example, and so we represented them as subhuman in order to pacify our "Christian" instincts. For generations we have convinced ourselves, and our sons, that black people may be badly treated without our staining ourselves because they are inferior creatures, like small children or dumb animals. The Third Reich never more convincingly sold itself on a bigger lie.

INTERVIEWER: Isn't the South a ghetto for some whites?

KING: It is for those of us who don't care to work at the grist mill, or who insist on having an original thought now and then outside the conventional dogma of the Rotary Club. Babbittism isn't the sole property of the South, as Queens and Chicago, among others, bear witness, but perhaps we own more than our fair share of it. For years I've been hearing of the "New South," the industrialized South, looking toward more prosperous and more civilized days. When I go back, however, I find the puritan ethic firmly in control and the same old money barons in the saddle. I find white racism polarizing and, thanks to the panderings of the Nixon-Agnew-Mitchell "Southern strategy," becoming more open than at any time since before the beatings at Selma Bridge or since Bull Connor's police dogs and fire hoses in Birmingham. I find a narrow suspicion of beards, or of any thought believed to have been imported from New York or Washington. I feel like a stranger in Jerusalem there.

INTERVIEWER: Except for some few small literary magazines, or some newspapers, where may would-be Southern writers serve their apprenticeships?

KING: We have no publishing houses, few magazines. Our newspapers are pathetic, with some scattered exceptions, content to coin money and whoop editorial platitudes. A man finds, working on many newspapers in the South and Southwest, that his publishers and editors are timid souls who discourage him from writing anything that might rock the comfortable community boat. They don't want him upsetting conservative advertisers or accepted social institutions by his critical evaluations or by bold use of the language. He ultimately realizes he has no forum in the South. So he heads for territory where better forums and superior intellectual opportunities may be available.

INTERVIEWER: You worked on newspapers for several years. Hemingway thought it was wonderful training. What do you think about newspapers writing as a training ground for the would-be novelist?

KING: It's good training to the extent that anytime one daily uses the language he will learn and discover, because writing is an act of discovery. The better the writing the larger the discoveries, and vice versa. Most newspapers, however, will not permit the writer to use the language inventively or to share his full perceptions with the newspaper audience. Editors and publishers hold to this silly myth of "objective reporting," though they quickly abandon it should they decide to defeat a politician odious to their purposes or to defend the mail subsidy they enjoy at the expense of the rest of us. Only recently have some few newspapers discovered that it's in the interest of good journalism to permit the writer to bring his own thoughts, his own personal observations, or comments, or even prejudices, to the page. So I think newspapers

offer a limited opportunity for the practice of real writing crafts-
manship. I suppose, however, that the man who wants to write
fiction is better off working on a newspaper than, say, he is shovel-
ing goat shit.

INTERVIEWER: Aren't you being a bit hard on newspapers?

KING: I mean to be. The shame of newspapers is that great gulf between what they are and what they have the opportunity to be.
Much the same may be said of Congress. Most newspaper experiences kill the writing spirit after a time, especially the ones of
small or middling circulations that are so prevalent in the South
and Southwest. I've known newsmen who fifteen or twenty years
ago wanted to seriously write, and I thought perhaps they could.
Perhaps they used words well, had a natural eye for life's absurdities, or had unusual perceptions. They often laughed or railed or
cried at the frustrating policies and limited ranges of their newspapers. The most driven ones left. The others stayed to wither in
the city room. Go back to those old haunts now, and inspect those
ole boys. They've become narrow, old, sour. Their spirit has been
crushed. They've given up. They've come to reject even the
thought of dissent, to fear new ideas. God, it's sad! They've become bank clerks in their souls. I've seen it happen to a dozen
individuals who once had in them better stuff than ever got out.

INTERVIEWER: We both know police reporters who have become more
like the cops than the cops.

KING: Exactly.

INTERVIEWER: How did you save your style after all those years on
newspapers?

KING: Perhaps my style developed later. I didn't publish anything outside newspapers until I was thirty-six. Early in my newspaper
days, when I was a sportswriter, I did get to flirt with style and
experiment with several variations. I would advise beginning reporters to work for a while on the sports beat, no matter what
their natural interests.

INTERVIEWER: Why?

KING: You simply have more freedom in use of language.

INTERVIEWER: No one cares what you write on the sports beat?

KING: Oh, sure. You'll catch hell from fans and athletes on occasion.
Generally, however, the publisher or editor doesn't take sports
seriously enough to worry about libel, irate advertisers, or the many

other fears indigenous to the breed. On most newspapers a sports columnist can reveal more truths, be more entertaining, and expose more absurdities than you'll find being done on the editorial page, God help us, or in the front page news story. His real influence on large events may be small, but at least he has more operating room.

On a police beat, a political beat, or any beat covering the social and political institutions, you encounter herds of sacred cows and forests of censors. The people you're covering are so uptight about their own little careers and images, and they have so much influence upon, and friendships with, your editors and publishers, that you're likely to be blue-penciled should you report anything outside "the plain facts"—the plain facts being those with which Establishment figures can live and prosper. You can't use ridicule, satire, black humor, or inventive language without inspiring heart attacks, city room sermons, or your severance pay.

INTERVIEWER: Do you speak with the voice of experience?

KING: Damn right. I only left one newspaper without being fired off it, and I was probably two days ahead of the posse when I quit.

INTERVIEWER: What was the problem?

KING: They said I was a troublemaker. See, I had this peculiar notion that a reporter should not always walk around blind—that when he saw something insane or deceitful or dangerous, he should be able to write about it honestly. If I may plug my latest book, *Confessions of a White Racist* illustrates the specific example in my case. Most newspaper publishers I have known, and too many editors, would make excellent Chamber of Commerce flaks.

INTERVIEWER: What about doing a stint at one of the desks in the city room?

KING: Nowhere is the air more inhibiting. Nowhere else do brains more closely resemble boiled peas. Unless it's in the publisher's office.

INTERVIEWER: Why this contempt for publishers?

KING: They're the prime source of most of the writer's troubles. They have a vested interest in their community. They are, after all, sizable businessmen therein. They're cronies and pals of the social, political, and economic wheels they *should* be professionally detached from and critical of. They belong to the same clubs, they harbor the same ideas—and the big idea is to coin money and control power. In town where a newspaper is most safely monopolistic, you'll find the shrillest editorials for free enterprise and the glorious competition of the open market. Bullshit! Let them practice what they preach. I honestly believe that newspaper publishers and their editorial hirelings in monopoly towns are the most hypocritical of the human species.

INTERVIEWER: Can you explain your political credo in twenty-five words or less?

KING: I can do it in four: "Don't fuck with me."

INTERVIEWER: All righty. Don't you think politics has something to do with writing if you're a Southerner?

KING: A hell of a lot to do with it, and I don't care if you're a Southerner or an Eskimo. We live in a political world.

INTERVIEWER: Nowadays, when you have an idea for a book, especially nonfiction, publishers want you to write an outline or, in effect, want you to give them a large percentage of the book before you've written it. And they ignore, I think, that even nonfiction writing is, as you put it earlier, an act of discovery.

KING: Writing an outline or a synopsis is the hardest kind of writing. First, because the writer generally has no idea as to the specifics of where a book will go—where his research, interviews, observations, or midnight thoughts may take him. I think outlines and synopses and sample chapters do little other than give nervous editors something to show if their bosses demand to know why they bought a certain work-in-progress. Good editors know that a writer can't be confined to some preconceived notion of a book. They don't even attempt to hold him to original outlines or concepts.

INTERVIEWER: After all, writers didn't move up from the general to the specific. They move upwards from the specific to the general. Perhaps many editors think, "Here you've got an idea for a book. It must be already in your mind, word for word, and what you're asking us to judge you on is a complete idea."

KING: The good ones don't. The good ones leave you to find your own voice and direction, intervening only if you confess to being lost on the way and ask them for directions. This is a strong point of Willie Morris, our editor in chief at *Harper's* magazine. My best work for Willie has been accomplished when I said, "Willie, I want to do a story on my congressional experiences," or maybe a piece on country music, or visiting my boyhood home, or on some obscure comedian he probably has never heard of. Willie Morris is smart enough to know that if the writer is engaged in a pursuit in which he has a high personal interest, then he should be given his head. "Do it" is about the only instruction he gives. He leaves the discovery of the work and its direction and basic length up to the writer. I think that's why so many writers of excellent reputation are increasingly eager to appear in *Harper's*. Morris doesn't make the mistake that some editors do, and that's expecting the writer to deliver a manuscript true to the concepts of the editor.

The best kind of writing, and the biggest thrill in writing, is to suddenly read a line from your typewriter that you didn't know was in you. Or you didn't know you felt quite this way about a certain thing. And maybe that will spin you off to dig into the thought a bit deeper. And a few hours later, you've birthed a personal philosophy you really had never consciously thought of before. Sometimes this can be the most powerful part of a piece or of a book. And a very successful book, a very satisfying book, will be a continuing series of such new adventures or discoveries. *No way* to put that into an outline!

INTERVIEWER: Right. And do you agree that sometimes in order to know how you think you must first write, or try to write, how you think?

KING: That's what I just said, John. Pay attention. And pass that Scotch this way again. I'll give you a perfect example if you're in a mood to suffer personal testimony.

INTERVIEWER: Certainly.

KING: My latest book, *Confessions of a White Racist*, is based on an article that appeared in the January, 1970, issue of *Harper's*. Now, I tried to write that article perhaps two years before its publication. Originally, the title was "How I Became Whitey." The piece was going to take a wounded tone: "Here I am, a white liberal who has always done the best he could within the racially split society to learn, to grow, to be an activist, to be of human stuff, to be a worker for true brotherhood. And now, suddenly, I'm being cursed as 'Whitey,' 'Honky,' 'Beast,' 'White Devil,' and so on. And I resent it." My purpose was to show how this foul thing had come about. Well, I started writing. And it just didn't work. The reason the article didn't work was that as I wrote it I realized I was writing and thinking pure white man's bullshit. I belatedly realized that I held the same attitudes that far too many white people harbor: "Oh, I have done so much for those poor downtrodden people, and now they throw rocks at me." The more I tried to write about what I had done for black people, the more I realized I had done zilch. The more I got into it, the more it dawned on me that I was guilty of the unthinking practices I had always assigned to other white bigots. So I thought, "How does one with my good intentions find out at this late and crucial time of life that he's *not* done a damn thing, really, in areas where he had considered himself accomplished? What forces in the society and what old poisons in my heart shaped me into such a disappointing and self-serving creature?" This sent me on a voyage back into my mind's most private country: When had I first become aware of black people? Who was the first black person I saw? What were my thoughts then? What did my social or political institutions and my family teach me of black people, by word or deed or example? As a result there evolved an article, and then a book, with the almost exact opposite viewpoint that I had originally intended to reflect. This was certainly the most basic and important discovery I have made about myself in forty-one years of living. And it was made at the typewriter by a man stumbling and feeling his way. I sat down to write a lie and truth got in the way.

INTERVIEWER: A lesser editor than Willie Morris might have insisted on your sticking to the original plan.

KING: I know some who probably would have.

INTERVIEWER: Care to name them?

KING: No, because it remains necessary for me to sell them an occasional piece. I have more dependents than the late Nizam of Hyderabad, who, when he died in 1967, was mourned by three wives, forty-two concubines, two hundred children, and three hundred retainers.

INTERVIEWER: Any publication you want to squeal on?

KING: How about *Time*? I hate committee journalism. It's too much like a Saturday night gang-bang. When I reviewed books on a free-lance basis for *Time* in 1965 and 1966, I would often, on publication, recognize two or three lines of my prose surrounded by acres of a stranger's prose—committee prose, if you will. Once they turned a favorable review I had written around by almost 360 degrees to make it carping and bitchy, yet somehow managed to retain several of my best lines.

INTERVIEWER: Did you have enough integrity to protest?

KING: I did not. I did bitch, however. Really hooted and danced. A few weeks later, after I turned down a full-time job with *Time*, they notified me in a stiff little note that since *Time* would no longer farm out book reviews to other than "potential staffers," I was, in effect, out on my ass.

INTERVIEWER: Did that do damage to your artistic soul?

KING: Yes, it wounded it by about seven hundred dollars a month's worth.

INTERVIEWER: It's been said that in modern-day America, we produce for the sheer sake of producing. *Are* there not publishing companies who will publish some writers for the sheer sake of keeping their presses running?

KING: Perhaps. People with bureaucratic hearts run almost all big organizations. Self-perpetuation is a strong instinct.

INTERVIEWER: There is a publishing house in New York today which has a reputation for publishing almost any fiction that comes across the board, and then does nothing for the writer.

KING: They publish *some* good fiction there. But you're correct, as I see it, when you charge that house with doing less than it could for many of its writers. According to its own claim, it has the most outlets for its books of any publishing house. They make a big thing of all the bookstores they own. This is an impressive consideration, especially to a writer who is new to the game or has had indifferent success elsewhere. So the writer spends a year, two years, three years writing his book. And while it may be the most important event of his life to the writer, it is merely number 702 to them. So they print 2,000 or 3,000 copies of the book and place them on the shelves of their many stores, where anyone willing to wrestle a salesclerk may buy one. Except in the cases of name writers or a rare book the house has unusual hopes for, this publisher seldom seems to strain its equipment either by making generous advances or offering large advertising budgets. The beginning writer or the semiobscure writer can have a half-dozen such experiences, can live half his productive life, without having much good happen to him. This house we're talking about isn't the only offender. Several big houses operate in that fashion: they put their money behind four or five big books per season and tend to let the remainder shuffle for themselves. By the way, I'm not speaking sour grapes: I haven't published with them, nor tried to. But book publishing is an inexact science, like soothsaying or chicken-sexing. I suppose each house has its reasons for operating as it does.

INTERVIEWER: Is there one novel, or any book for that matter, that you think was almost classically misinterpreted by critics or almost unanimously ignored by them, in which you personally found unusual merit?

KING: I could name several. Edwin (Bud) Shrake, a fellow Texan, wrote a novel called *Blessed Macgill*, published in 1968. It's a fine little novel, and it was almost wholly ignored by the critics. And in addition, Shrake's publisher didn't spend much more than fifteen cents for promotional purposes. I think it sold less than 2,000 copies, which is a goddamned shame. Because it *appeared* to be a story about a raunchy old Texas buffalo hunter, the reviews said, in effect, "Here's a novel about a buffalo hunter in early day Texas." In truth, *Blessed Macgill* is a subtle allegory on the absurdities of organized religion, and of that pomposity in man which inspires him to hold in high regard his more foolish myths and cultural habits. It makes comments pertinent to the universal condition of man that were relevant not only to frontier Texas, but that are relevant today or were relevant in the time of Christ. The mistaken concepts of frontier Texans toward Indians, for example, and their treatment of them, finds a parallel with our national attitudes toward black Americans today. I don't know that a single critic picked up on the social messages in the book or caught the comic justice in a crusty old whiskey-drinking, Indian-

killing, foul-smelling buffalo hunter being beatified after his
death on the basis of a self-serving diary apparently written in his
final days.

INTERVIEWER: Any other Southern writers whom you feel have been
shamefully neglected?

KING: Larry McMurtry, another Texan, has not exactly been ignored,
though I think he's better than is generally realized. His *Horseman,
Pass By*—very well mutilated by Hollywood as the movie *Hud*—
says as much through Hud Bannon, a Panhandle cowboy, as
Arthur Miller said about our crazy society through Willy Loman
or as Saul Bellow said through Professor Herzog. I think
McMurtry's best novel is *Leaving Cheyenne*. Who has heard of it?
Possibly because of McMurtry's root connections with the cowboy
life, and an unfortunate title that may have prompted people to
think of a TV series or a pulp Western, that book has remained for
most people a closely guarded secret. In 1968, he published *In a
Narrow Grave: Essays on Texas*. It appeared to a deafening critical silence, though it's as impressive a work on a time and a place in
America as is Alfred Kazin's haunting recollections of a Brooklyn
boyhood, *A Walker in the City*, or Norman Podhoretz' excellent
study of life in the New York literary jungle, *Making It*. Incidentally, Podhoretz was pretty foully treated by his fellow literary
critics who reviewed *Making It*. I guess a lot of old scores were settled.

INTERVIEWER: One more example of a miscarriage of literary justice?

KING: There are dozens. "Life is unfair," John F. Kennedy said shortly
before they shot him. Babs H. Deal published a novel in 1969,
High Lonesome World, about the life of a country music star. I've
never read a novel as knowledgeable about that native American art
form, or the poor, unlettered people who spend their lives in it. She
also perfectly captured the small-town mentality in her book, writing in the first person on behalf of perhaps a dozen major characters. Both male and female. And each time the voice rang true.
Really, it's quite a good job. I recommended that book to a certain
New York critic over drinks. The moment he learned its subject
matter he flared his nostrils as if he'd caught a whiff of something
malodorous.

INTERVIEWER: Back to this thing about publishing houses that ignore the writer—what can we do about it? How can the writer choose the publishing house best suited to his work and temperament, the house where he may drive the best artistic or financial deal for himself?

KING: He might try rolling the dice, or seek the services of fortune-tellers. No, seriously, it's a power game. The beginning writer is disadvantaged in such a game. He has little control over his own destiny. Generally he's so eager to publish he'll sell for a song and a promise. He really has no options. He knows less about the individual merits or demerits of a given publishing house than he knows about bringing in oil gushers. Once you've published a book or two and learn the game, then experience teaches what editor is good in this house, or what editor might be poison for him in that house, and so on. As in Congress, one soon learns where the power lies and also where the windbags are. He learns what house, or what editor, really loves books as opposed to those who love money best. As one learns, or his reputation improves, he finds more options open. The "successful" writer can go a long way in dictating his price, advertising budget, editor, promotional control, and, most importantly, the literary direction of his book. Especially if he has a hip agent.

INTERVIEWER: Should all writers have an agent?

KING: Yes. They're worth their 10 percent. They're professionals in a very tough game. They know how to get the best prices, the best exposure, they know all about escalation clauses, deferred payments and other business mysteries that terrify most writers. The only writer I know who doesn't need an agent is John Kenneth Galbraith. And he's not only an outstanding economist, he loves the confrontations of negotiation. Most of us are helpless lambs in such circumstances.

INTERVIEWER: People in writing classes sometimes tend to forget that this is not a wonderful, aesthetic pursuit wherein you write a book and forget about it.

KING: As Jake Barnes said to Lady Ashley in the final line of *The Sun Also Rises*, "Isn't it pretty to think so?" If you make your living writing, however, it doesn't work out that way. There are economic realities in publishing. Promotion, scheming, hustle, and midnight tears are part of the bit. I hate it. But, up to a point, I do it.

INTERVIEWER: Have you ever inserted anything in a book for purely commercial reasons?

KING: Daddy, you ask hard questions. How did they keep you out of the Gestapo? The answer is "Yes." In *The One-Eyed Man*, I was studying political power and the application of that power for good or evil. I really had no room in that book for sex. It was simply not a natural part of my theme. It was my first book, however, and I was eager to succeed and I therefore became easy prey for an editor who told me that if I didn't inject a few sex scenes I would lose 3,000 readers. That seemed like multitudes at the time. I allowed myself to be persuaded.

INTERVIEWER: Do you want to mention the editor's name?

KING: No, because I like the guy. He hurt my book, but then I should have been stronger. And I think he believed himself correct. Editors make honest errors the same as we natural geniuses.

INTERVIEWER: Did he *really* hurt your novel? I mean, wasn't it a selection of one of the major book clubs?

KING: Yes, but the sex was synthetic, inefficient, forced. Ken Galbraith wrote that my novel was the best political novel since *The Last Hurrah*, but in a private note to me he added that the sex scenes were "simply terrible" and that I had been wise to keep them short.

INTERVIEWER: I believe you read with some interest William Styron's *The Confessions of Nat Turner*. What are your opinions of that book?

KING: Let me first talk about Styron.

INTERVIEWER: Okay, fine.

KING: I was as much influenced by Bill Styron's first novel, *Lie Down in Darkness*, as any novel I've ever read. I read it in my early twenties, when I was aspiring to write without knowing whether I would ever publish a word. I loved it then, and when I reread it a year or two ago it stood up as few books do. I've read all of Styron's books. Critics jumped on *Set This House On Fire*, but it was a powerful story of human depravity and of evil in man. *The Long March* was a short and simple story, but stark and moving in its revelations of military brutality. Styron is a careful craftsman, a patient writer who gives years to his books—I think he worked on *Nat Turner* for something like seven years, and he had thought about it for twenty years—and when it comes to poetic prose few of his contemporaries can touch him. Passages in *Nat Turner* show again his rare gift for beautiful use of the language.

INTERVIEWER: I have the notion you are about to say, "But—"

KING: Right. *But,* the Nat Turner book doesn't make it for me. On first reading, I rather liked the book. I guess I wanted to like it, because I had long admired Styron's work and had shared the cup with him late into the evening on several occasions. A second reading and much thought changed my mind, however. I think Mailer put it too strongly when he said something to the effect that Styron writes like an angel about landscapes and like an adolescent about people, though I do think Styron is handicapped by romantic notions of the Old South. I think perhaps he has bought too much of the Southern myth about the general benevolence of slavery, about the nobility of the Southern heritage. He has a gentle and somewhat myopic view of Southern lore.

INTERVIEWER: What do you say to the criticism that in writing *Confessions of Nat Turner* Styron was guilty of an act of conceit or vanity in making himself, a white Virginian, into a black revolutionary like Nat Turner?

KING: That's a horseshit criticism. The artist has the right to place himself in any role he wishes to depict. He also has a right to tamper with historical fact in a work of fiction. Of course, he's also responsible for how well he pulls it off. I don't think Styron understands much about revolutions or the revolutionary mind, or, more specificly, black revolutionary minds. Not much of the revolutionary or social critic lives in Bill Styron's heart. He likes an ordered society. He's rich. Maybe he's too rich for the good of his art.

INTERVIEWER: I once had an interesting proposition put to me that all novels are historical fiction. That the good novels put things at a distance, at arm's length. Don't we need a stiff arm, what they call in more polite language an aesthetic perspective, to really do that? In other words, don't we need time and distance and a mulling over of history to write effectively in the novel form?

KING: Yes, that's what I meant earlier when I said that people with contented minds usually write the lasting novels. Though in order for any writer to understand the past, other writers earlier had to have accurately recorded the present in which they lived. Our best writers of this generation somehow seem to have exhibited a common quality—that is, an uncommon ability to record the nihilistic madness of our age. Traditionally in the novel, the protagonist meets and conquers. Beginning with the novels of the 1950's—though Norman Mailer was doing it as early as in the late 1940's with *The Naked and the Dead*—our fictional heroes routinely came, saw confusion, conquered not. Pick up John Barth's *The End of the Road* and—

INTERVIEWER: I just finished reading it.

KING: And you find no action in the early pages. None. Jacob Horner is little more than an inanimate object. He, as narrator, describes in minute detail the chairs, the commonplace objects around him. He reveals himself a helpless observer rather than an active force. He's describing a harsh and stark hospital-type room where he's waiting for a bullying and somewhat mystical quasi shrink on whom he's totally dependent. Barth transmits here some sense of what it is like to be wholly alienated in the society, wholly lost. Horner is a victim of his time, of changing values, of a world to which he can no longer relate, as was Willy Loman, Hud Bannon, Alex Portnoy, Professor Herzog, Tommy Wilhelm, Frederick Exley. These are lost men, men with whom the angry frantic world is impatient and unforgiving. "Heroes" in modern novels are men in extremis, Spender, I think it was, said. They are men in emergency situations without obvious connections in time and space. Rootless. Drifting. The opening paragraphs of James Joyce's *Finnegans Wake* suggests war, death, copulation: *everything* is happening. Contrast this with Barth's opening in *The End of the Road*, or Gunter Grass's beginning in *The Tin Drum*, or Beckett's start in *Molloy*. Hell, you can't even *guess* what is happening to the poor souls being presented as heroes. Hemingway would have pissed on such men and called them weaklings, cowards. For at least twenty years our best writers have been reflecting the "new" uncertainty in America. I'm impatient with critics who continue to demand loyalty to traditional concepts of plot and action. Some of them complain that modern novels fail to proceed in an orderly march from point A to point B to point C. Of course they don't. They can't. The goddamn *world* doesn't. The world is chaos and confusion and uncertainty, moving and changing more rapidly than ever before, rendering logic senseless in its headlong mad flight.

INTERVIEWER: You don't groove on critics, do you?

KING: Do mice groove on cats?

INTERVIEWER: How have critics generally treated you?

KING: With minimum high regard with respect to *The One-Eyed Man*. Generously, indeed, with . . . *And Other Dirty Stories*. My third book is at this moment some months away from publication, so we do not yet know how the rubber match will come out. It is an existentialist moment.

INTERVIEWER: Whatever that means.

KING: Get Mailer to explain it to you.

INTERVIEWER: Who's doing the best writing in America right now?

KING: Norman Mailer. He's king of the hill. I think he's doing his best work in nonfiction. I don't know your opinion of his latest novel, *Why Are We in Vietnam?*, but after three dogged readings I'm still at sea. That novel is as crazy as the times. And maybe, come to think of it, therein lies its claim to art. But I still don't understand it. Mailer seems, to me, to be uncomfortable in that novel. Perhaps his game was to reflect national confusions through the deliberate confusions of his prose.

INTERVIEWER: What of Mailer's nonfiction is your favorite?

KING: *The Armies of the Night* said more to me about my society and my time than any other contemporary book. *Miami and the Siege of Chicago* supplemented it. I recently heard Mailer read from the still-unpublished manuscript of his moon-shot book, *Of a Fire on the Moon*, and I think it may prove to be the first good literature on the Space Age. If one is interested in discovering more of Mailer-the-writer, with respect to his thought processes, he must list *Advertisements for Myself* at the top.

INTERVIEWER: What can we say about Southern writers, other than that we love them all? Now, who's the best?

KING: I nominate Faulkner. No man has better understood that part of the world in which he lived, or written of it better.

INTERVIEWER: Whom do you like among contemporary Southern writers?

KING: Eudora Welty. Robert Penn Warren. George Garrett. Georgia McKinley—

INTERVIEWER: Georgia McKinley? I haven't heard anything about her.

KING: She wrote a book of short stories several years ago, *The Mighty Distance*. Her new novel is *Follow the Running Grass*. She has a great feel for the land, for the Southern idiom. But where Georgia McKinley is merely good, Eudora Welty is simply great. Her short story "Why I Live at the P.O." is a classic.

INTERVIEWER: She's probably pulling her hair if she's reading this, because everybody in the world loves that story. Unfortunately, she's being remembered for that.

KING: Where is the misfortune in being remembered for an exceptional story? That one just jumps out at you—much as if you consider the work of Shirley Jackson, "The Lottery" is bound to jump out at you.

INTERVIEWER: Any more Southerners-of-letters you wish to nominate as exceptional?

KING: Let us not slight Styron. Nor Reynolds Price on his better days. William Price Fox, whose *Southern Fried* is funny thrice over. It's a collection of short stories. I also liked his novel, *Moonshine Light Moonshine Bright*, about two teen-agers who go in the bootlegging business. And, of course, I'm extremely partial to the work of Mrs. Henrietta P. Lazbuddy.

INTERVIEWER: *Who?*

KING: I just made that up, John, to see if you're alert. For the record it's 3:35 A.M. Let me move out of the South to say a good word for Fred Exley, too. Have you read *A Fan's Notes?*

INTERVIEWER: I have, and I loved it.

KING: Do you know what that novel sold, Professor Carr?

INTERVIEWER: No.

KING: It sold something like 7,500 copies. Didn't much more than pay for the paper. Goddam shame. I was tossing a few pots with Jimmy Breslin recently, who was out huckstering his best-selling *The Gang That Couldn't Shoot Straight*, and Breslin said he was almost ashamed to accept the money for his sales when a book as beautiful as *A Fan's Notes* did so poorly in a box-office sense.

INTERVIEWER: I was so enthusiastic about that novel that I bought spare copies and sent them to my friends. I told them to read it or never speak to me again.

KING: I did that years ago with Styron's first novel, and didn't do it again until A *Fan's Notes*.

INTERVIEWER: This conversation is germane, I think. A *Fan's Notes* won the Faulkner Award.

KING: It deserved the National Book Award *and* the Pulitzer. Here's a copy of it. How is it described in the subtitle?

INTERVIEWER: "A Fictional Memoir."

KING: Right on. Not pure fiction, right? Not a conventional novel. Your honor, I submit this beautiful book as Exhibit A in my contentions that contemporary writers find the straight novel insufficient to these times and to the deeds of these times.

INTERVIEWER: A *Fan's Notes* is, maybe, a book about a guy writing a book, or trying to write a book.

KING: That's what it is on the surface. It's really about a man trying desperately to maintain a grip on his slipping sanity.

INTERVIEWER: It has that in common with other contemporary novels we've discussed.

KING: Frank Conroy's *Stop-time* is another of those books that one reads with an increasing understanding of one's own limitations. And, back to Southern writers, Willie Morris' *North Toward Home* is a beautifully wrought thing. If you have lived in Texas and New York, as I have, and know something of life in Mississippi, as I do through a number of visits there, then you can make a value judgment about how well it captured each of those places from a period covering, roughly, the 1940's to the late 1960's. And it captured them very well, indeed. It's an important sociological study. Incidentally, David Riesman is teaching it as such here at Harvard this year.

INTERVIEWER: If I had to die tomorrow but could give some friend from the planet Mars the book he should remember us all by, I think I'd give him *Absalom, Absalom!* What would you give such a friend?

KING: A 10 percent discount on whatever work I had in progress.

INTERVIEWER: Oh, can't you ever be serious?

KING: I was never more serious in my life.

INTERVIEWER: Before the tape and our mutual patience is exhausted, will you name the writers who have influenced you most?

KING: It's an ever-changing list. But, at various times and in different periods, I have been influenced—perhaps overly influenced at times—by Twain, Mencken, Styron, Mailer, Faulkner, Warren, Ambrose Bierce, Ralph Ellison, Vance Bourjaily, H. Allen Smith, most of the biblical scribes, and one W. C. Brann, who had the honor of being murdered in a journalistic rivalry in Texas at the turn of the century. Right now I'm turned on by Kurt Vonnegut, among others.

INTERVIEWER: John Steinbeck?

KING: I liked him, but I can't say I was really influenced by him. Ditto for Hemingway, and for Faulkner. It's dangerous for any writer to let himself be strongly influenced by another writer when he sits down to do his thing. Robert Penn Warren should sue me for what I stole from him for *The One-Eyed Man*, and maybe A. J. Liebling's heirs have some small right to legal recourse. In fact, after reading an advance copy of my novel, Warren wrote our mutual editor that "It appears your new writer has been writing in my sleep." I'm much more my own man now.

INTERVIEWER: By way of discarding our last remaining friends, how about naming two or three writers you really hate to read? You can exclude the obvious hacks like Jacqueline Susann.

KING: Celine. Malcolm Lowry. John Updike. J. D. Salinger.

INTERVIEWER: Why?

KING: They depress me without giving the slightest bit of exhilaration.

INTERVIEWER: Do you think life is all laughs?

KING: No, it's mostly strangled cries.

INTERVIEWER: Perhaps that's a good one to quit on. Thank you, Mister President.

KING: Go and sin no more.

II

INTERVIEWER: What happened at *Harper's?*

KING: I'll quote Willie Morris: "It was a battle of the literary men against the money and, as always, the money men won." Perhaps that oversimplifies it a bit, but it's the basic truth.

INTERVIEWER: Were the money men really so disappointed they would bring about the confrontations that caused the resignation of all that talent—you, David Halberstam, John Corry, Marshall Frady, Midge Decter, Bob Kotlowitz, and John Thompson?

KING: They didn't like losing money. Actually, the business side of the magazine—headed by William Blair—tried to make the editorial side the fall guys. You see, mass periodicals have fallen on hard times. They go under one by one: *Collier's, Saturday Evening Post,* and now *Look.* It has to do with a changing America. Television grabs the advertising money now, or specialty magazines geared to a given audience. Add to that, we had the Nixon recession and, frankly, I think *Harper's* management panicked. Blair, whose title was publisher, but who was really business manager, sold the owner, John Cowles, Jr., on the idea that the magazine was in financial trouble because of the editorial content or because of loose spending practices on the editorial side. But all of us worked more cheaply there than we would have at any other magazine, because we believed in what Willie Morris was trying to do: publish the most exciting, the most literary magazine in the mass market.

INTERVIEWER: What did they pay you contributing editors?

KING: We all worked our own deals, so I can't speak for the rest of them. I wrote five articles per year for $12,500 plus expenses. That's nothing like big money. Since we all quit, I've made more money free-lancing, but I've enjoyed it less.

INTERVIEWER: What appealed to you about the Willie Morris crew at *Harper's?*

KING: First, Willie blazed the way in free use of the language. No subject was taboo, no word taboo, the writer could keep his integrity. Willie was a trailblazer in that respect. Second, we knew that we could take, within reason, whatever length we needed to do a story—10,000 words or 14,000 or 25,000 or whatever might be needed. You could really plumb the depths of your subject. The editors cared about what you said, cared about the prose. They didn't try to cut it down like a cable. And the association with those guys—Halberstam, Corry, Frady, Willie—hell, it was like a family, like a band of brothers. We are all terribly interested in fine writing, in reporting the world as we see it from our own private visions, in blowing the whistle and calling institutions to account. And we all held our whiskey pretty well. It was a great group.

INTERVIEWER: What's happened to the group?

KING: Frady hooked on with *Life,* and he's by far their best writer. Corry went back to the New York *Times.* Kotlowitz is in television news. The rest of us are free-lancing and writing books.

INTERVIEWER: Was there any way the group might have stayed together, had certain compromises been made?

KING: I doubt it. There are not many compromisers in the group. After John Cowles accepted Willie's resignation, the rest of us met with him to see if anything might be salvaged. But he walked in and coldly read us a 1200-word statement MacArthur might have hesitated to read to the Japanese on the U.S.S. *Missouri.* In effect it said, "You are a conquered people, and we have taken your emperor away, and from now on you only have those rights we choose to give you." We told him to fuck off and walked out. He really left no room for negotiations. It almost seemed a deliberate ploy to force us to walk out, but when we did—after about three hours of shouting at him—he grabbed Frady's arm and begged us to stay for more talks. I don't know. I couldn't rhyme his words with what he claimed he wanted. Halberstam said it was as if Cowles talked in Chinese and we listened in English, and vice versa.

INTERVIEWER: How did the whole *Harper's* affair come to a head?

KING: It's complicated. Let me go back to 1966, I guess it was. Willie Morris was then one of several editors at the magazine and early on, it appeared that John Fischer—then editor in chief—was grooming him as his successor. Fischer routinely threatened to retire on the first day of each January, effective the next July first, but never did. He just couldn't let go. Well, it rocked along that way for about three years. Then, in early 1966, Cowles met with me and Willie Morris to say he intended to buy the magazine and install Willie at the top. He—on Willie Morris' recommendation —wanted me and David Halberstam to come aboard as the first contributing editors, of which there would eventually be about ten.

We encouraged Fischer's retirement—Cowles, especially—and attained it. The magazine under Fischer had gotten rather old-maidish and cautious: articles like "Whither Abortion" and so on, none of them very bold or reaching any conclusions. Cowles told Willie he could have a free hand, and indicated we had five or six years to make it. I guess it was '67 by the time Willie actually took over and put together his team. Originally, John Cowles was very enthusiastic. He wrote us notes or called us, and came from Minneapolis to New York quite frequently. The future looked rosy. Well, we became the hottest book in the trade. You could hardly pick up the news mags or the newspapers or turn on a talk show without everyone saying what great things were happening at *Harper's*. And Cowles was all for it. When Willie proposed paying Bill Styron $7,500 for his long excerpt from *The Confessions of Nat Turner*, Cowles said, "Let's pay him $10,000 because it will sound better when word gets around. It will attract more good writers."

So we were on top of the world. Then Cowles—his family owns the Minneapolis newspapers—succeeded his father in running them, and had less time for the magazine. He sent in Bill Blair, an old ad salesman, who didn't have any appreciation of good writing. He just never understood what we were doing. Here was Willie getting Styron, Mailer, Frank Conroy, Feiffer, Plimpton, James Dickey, Irving Howe—God, you name 'em—in the magazine, and turning his own literary wrecking crew a-loose on the world, and Blair didn't know what was happening. He was a big man for staff meetings and paper-shuffling and all that, and wanted everybody to keep office hours. Willie is a great, great editor and a fine writer, but he has no more use for all that phony office politics than a bull has for teats.

So, in effect, he told Blair to go butt a stump. Blair ran to Cowles—and I wouldn't be surprised if John Fischer helped push us over the edge, because he never really seemed to approve of his protégé's success—and began to lay all the troubles of the magazine at the feet of the editorial department: the Morris Wrecking Crew. That's what they called us privately, we learned through a secretary. Next thing you know, Willie is asked to appear in Minneapolis periodically and justify his existence. He didn't have the patience for it, or the belly for it. Soon, he just abdicated Cowles's right ear, and Blair captured both of them.

INTERVIEWER: Was Willie's resignation the result of one of those Minneapolis meetings?

KING: Exactly. He came back from there steaming mad, saying he'd been attacked by Blair, Cowles, and several other of the money men and he wrote Cowles this tough letter saying he could not, and would not, go along with the scheme proposed at that meeting.

INTERVIEWER: What had been proposed?

KING: Fold the magazine immediately, fold it slowly, or drastically change its direction. Make it a specialty magazine. "Like *Ski Magazine*," Blair recommended. Willie's sense of history was offended—after all, *Harper's* was the oldest and perhaps the most respected periodical in America. He just couldn't preside over its becoming an organ for ski enthusiasts, or hubcap thieves or female impersonators, or whatever other narrow group they had in mind.

INTERVIEWER: What specific complaints did Cowles have when he met with you contributing editors after Willie Morris resigned?

KING: It's damned curious. All he could say was that he had asked Willie for an article on population control, and didn't get it, and one on the inner tickings of the FCC, and didn't get it. He had no other specifics, other than to complain we didn't have the proper "editorial mix." But he couldn't give us any clue what that might be. And he even suggested that some fool readership poll might be consulted to ascertain the future of our editorial content. Silly. A magazine must reflect some point of view, some sense of mission and coherence. Can you imagine what a mishmash you'd have leaving it up to the man in the street? Probably a lot of real snazzy articles about Popsicle vendors and patchwork quilting.

INTERVIEWER: I think you made an even more direct statement.

KING: Yeah. I said, "John, when I had absolutely no useful function to perform for the Free World one day, I read one of those silly readership surveys. One of the questions asked how they liked the new stitching and binding of the cover, and hell, I *work* there and hadn't noticed the difference. And as for using your poll to determine the editorial content, John, I've written for maybe thirty periodicals and *never once* have I been asked to tailor my work to some goddamned poll. And John, I'll kiss your ass till your nose bleeds if I'll stand for it now."

INTERVIEWER: And then?

KING: Well, that's when the shouting started. You just don't talk to rich men that way.

INTERVIEWER: What is *Harper's* future?

KING: I think after the press coverage our resignations got that they'll try to hang on, roughly, to the same format for a while. In the end, they may not make it. I do think they'll attempt the gesture, if only to salvage pride. Eventually, if it remains in the same hands, I think they'll fold it or go to a special audience.

INTERVIEWER: I still hear a lot of talk about how great the magazine was under Willie Morris. Do you think the Morris years will be remembered?

KING: Yes, damn right I do. He opened the magazine up to "New Journalism" in a way that nobody had before him. Other magazines became more bold by following his example. Jesse Hill Ford told me recently that he thinks our crew at *Harper's* will be remembered past the memory of the old "Fugitives" group—Red Warren, Allen Tate, *et al.*—because we were national, not merely regional, and really broadened the scope of mass periodicals. It would be pretty to think so.

INTERVIEWER: Is virtue its own reward?

KING: Of course not, fool.

INTERVIEWER: Is there sex after death?

KING: Not among Baptists.

INTERVIEWER: One more serious question: did the Norman Mailer article "The Prisoner of Sex" play an important role in bringing the *Harper's* situation to a head?

KING: Not really. That made good propaganda at the time, but not really. Oh, I think old John Cowles, Sr., disapproved of it, and there was some minor carping, but such a deep disenchantment existed between the money men and the literary men that it had to explode eventually. I will say for Cowles that he never once, to my knowledge, censored an article or tried to. Perhaps he just didn't appreciate what he had. Neither he nor Willie are very good politicians, and Blair is, in a Machiavellian sort of way, and so we were shot down.

INTERVIEWER: Who, in your opinion, was the best writer of that old *Harper's* group?

KING: I think Marshall Frady was the best writer, and Dave Halberstam the best journalist. Frady can make the language sing and hum and dance. He's like reading the Old Testament. Halberstam is the toughest-minded man I know, and when he gets the facts, he knows how to lay them out in a very effective, very controlled way. He's great at interpretation: telling you what the facts really mean.

INTERVIEWER: Then where does that leave you, Corry, *et al.?*

KING: Drunk at Table One at Elaine's, lamenting the dearth of talent at Table Two.

The Unique Voice:
❧ DORIS BETTS

Interviewed by GEORGE WOLFE

Doris Betts is a good-looking woman. She is small, about five feet four. Her shoulder-length auburn hair frames a lively face animated by two chocolate-colored eyes. When she smiles, she usually laughs. During this interview, she wore a green turtleneck sweater, and greenish, tightish jeans and buckled, calf-length boots made of some sort of animal hide.

The interview was conducted on Saturday, November 23, 1969, in the Betts home in Sanford, North Carolina. The paraphernalia of two teen-aged children, a nine-year-old, and two dogs was scattered about, including two motorcycles. The family owns two of the 90 cc hill-climbing variety, and Mrs. B. is an avid rider. One is certain she would be. She told me, laughing, that her highest ambition was to own a 500 cc Triumph motorcycle because "I find that what I like most is to get out on the highway and really open it up." A 500 cc cycle would have a top speed of about 120 mph.

Of her own schedule, Doris says she writes "whenever I catch time, which means anytime." She feels that she writes best fairly early in the day, and at one point in her life was rising at 5 A.M. to write for two hours. She has no particular retreat or special writing place and says she can write anywhere, in the dentist's office, laundromats, or wherever she must. "I once wrote a very bad novel during lunch hours in the restaurant of a Chapel Hill shopping center. Terrible place to write."

Doris Betts was born in 1932 in Statesville, N.C. She is the author of three novels, Tall Houses in Winter *(1957),* The Scarlet Thread *(1964), and* The River to Pickle Beach *(1972); and two volumes of short stories,* The Gentle Insurrection *(1954) and* The Astronomer and Other Tales *(1966). She has won many awards.*

INTERVIEWER: With your family, are you able to concentrate to the exclusion of things like dogs barking, children coming and going?

BETTS: Pretty much. The only thing I cannot disregard is a direct question. And that doesn't break my train of thought too much anymore; but that took time. That's one reason I get out of patience with students who say, "Oh, if I only had ideal conditions." And that's why I snarl. There are no such things as ideal conditions.

INTERVIEWER: Are you required by your editors to do much rewriting? Say on *The Scarlet Thread*, specifically?

BETTS: Yes, I did a pretty thorough rewrite of that, because they couldn't decide where the book was going; it didn't seem to have a recognizable theme. To begin with, this has something to do with the fact that novels are not my field. I do not do them well, and I seem to have to write a novel before I myself know what it's about. Whereas, with a short story, I usually grasp hold. This novel (the new manuscript in her hand) which I am revising now, is under contract. . . .

INTERVIEWER: Does it have a title yet?

BETTS: *The River to Pickle Beach*, which it's had for two or three years. It's going to require a complete rewrite of, I think, the first section, and some sharpening of the theme.

INTERVIEWER: How do you go about writing a story? Do you begin at the beginning, at the end, or do you take an incident and work backward to a critical point, something that would generate the story?

BETTS: At one time or another, I've done all those things you mention. I've written a few stories because I had what I thought was a lovely last line, or a last scene. But most of the time I start a story and I do not know at that point where it's going or what it's about. I have only an opening scene, and usually a character. But it falls in place out in front of me so quickly, that it seems to me that I knew it all the time. I am comfortable with short stories.

INTERVIEWER: How long has it taken you to do a novel, either one of the published ones?

BETTS: *Tall Houses* probably took about a year of steady work. And it's an extremely bad book. *Scarlet Thread* took maybe two or three years all together; although some was reading about the historical period, very little of which I wound up using. It's not a very good book either. This one has been thought about for as much as ten years, but has been written on in a concentrated way, for only about a year or one and a half. I'd never do a novel, by the way, if I didn't have to.

INTERVIEWER: Have to? Psychically or . . .

BETTS: No, financially and in a publishing sense. Because they don't really like short stories. They don't make any money off them. And they take the short stories, in order to get a novel. So for me, the novel is like the bread on the sandwich, I just slip in the bread so they'll let me do the filling.

INTERVIEWER: Do you make charts and diagrams for character deployment and plot? The sort of thing that Faulkner did for *A Fable*, on the wall?

BETTS: [*Laughing*] Well, the first time I did a book, I thought I had to do that, because Faulkner did it. And I did have things pasted up. It didn't help me very much. The second time, I forgot about doing it, and I got everything all screwed up. Really. I lost track of when people had been born or died, how old they were, what color the curtains were three chapters back. And this last one I went ahead and finished before I looked back to see the inconsistencies. It depends, I think, on the kind of novel . . . In *The Astronomer*, as a matter of fact, in the first version, I had her pregnant for something like eleven months. And that was not caught until the copy editor caught it. I *should* keep track, that's why I laugh. I don't, but I should.

INTERVIEWER: Lawrence Durrell says he 'pinches' or steals from certain writers. Do you do that, and if so, consciously or unconsciously?

BETTS: Yes, I do think I do that. I make students at Carolina keep journals. And I keep notes and journals too, most of which I lose. A lot of what goes into a journal, such as a quote, or a scene that impressed you, you wind up using, not consciously. What happens is after I've finished it and sent it off, I find an old notebook from six months ago; then I am aware that I have pinched. It's often a situation, maybe, or a quality, an aspect of one character. I doubt very much if the writer I stole it from would be conscious of it. I hope not.

INTERVIEWER: O.K., let's get down closer to the nitty-gritty. What about the subject of being a Southern writer, specifically a Southern woman writer? Could you comment on the nature of Southernness in your stories and novels?

BETTS: I think to think of oneself as A Southern Writer is to come by hindsight and to pick up the characteristics everyone else applies to you. I never really thought about it until, oh, about four or five years ago. I began to read literary criticism for the first time in any kind of serious way. It fascinated me very much about other writers, until I had the opportunity to see a little bit written about myself, which I thought was so awful. Eudora Welty said one time it was a little like a woman with her petticoat tail cut off, who said, "This is none of me." And I suspect this is what all writers feel about the categories they're put into. I'm a Southern writer in the sense that this is the landscape I know, and the climate, and the people, I'd be a fool not to make use of that. But I'm not so certain that people are that different in one part of the country from another. I can't as a matter of fact imagine my people set down in Indiana, as Hugh [Holman] said, because Indiana is only a word for me; I don't have any . . . hills, or temperatures to go with the idea. But I'm not aware of being anything except someone who writes from the things she has seen and heard.

"Woman writer" is even more offensive to me than "Southern writer." I don't know why, exactly; I don't like it.

INTERVIEWER: It implies, perhaps a certain weakness in the way it's asked.

BETTS: Well, no, I don't think it should imply a weakness, unless, of course, you happen to believe that women are weaker, which to begin with, I do not. I really think [*pause*] that more women should have been writers, good writers, than are, since the subjects which interest fiction writers are the subjects with which women have been forced or have chosen to spend their lives: that is, very close relationships with other people, both the young and the old. And they do tend to spend much of their life in personal terms, which I think is what the fiction writer is doing, unless he is a huge novelist like Tolstoi and can really think about society. Which I cannot anyway. That may be feminine.

INTERVIEWER: Do you think there is any such animal as a Southern mystique which inheres somehow mysteriously below the Mason-Dixon line, with which the writer can work?

BETTS: I seem to have what people like W. J. Cash said was a Southern mystique, which is a strong sense of family, and of land, and of seasons, and the old biblical traditions, and a rather stern sense of morality, as a matter of fact. I'd like to have a deeper look at other regions of the country before I'm persuaded that that is not fundamentally American and hearkens back to the pioneer spirit, rather than just this region. I mean, how else would I have been, being outdoors nine months out of the year, at least? Of course the seasons matter, and I did happen to grow up with farm people, or one generation removed from farm people.

INTERVIEWER: It seems apparent that the Bible plays a large part in your writing. In *The Scarlet Thread*, for instance, there are introductory quotes from Joshua and Genesis, and you have named four characters Esther, Thomas, David, Samuel. Would you comment on that, on the significance of that, if there is any, in your mind?

BETTS: Well, part of it is from having looked back into that period of North Carolina history. People did then still name children from biblical sources. The Bible is a strong source in my writing because I grew up in a strict religious family, strongly fundamentalist. I must have spent the same equivalent number of hours in church or church-related things as my children do now at television. I mean, morning and evening services, choir practices, prayer meetings, and the whole bit.

INTERVIEWER: Not to mention revivals.

BETTS: Not to mention revivals, for which I played the piano. My mother greatly wished that I would grow up to be a missionary. In fact she saw herself as Hannah, and me as Samuel, to be given to the Lord's service. I've let her down rather badly in that regard. But you don't get away from anything you breathed in and out over that long a period of time. Often the Bible stories themselves are marvelous, really marvelous, background for a writer—a lot of the rhythms, to begin with, in the Bible. And secondly, all those stories are very physical, very specific and concrete. Some of them are dreadful stories. There is no pretense or Pollyanna quality in the Bible any more than there is in Grimm's fairy tales. And you come out of them with a great sense of the flesh, and the blood, and the same material which

I did see about me, and about which I have written extensively.

INTERVIEWER: Are you Esther? And are you ever a character?

BETTS: I've been parts of many characters. I've been told that I write better about women characters than about men. We're back to the feminine business. That may be because I'm using things I know without having to think about them, which is, I think, what one does best with fiction. What you know with your bones and corpuscles is better than what you know rationally and by research. I've been in many characters. In this last book of short stories, there are two stories about a girl-child, which are autobiographical events, completely. And various other things in the books are.

INTERVIEWER: Let's pursue this a moment. Generally, how much autobiography is present in your work? For instance, the story "The Spies in the Herb House" in *The Astronomer* volume is so well done, it is difficult to think the re-teller could be anyone but yourself.

BETTS: Yes, that was me, and a rather stupid child, too. I read part of that story at the Governor's School. And we had a number of black students there. When they finally realized that I was so dumb, that it had taken me forever to figure out what those four letters were on the wall, they literally fell out of their desks laughing. And I felt very, very old.

INTERVIEWER: What writers do you admire, and have they been the same ones who have influenced you directly?

BETTS: No, no they've not been the same. I'm changing all the time. When I first began writing short stories, I strongly admired Katherine Anne Porter, partly, I know, because I met her in college, and she gave me some advice on revising a story, "The Sympathetic Visitor," which did appear in *The Gentle Insurrection*, in her version, not in mine. She made an enormous impression on me, and I do admire her stories. She was my long-time heroine; since then, I have come to like Flannery O'Connor better, and I like a writer like Muriel Spark, whose precision I admire. I like many of the new writers who write not at all like me. Donald Barthelme. I still read Chekhov a great deal. Some of John Barth when he's not too cute. I read so much that it's hard to give an answer. Oh, Rilke, especially *The Duino*

Elegies and *Notebooks of Malte Laurids Brigge.* Also Wright
Morris, because he writes so fluidly and plays with time.

INTERVIEWER: Have women writers influenced you more than men?
Do you feel, for example, any sort of especial connection with
Flannery O'Connor, Carson McCullers, or even Harper Lee,
all of whom are Southern and women?

BETTS: No. No, very strongly. Male writers have influenced me more,
I think, by and large, although I did happen to name some
women writers. Just as in my personal life, I think men have
influenced me a great deal more than women.

INTERVIEWER: Do you feel any particular connection with any of
your contemporaries? Do you think anybody's doing rather the
same thing you're doing, or are they *after* the same thing, men
or women?

BETTS: I don't really believe any writer feels much connection with
other writers, as such. It's such a by-yourself business, that if you
turn out to be writing about similar themes, it's almost by luck,
or accident, or over such an unbelievable pattern that you don't
even examine it. What I feel sometimes is a kinship with other
people's books, or something in them. But with the writers themselves, no. In fact, I don't want people reading my book and
thinking about *me*, individually, and I try to pay other writers
the same compliment. I would never put a picture on a dust
jacket if I had my way. I think all that's very tacky.

INTERVIEWER: All right, back to the religion a minute. First of all,
what religion are you, how were you raised? Does this affect you
by giving your thought or your approach a slant?

BETTS: I was raised an A.R.P., an Associate Reform Presbyterian,
usually known in my family as "all right people." It was a very
fundamentalist church—sang only the Psalms, for after all, they
were all inspired by God, whereas the hymns were written by mere
human beings. I had so much church and religion in those days,
that as to what I am now, I am an expatriate, and gladly.
However, the influence was enormous and continuous, and I will
never be free of the ethic, nor of the emphasis on emotion in
people, which really, I feel is stronger than reason in people.

INTERVIEWER: Then the biblical names I mentioned don't seem to
have any larger significance, à la *Grapes of Wrath?*

BETTS: No. No more than that Queen Esther was somewhat in mind. She was the queen of the family, more or less. No. Other than that, no significance.

INTERVIEWER: I'm not certain what a mythic background is, but it seems to me an interesting question. Do you think there is any mythic background in your work, any Southern mythic thing, or are you working in terms of any sort of myth at all? Archetypes?

BETTS: If so they are more apt to be biblical than "Southern." I do tend to work in families, father-son. And in salvation loss. Even though all that is really hindsight. I am engaged in telling stories, more than anything else, and I don't like all that nit-picking which goes with it. I feel that for a writer to be drawn into that kind of discussion is both to give himself away, and to besmirch what he is doing. You spend all your life learning to write many-layered, so that the story is there and the echoes and shimmers are there underneath it. Then when you are asked to stop synthesizing and start analyzing, it is a process of taking all those threads apart, which, as a matter of fact, the analyzers don't know how to put together anyway, so why should you play their game when you've spent most of your life learning how to speak in unison?

INTERVIEWER: Very good. Are you interested in employing symbolism? And if so, do you, and where?

BETTS: I do employ symbolism. Do you know the story Mary McCarthy tells about the student who took her paper to the creative writing teacher, who told her it was a fine paper, but now she must go back and put the symbols in—which does make any writer's blood run cold. What usually happens in symbolism in a story, is exactly what happens in your dreams. First the real thing is there, or the real experience, and as you go back and shape and put in the layers you are using symbolism whether you will or not, because symbol is a part of our lives. But to set out to do it in cold blood . . . To do it in cold blood, consciously, is to bend the story to the purpose, instead of bending the purpose to the story. On second and third drafts, I sometimes sharpen symbols, although I am not always conscious they are symbols. They are really things that are alive in the story, that mean more than one thing—that ring.

INTERVIEWER: Would you comment on the regionalistic characteristics in your work? Please use this definition or guide: The type of fiction wherein the action and personages of a work cannot be moved, without major loss or distortion, to any other geographical setting.

BETTS: If you wrote about people who could not be moved to another setting, then regionalism would not be much better than the fantasies that one tells oneself in order to go to sleep on a tense night. The kind of fiction that comes out of a region and lasts, lasts not because of the region nor the latitude in which it is cast, but because of whatever is in the story that is human, that is sustained over more than a geographic area. For instance, the Irish as writers are not significant because they are Irish, although there is all this specialness of the Irish heritage. Someone said of Chekhov, "He wrote the universe into Russia." Now, *that* is what good regionalism is, using what you have and what you know, in such a way that you can *get it all in* . . . into a parable of some kind, that will be just as meaningful and will not have to have too many footnotes anywhere in the world at any time.

INTERVIEWER: Fair enough. A couple of questions about your connection with the students and the university. You have the reputation among your writer friends here as being a first-rate editor—a person who can and will tear a story apart and find most or all of its flaws, and give it back with a smile. Does this talent help you in your own writing? Are you a good editor of your own work?

BETTS: [*Laughing*] I think I've *become* a good editor of my own work. I have had good editors, and have learned a great deal from them, in the newspaper field, where I learned about never using two words when one can do double work. But also in publishing houses in New York. I have a copy editor so meticulous at Harper's that she will mark a sentence such as " 'Don't do that,' he hissed." She'll say, "There are no *s*'s in this sentence, so they cannot hiss." To me, that kind of attention to detail shown an appreciation for what proper detail can do on a big scale. Because when the details are done right, you never notice them. They become invisible. Only that which is beautiful and lasting comes through. And I do think your style should be like that pane of glass through which you can see the heart of the story absolutely clearly without distortion.

I like editing. I feel that editing students' stories has helped me edit my own work. Although even now, I do not like to go back and look at anything I've published, because I always see more that could be done with it. And a split infinitive left in print just gives me the hives.

INTERVIEWER: You teach creative writing at UNC–Chapel Hill. How does this affect your writing? (You just mentioned something about this.) Does it make you more cautious in your own work?

BETTS: I've been warned that that's going to happen. The effect it's had on me so far is to open me out. And the two books I have recently done, the collection of short stories which is not yet published nor contracted for, and the novel which is contracted for, are both for me new things either in style, device, or subject matter. I particularly feel it in the last twelve or thirteen short stories which I have done—that my style has changed a great deal, and I think the university has been the cause of it. For one thing, I am writing more, umm, snide humor than comes easily to me. And I am enjoying that. I seem to be a looser writer. The risk for a short story writer, is always that he may become rigid and close himself into some kind of a box. The university has prevented that. It has made me more experimental, in fact. I may be now more careful about each sentence, but the overall freedom is greater.

INTERVIEWER: What do you look for in your young writers' work? Do you find their mistakes to be uniform, such as adjectival and adverbial fixations? Or do you find that their mistakes range over the whole spectrum?

BETTS: The first thing I find among young writers today is that they have read abysmally little, as a background. Some of the predictable stories that one gets every semester you can look for: the boy and girl story written by the girl. There is a lot of mental activity in a chintz bedroom. A lot of thought and no action, a lot of thinking about romance in one of those teaster beds. A horse story occasionally. Max [Steele] says he gets suicide stories; I don't and that makes me feel much more mentally healthy as a teacher than Max does: [*laughing*] I feel that maybe I have an uplifting effect.

Most of the students tend to rebel against form—which I think is very healthy, but it's not very good for a short story writer who first has to learn the form, and then how he can break it. . . . Well. I wish they would read more. It makes it very hard to discuss ways of doing things because you have not enough common ground between you. This is particularly true in the short story field; they've read *very* few short stories. And they want to write stories like novels.

INTERVIEWER: Is there any particular background that's better for an aspiring writer, do you think? Faulkner once said that all you need is a penny pencil and a nickel pack of paper. If you have something to say, it'll come out.

BETTS: I just gave half my answer to that—about reading. The best background I ever had was when my mother went uptown to shop on Saturdays. She couldn't afford a baby sitter, so she took me to the library. Since she was shopping for everything, clothes, groceries, everything, it took her hours and hours. It didn't take me long to realize that you could cut through the employees' bathroom and get into the adult section. Therefore, I read and read and read. The librarians were strict censors, and you couldn't check out anything that was above your age level, but you could go back and read anything.

I feel that if you do not read, you are always comparing your own work to life; and in truth the short story, in particular, is not the same thing as life. It compares to other fiction, but it does not compare to what happens to us day in and day out. You don't know what world you're really working in if you're not well versed in what has been done before and what has been done so well that it comes down and rings in your heart after a thousand years.

INTERVIEWER: You're on the school board of Sanford, North Carolina, a town of thirteen or fourteen thousand. Does this have any effect on your writing in terms of black-white confrontation as it obtains in 1969?

BETTS: Well, I think the times have had more effect on that. I sat down not too long ago and looked back at the first novel I wrote and I found the black characters to be extremely embarrassing to read back on. I was hoping the black friends I have would never check out this book anywhere. And yet, I was not conscious of working in stereotypes. I am not sure they were stereotypes; because that's what I knew then. The times themselves have had the biggest effect. I've written very little about schools and about students and about teachers. I don't know why.

INTERVIEWER: Now, in 1969, political activism is terribly important to a large group of "artistic" or "sensitive" people. Do you see any sort of Marxian responsibility of the artist in this regard? And what function does the artist have in this uniquely disruptive, antiwar, anti-intellectual, anticompetitive, group-therapy generation?

BETTS: First of all, I don't think the artist has any more or less responsibility than anyone else, and whether or not he becomes socially involved is not a matter of his profession, but of his temperament. Now, there are writers who I think are better off if they stay home in the garret working on their fiction, or whatever. But there are other writers who, because of the way they are made, and not because of the fact that they happen to be artists, feel that they *must* get involved. All right, for someone like me who is no longer going to Sunday school every week, I am by personal temperament stuck with doing something else to placate that old-timey conscience they built into you. I do think it is possible to get so involved in this that you do not write at all, but to me some involvement in your society feeds your sources, in the same way that the university feeds our sources. I won't comment at all about what other writers do or don't do. That's their bag.

INTERVIEWER: An old question—but as a woman, a mother, a wife, are there peculiar problems you face, ranging from the sheer problem of time, to any feminine hangups, obstructions, which you could define as singularly female?

BETTS: Give me an example.

INTERVIEWER: Sex, for example. Your literary approach to sex as opposed to a man's.

BETTS: I always took for granted that if you wanted to be a writer in this century and age, you had to work harder than if you didn't, because it usually led to a minimum of two jobs. If you're a woman and want to be a writer, you have to work harder still, because you have to do a minimum of three jobs. That's the main thing. Most of the hangups are vested outside you; in other words, the question of sex, for instance, if you're happy yourself, doesn't come up. What other people think about you doesn't concern you. I get a lot of flak sometimes, from people who are horrified because I write about some things, but I don't know that they'd be any less horrified if I were a man. And if they think it's any worse because I am female, well, then, you see, that's *their* problem, it's not mine.

INTERVIEWER: What about the creation of male characters? It's often said that women run aground on them. Jane Austen for one.

BETTS: I don't think I do male characters very well. I think I wanted to, to prove to myself I could. One of the things about writing about men which trips you up are the very little things. One thing, I always forget to let men shave. Writing from their viewpoint, I simply forget about it entirely. The little things I think, more than the big things. However, when I write about a male character, it seems to me he has a feminine cast. There's one of the few times I would admit to femininity. There's usually something . . . if I met him, he would not attract me; and I think that's because of a certain femaleness that is in him.

INTERVIEWER: Do you write poetry?

BETTS: I began by writing poetry—most of it very bad—and had the good fortune to have a teacher at UNC–Greensboro named James Painter who told me, your poetry is terrible, but your prose is not bad. So I switched to prose. I still write poetry for myself, and keep notes in poetry. It's not a bad idea for a short story, because you tend to condense an emotion even more, and it's like a seed for a story.

INTERVIEWER: Do you write plays?

BETTS: I've written several plays. They've not been very good either. I haven't done anything with them. There again, that's a discipline that makes you do everything in a dramatic way without commentary, and I think it's a good discipline.

INTERVIEWER: How do you react to criticism? Do you bother to read reviews?

BETTS: I read them all, and although I think it's a shame to admit it, I bleed profusely over every one. I think one should be above that, and I'm more above it than I used to be. I don't write angry letters. I do occasionally write a letter to someone who has done a review that is perceptive, not to thank them for it, because I think that's gauche, but simply to let them know that it was good reading. Because I think there is a difference between good writing and good reading, and I think there are not enough readers.

INTERVIEWER: Are there any other writers in your family?

BETTS: [*Laughing*] Lord, no. I do not come from a bookish family at all. That's really so funny. I'd love to go home at Thanksgiving, and tell that around the table, and hear the hilarity.

INTERVIEWER: Do you paint?

BETTS: I fooled with it this summer and put up with so much criticism from my family about how much I should be doing other things. I wish I could paint. How did you know that, why did you ask me that?

INTERVIEWER: God knows. Just wondered. But, Aldous Huxley had Philip Quarles say in *Point Counter Point*, "I am not a congenital novelist." Do you think you are? You are divided equally between two volumes of short stories and two novels.

BETTS: No, I am an artificial and contrived and forced novelist. It is entirely a matter of economics. I think there is a different temperament that goes with writing novels than with writing short stories. And if the Guggenheim Foundation spent one year testing all novelists and all short story writers, they would find that they all have a different metabolism and rate of breathing and different thought patterns and different blood pressures and different body temperatures. For me to be a novelist is entirely a forced action. I have not yet written a good novel, and I should be very much astonished if I ever do anything more than a competent novel. I would like never to have to do one.

INTERVIEWER: Again to current cosmology. What place, if any, do you see for the mind-expanding drugs now in vogue, especially among the young? Do you think it—the experience—is valid, artistically?

BETTS: Well, it would never do for me. That's the first thing. Since most writers I know have been "turned on" always; and if anything, it's trouble enough to turn "down" enough to put it on paper, instead of going around engulfing everything. My experience from observing people I know who have dropped acid and everything else is that it is an illusion, because if it's pursued long enough—and this is the thing that I see that frightens me the most—it destroys particularity in a writer. He does come out with some amorphous and magnificent feeling which he finds very difficult to communicate. The more he is absorbed in drugs, the more he thinks he has achieved a beautiful insight. And for all I know, he has. I do know that his communication of it becomes more and more incoherent; thus, we never catch the glimmer of it that he feels. And he has bought it, I feel, at the price of being a writer. I think he should know that before he sets out on the bargain, that's all.

INTERVIEWER: Have you ever dropped any acid, smoked any pot?

BETTS: Obviously not.

INTERVIEWER: When you reread early stuff, how do you react to it?

BETTS: I never have liked anything after it was written. I do not go back and read, except in agony and with regret. Always what's coming seems to be what's worth doing.

INTERVIEWER: How deliberate are you in the matter of technique?

BETTS: Not at all, while I am writing. That's like Katherine Anne Porter, who said she spent all her life learning about technique, so that when she sat down to write, she could forget it. I think that makes a great deal of sense. It's like learning to dance so that you no longer have to count the notes or watch your left or right foot.

INTERVIEWER: Some psychologists have suggested the creative urge is a kind of neurosis. Comment?

BETTS: Well, if most of the people I see every day are normal, then, yes, I am neurotic.

INTERVIEWER: Have you written anything under a pseudonym?

BETTS: No. No, and I would like to. But I haven't quite figured out how you would cash the checks.

INTERVIEWER: Do you review, and if so, what and for whom?

BETTS: I used to do a great deal of reviewing. *Saturday Review* and the New York *Herald Tribune*, four or five newspapers. I finally quit it; it took a great deal of time, and I found that I had to review a great number of terrible books in order to get one or two that I wanted to keep. Also, if you review for anything in New York, they send you what *they* think are Southern novels, which by and large are corn pone fakes. I couldn't stand reading those one after another. Really tiresome.

INTERVIEWER: What are the favorites among your stories?

BETTS: Back to old work, I don't have any favorites there. My favorites are two stories. . . . I like the story that is in the *Red Clay Reader* this year ["The Ugliest Pilgrim"], and I like the story which I haven't been able to sell to anybody, called "Beasts of the Southern Wild." Next year I won't like them either, though. But that's what I like now, because that's recent.

INTERVIEWER: The length of *The Astronomer* story is peculiar. What do you call it? Why this length? [110 pages] Did you start out to write a novel which got shortened or a short story which got lengthened?

BETTS: I did start out to write a novel. *The Astronomer* and *The Scarlet Thread* were both begun under a Guggenheim Fellowship. At the time I was supposed to be working on two novels, and they were the two. It's just that *The Astronomer* would not be any longer than it was. Which meant it was absolutely unpublishable except eventually in a book. Therefore I wound up publishing *The Scarlet Thread* first, and *The Astronomer* second, together with some stories. It is an odd length. As I look back I think it was good training for me. I still say I'm not a novelist, but I think I learned something from writing that which has helped me in working on this novel, which is a shorter length than the novels I've done before. I think I'm sort of working up to a form that does not come naturally to me.

INTERVIEWER: What are your feelings about the responsibility of the writer to language and its living quality? Does a thing like *Webster's Third New International Dictionary*, which quotes such luminaries as Elizabeth Taylor and Willy Mays, bother you?

BETTS: Yes, I'm afraid I'm a purist about language, since I think that's all we have. It takes so long to learn to use words that when the world at large blunts the meaning after I've spent years trying to get more and more and more precise and exact, I am as incensed as a surgeon would be if someone came in and blunted his scalpels while he was out to lunch. I think that is a very unfair and irrational reaction, but I do have it.

INTERVIEWER: Again, a woman question. You have several times written about the pain and, for a man, unknowable agony and sublimity of childbirth. In the case of Rosa Bennett in *The Scarlet Thread*, the abortion of Eva in *The Astronomer*—are these the especial provinces of women writers? Not the provinces perhaps, but the peculiar areas in which a woman excels?

BETTS: Well . . . .

INTERVIEWER: You have three children. . . . I mean, I don't want to remind you of that, but . . .

BETTS: Until you said that, I was going to say that I'd only written one story about that. Which proves that I really think of stories first. I have written one story about that which is in this new collection. Both those times you mention, the child does not survive. And to me that is what is ultimately painful and what casts back a painful air over the whole physical experience. The physical experience of childbirth for me has been, as a matter of fact, relatively comfortable and uncomplicated. I think the body is so constituted that it's very difficult for women to remember once the birth is accomplished, because your attention is then focused so much on the future and on the product. I do think it is something that I know and that I can write about in the sense that I cannot write about a man shaving, for instance, or other, sexual activities from a man's viewpoint in quite the same way—having been there.

INTERVIEWER: Thomas in *The Scarlet Thread* is a very destructive character. He kills the old black savant, Miss Bethesda Lee Michael. He bites his wife in making love to her, he hurts people rather indiscriminately after he grows to manhood. Would you comment on his perverseness—on his nasty nasty nature?

BETTS: Only that I tend to polarize, again perhaps from a religious upbringing. If you had asked me what I thought the two greatest human virtues were, I would probably have said intelligence and kindness. Therefore when I make a villain he is almost inevitably . . . It is hard to make a villain stupid, for then you feel sorry for him, he can't help it. But he is almost inevitably cruel. To me this is what is heinous in man. I think man is the only creature who can be willfully cruel to his fellows.

INTERVIEWER: David Allen in *Scarlet Thread* is a strange and fascinating character with his artistry and woodwork, his gentleness and strength. Would you comment on him?

BETTS: What finally interested me was what kind of individual in this society, this kind of society, can make a life for himself within what I think is the oppressive nature of cotton mill towns and even the grinding poverty of many small farms, which is what I know best. There were two: there was the rebel Esther who ran away and then, the one who was some kind of an artist if only a local craftsman or artisan. He just developed as a woodcutter and a stonemason more or less by accident—partly because we had a sculptor friend at that time whom we saw a lot of, Robert Howard. I think he is extremely good. I called up a big old chunk of sandstone in the yard and a wood chisel and a hammer and went out and beat on it so I would know just where you get hit and hurt when the mallet misses, and where you get sore. So that's what David became. And the tombstones, just because death and cemeteries sooner or later get into everything I write.

INTERVIEWER: Have you ever drunk moonshine whisky? Most of your characters prefer it exclusively to the bonded variety.

BETTS: Yes, I've drunk it, and it's terrible. Even with a peach floating on the top, which is supposed to help it.

INTERVIEWER: Are there any bootleggers in your family?

BETTS: We'll never tell.

INTERVIEWER: Did Thomas Allen in *Scarlet Thread* really, "never had a chance" as he says?

BETTS: Of course he had a chance. I was just doing what a writer does in fiction which is to make the characters' excuses for them.

INTERVIEWER: There is also a good deal of sex or visceral activity in your work, for instance, in "Spies in the Herb House" where the children's total innocence is juxtaposed to the depravity of the graffitti; the Mandarin is very aware of her sexual uselessness. "Clarissa and the Depths" deals with a black girl who is about to have her first sexual experience, obviously wants it and fears it. In "Proud and Virtuous," the woman watching the road gang is apparently sexually aroused by the thought of half a dozen sweaty, strong, lawless, horny convicts gathered at her back door drinking lemonade. And others. Would you comment on sex in your work?

BETTS: Max [Steele] said not long ago that Hugh [Holman] had said to him that the one thing that I had not developed fully or given full attention to were my proclivities for writing about sex. As it turns out, this past year I think I have written more material that has a sexual center than ever before. That may have something to do with my advancing age. I'm not certain about that. Or that I am no longer disturbed by what anybody would think about it. I may have at one time been bothered by that.

I have the feeling that fiction works best when it springs from the body and from the senses rather than from the cerebrum, and that most of the symbolic quality of fiction ultimately gets right back to a nerve ending or a sense or a texture, or a sensation, rather than to an intellectual thought. I like writing physically, which I do all the time, but not so much sexually because I believe most other scenes are physical, and that has been increasing in what I have written. And the last stories I have written in this book are probably even more physical. Also, when you do reread old work, the more you have philosophized, the more you will be embarrassed; and the more you've dealt with what people feel in the body the more you are apt to have been true, if you weren't faking it in the beginning.

INTERVIEWER: Are you particularly interested in astronomy?

BETTS: I wasn't a bit interested in astronomy as such except for the purposes of that book, and I had to do a good bit of reading at the time. In a small town your life is likely to repeat the same patterns anyway if you are not careful, and if you are an omnivorous reader you do tend to incorporate into what you are writing whatever interests have sprung up in you like a brush fire for the time being. At one time or another I've been interested in 5,000 different things and it's helped feed the books. I don't mean it in the sense of Ian Fleming where you learn all about golf in one chapter. And yet, there is the sense of constantly making the work have more substance or weight or even fact. There's something precious about fact if you don't let it get out of hand. I got interested in birds some time ago and that's been in some things I've written. I'm interested in growing flowers from cuttings; that's been involved in it. Lately I've been reading a lot about fictional technique, therefore it's no surprise to me that in this [new] novel there will be a chapter in which fictional technique is explored, and so on. That's just a matter of what interests you spilling over.

INTERVIEWER: Are you interested in mythology? Greek, Roman, or other?

BETTS: Greek intensely. The only things you had in my house to read were the Bible and associated books, the farmer's almanac, Zane Grey's westerns, and Edgar Rice Burroughs' Tarzan stories; and one old book of Greek myths which I began to read when I was about seven or eight, I suppose. They enchanted me for the same reasons that Old Testament stories did except they are a much airier, much less human kind of mythology. A winged horse is not quite the same thing as the stories of David and Tamar. I took Greek in college, read a great many Greek tragedies, and still do.

INTERVIEWER: Would you explain the map versus the labyrinth bit in *The Astronomer*? I don't really understand that.

BETTS: You're the only person who has ever asked me that, and I'm rather pleased at that. However, it's been so long since I've looked at it that I doubt if I can do much with the question; except to say that at the time I was interested in the people who go through life as if it is preset, as if . . . By preset, I mean either by religion or by their parents' standards, or whatever way you think you can come in and it's all set up for you, and if you follow it, you come out all right. That's the map. The labyrinth is my preference: that everyone is in here all by himself for the first time and the only time, and he has to make it up as he goes along, he has to blaze his trees as he goes along entirely. And that there is no certainty—ever, as to how he will come out, and he can only learn so much from the map makers. That kind of distinction interests me. [*Pause*] Let me say more about that.

INTERVIEWER: Go ahead.

BETTS: All right, a long time ago, at least, and I've changed somewhat, but not too much, I thought the reason I was interested in writing was because I was fundamentally interested in mortality —in Thornton Wilder's having said, "Every human being who's ever lived has lived an unbroken sequence of unique occasions. It's the unique occasions that interest me." And that's what fascinates me about character. I think it's true that I write about the lower and lower-middle class, because the mortality is much closer to the edge of the veil there. It's a more primitive way of living, and one is conscious every time you sing old down-home, thumping hymns that death is always present, and that one is talking about it in terms of blood, flesh, and perishing. And I do think every human being is so unique and is not going to be duplicated. He's the only one who ever was and ever will be. It's like William Saroyan saying, "I began writing in order to get even on death." I think that's not a bad reason, really. You pick the place where you think you have the best chance of getting even, and it turns out to be either where you grew up, or these people with whom you grew up, because they are the ones whose death will hurt you deepest; and if that is what you are against, then that's where your material is apt to be most accessible.

INTERVIEWER: Does "getting even on death" mean beating old man death at his own game? Also, does your interest in mortality and time derive from the highly fundamentalist background in which you were raised? Is the always implicit retributive disposition of Jahweh / Jehovah carried over in your work from an early scare-training in religion—with death usually the reward (wages) of sin?

BETTS: Well, there's nothing a bit original about creating stories which are greatly affected by a contemplation of death. I take for granted this is one of the incentives of all people who want to leave something behind them. When Albert Camus contemplates death, he gets a different kind of fiction from me, and so on. I'm sure you're right that religious upbringing has affected me here, but not in that simple wages-of-sin-is-death business, because I rejected that when I was very young. Not for any sound rational reasons. I just didn't like it. But in the Bible the themes of living and dying are so entwined, and in a close-knit family of all ages with its roots on the farm, the cycles and rhythms so steady and visible . . . It all went through me and through me, as Charlotte Brontë said once, like wine through water and "affected the color of my mind."

The big effect has been in characterization: the feeling that no moment can ever be duplicated, that even this one with the tape recorders could never be exactly reproduced, so that every moment is marvelous. Unique. All my early stories are about lonely people, each full and running over with that uniqueness.

Then the next thing that hits you is that every one of these remarkable people is mortal and will die. That no one is exactly like any other, has never been on the earth in just this form, will never be exactly duplicated, and will die. I find William Saroyan a sentimentalist, but he wrote about this in the introduction to one of his story collections, pinning it to his father. And after a while his father did die, and he saw how quickly the individual, special part of him would be forgotten. That the race and species could stay, but the individual could not stay—so he began using his father in stories as a way of preserving him. And that's when he said, "I began writing in order to get even on death." Which always makes me think of Faulkner's Nobel Prize speech: "The aim of the writer is to uplift the heart of man . . ." Then, something else which indicates that whenever he is able to do this, "the writer says *no* to death."

INTERVIEWER: Preserving individuals and robbing graveyards?

BETTS: Yes, writing is a way of preserving individuals, a running guerrilla warfare with death, a snatching of personality out of his jaws. And right away you have stopped dividing people into good characters and bad characters, because the common denominator is uniqueness. The mortality of strangers and villains matters, also.

So, you're right. There are graveyards in most of the landscapes I have invented, and the living go there to visit. There's one in the new novel, with an old-timey cemetery-cleaning where the people sing songs. There's an argument in *Scarlet Thread* between Mildred and Esther about which way the Bible quote really reads: "In the midst of death we are in life" or, "In the midst of life we are in death"? And it's very logical that the novella I'm writing now takes place *after* a man has died, in some specialized version of the Elysian Fields.

Because that's the central fact, isn't it? You look at life differently from how the chimpanzee looks at it, because you know in advance that it ends, right? And after you know that, what?

It seems to me everything I have written has been along two lines of development. . . . Maybe they're the same line . . . mortality and time. To overlap viewpoints, to feel the weight of past time enter the present and influence action, and with Benson Watts to go through the membrane and tell a story on the other side—it all seems very linear and simple to me. Predictable.

You know, the man who painted the bison on the cave walls survives in a way his cousin, the hunter, does not; and the bison survive, too. The way Henri Rousseau's *Sleeping Gypsy*—once he painted it—will always be in present tense. To me, that's a big challenge for a writer, almost bigger than for a painter. How to make people, events, and story, using accurately the world he knows, in such a way that its effect will always be in present tense.

I've been accused of being a gloomy writer. Maybe death broods too much in my prose. That's one reason Rilke's poetry, especially the elegies, affected me so much. . . . I wanted to move, as he did in his later *Sonnets to Orpheus*, to a mood of praise. In spite of everything, praise. One story published this year grew out of that, "The Ugliest Pilgrim," which is built like a folk ballad and intended to end on that high, piercing Joan Baez note, and maybe my shift to comedy and fantasy are part of that, too. The only trouble is that Rilke's elegies are so much better *poetry* than his praise-sonnets. But I don't want to be gloomy about death, just persistently aware of it.

One of the most obvious things to be said about the short story as a form is that it seems to *stop* time, to gather it together, to make it dense and glowing. No wonder I liked it best of all.

INTERVIEWER: Very good. You've just had another novel accepted, you told me. Is Harper's going to do it?

BETTS: Harper's is going to do it. It's a contemporary novel. Nineteen sixty-eight, in fact. It opens pretty close to the point that Bobby Kennedy is shot, and is dealing with time and violence, the effect of time on the present and a specific act of violence which will take place, a murder, in fact, on this imagined resort beach located on a nonexistent piece of land in Brunswick County, North Carolina.

INTERVIEWER: Know when it will be coming out?

BETTS: No. Depends upon when I finish the revisions. I'd like to think it would be out in the spring, but it may not.

INTERVIEWER: Want to boost it?

BETTS: Hmmm. I don't know. Not so much. I'm apprehensive of boosting in advance and praising afterward. It's only the moment that you're right there. . . . That's a typical short story writer's remark: "right there." I'll just say there are three main characters, and I'm switching viewpoints between them, and the character whose present time is strongest tells her section in present time, and the others in the past, which has something to do with the theme. It's shorter than usual.

INTERVIEWER: What's next for you?

BETTS: Well, right now, I'm working on this revision, and on several short stories. I'm writing a novella which is called *Benson Watts Is Dead and in Virginia*, which literally takes place after a man has died. It's his experience after he has died, and it's a logical extension of things that interest me most in fiction, which, as I say, are mortality and time. These are the big things that interest me. And so it's a fantasy, which is another area which I think I have been getting into more and more and more, especially in the short story lately. I'm inclined to think now that it will run the length of *The Astronomer*. But it is a bit different from what I have been doing. But I am having a lot of fun doing it, which means I am now reading a great deal about metempsychosis, reincarnation . . . which I don't believe in, but which by a long shot I prefer.

INTERVIEWER: The short story is your bag; how would you define it?

BETTS: I wouldn't, but I would steal from the letter of Chekhov in which he said, "I can speak briefly on long subjects." That's my favorite definition of the short story and of what it can do better than any other form, because I think it can speak on longer subjects even than poetry usually can. Whereas the novel speaks at length on long subjects.

INTERVIEWER: Why, do you think, has the short story always been seen as largely an American art form?

BETTS: Well, someone has already said that the short story is the art of the short expectation of life. It does have something in common with the quickness of journalism and the brevity of the thirty-minute teleplay. It has the temptation of catching things on the fly. . . . In truth I don't think many Americans read literary short stories very much, nor like them very well. The short story, although it is supposed to have something to do with the brevity and speed of American life, is not a form which Americans like very much, because they have not the patience for its intricacy, any more than they have ever gone very much for string quartets. I think it's the same kind of format: they'd rather have a symphony any day, or a long novel. Complicated, teeming, as New York City teems.

INTERVIEWER: Would you comment on contemporary literature?

BETTS: If there is a trend in contemporary literature which I do not like, it is the tendency to be antirational all the way in modern fiction. It is to assume that there is never a point at which the reason and the intellect act upon these experiences. I think the ultimate result of that is just self-expression, or a kind of intellectual masturbation, instead of experience which is shaped and directed and lasts beyond the telling of it to oneself. That is one of the things I don't like about some student work, and some mod work, pop art work. I think it grows strictly out of the immediate, and dies away back into the immediate, and has nothing that will make it persist.

Kite-Flying and
Other Irrational Acts:
❦ GEORGE GARRETT

Interviewed by JOHN CARR

*George Garrett has had a prolific literary career for such a young man,
and a frenetic life—and shows no signs of letting up. Those who
know him often have the impression that they know not just one
man, but several: George Garrett, Literary Impresario, he of the
fulsome publications list, junketing around from the North Dakota
Conference on Southern Writing to the Carolina Coon Dog Villanelle
Contest to the Fifth Annual Reunion of the Girl in the Black Raincoat anthology, and busy in between times with a novel here, an
anthology there, poems everywhere; George Garrett, Kindhearted Mega-
lomaniac, in personal charge, Lee Roy, of the I*n*c*r*e*d*i*b*l*e
Hollins Conference on Writing and the Cinema; and, the persona
that underlies all the others (there are more) and becomes more
and more cherished: George Garrett, the boon companion and friend,
stand-up comic, ex-boxer and football coach, and mender of verses
and paragraphs, able to recount the Portuguese expedition to Ethiopia
in 1541, act out Gregory Corso leaping out of the bushes at W. H.
Auden (playing both parts), and put grad students to work raking
his cantilevered lawn at a single bound.*

*In fact, I began this book while I was one of his graduate students
at Hollins College and wouldn't have been able to finish it without
his help and encouragement, to say nothing of the writing I was able
to get done at Hollins because my interview project was being counted
as a seminar in modern literature (which it certainly was, and it lasted
not just a semester, but three years). His own interview took place in
his house in Roanoke, Virginia, where he and his family were then
living. We got down to business the morning of December 19, 1969,*

after having sat up to watch Tiny Tim's wedding the night before (the marriage lasted less than the time it took to bring this book to publication).

When Garrett was twenty-eight, "The Reverend Ghost" was published in Poets of Today, IV, edited by John Hall Wheelock (1957). King of the Mountain, *a collection of short stories, and* The Sleeping Gypsy and Other Poems *came out the next year. His first novel,* The Finished Man, *appeared in 1960.* Abraham's Knife (*poems*) *and* In the Briar Patch, *another collection of short stories, followed in 1961. His second novel,* Which Ones Are the Enemy?, *was also published that year. In 1962,* Sir Slob and the Princess, *a play for children, was produced. In 1964,* Cold Ground Was My Bed Last Night, *another collection of stories, was published. His third novel,* Do, Lord, Remember Me, *appeared in 1965, and two years later* For a Bitter Season: New and Selected Poems *was published in the United States and* A Wreath for Garibaldi and Other Stories *came out in Great Britain. The latter book has never been released in this country, although it contains some stories which have not been printed here.*

In the fall of 1971, Death of the Fox *was published and immediately praised as one of the best books of the year and the best novel Garrett had written. And the last is some praise.*

He is now professor of English and teacher of creative writing at the University of South Carolina, living in Columbia with his wife Susan, daughter Alice, and sons Bill and George.

INTERVIEWER: What I wanted to talk about first was the latest novel; then we can get to "Art Is for Kids."

GARRETT: You mean *The Death of the Fox?*

INTERVIEWER: Yes.

GARRETT: Well, that's a long story. It started back when I was an undergraduate at Princeton and was about to graduate—about 1952. I guess I did the first fifty pages then. I'd gotten really interested in Sir Walter Ralegh, but thought at that time that it would be a biography. So I fussed around and did about fifty pages and then kept on doing research—off and on—while I was doing other things. Then all these biographies of Ralegh came out. They certainly had needed a good biography of Ralegh, and some very good ones came out—and continued to come out, right up through last year. So that eventually, the facts, short of someone turning up a trunkload of mysterious papers, had been pretty well rehashed and worked over. *Now*, along about 1963 I had done this novel *Do, Lord, Remember Me* and it had been accepted by Mr. Duell of Duell, Sloan and Pierce after another publisher had turned it down—they had had the option on it and the guy wrote back, I think two days before Christmas, and said, "Merry Christmas. Fuck you." He went on to explain why he declined the book, and I had to look up both words: "scabrous" and "orotund."

INTERVIEWER: Is this guy still with them?

GARRETT: No. Now he's the head man at another house. Nothing succeeds like success, huh? If you've got a Bennett Cerf jokebook in one hand and a Roget's *Thesaurus* in the other, you can go a long way in that trade. So I thanked him for his Christmas gift— they had held on to it for about eight months or something—and then Mr. Duell looked at it and made a very quick decision and said he'd be glad to do it. He liked it and we were set.

Now about this time, Mr. Duell had merged with an outfit called Meredith Press, that, prior to this, I gather, had been a printing outfit, and had also published *Better Homes and Gardens* and all that line of Better Homes and Gardens cookbooks and Better Homes and Gardens gardening books and Better Homes and Gardens grooming books. . . . And Mr. Duell didn't realize that in merging he would lose a certain amount of power. Well, he called me up and he was very upset. I had known him for a long time, not as a publisher, but as a friend. He was very upset because it was very shortly after he had sold his publishing house that they said no on my book. They weren't going to do this, ordinarily, but on this book, NO, NO, NO.

INTERVIEWER: What was the matter? I don't recall that you called for the overthrow of the government in *Do, Lord.* . . .

GARRETT: They said it would really offend their *Better Homes and Gardens* readers. Of course, it wasn't particularly *intended* for that audience, but . . . and they were very adamant about it. But they had to reach a compromise, because Mr. Duell was very upset. Finally, he gave in to them under this condition: that anything else I would write for them would be okay, and they'd make exactly the same contract. And I would also be free to publish *Do, Lord* elsewhere. That was very nice. And then, to my surprise, Mr. Duell got on the phone and said— I'm afraid this is like Irving Wallace, who brags about putting three lines on a piece of paper and then selling the book—he said, "Is there any subject you want to write about?" I couldn't think of anything at the minute; there were a lot of things in my head and lying around, but they were all unsuitable for *Better Homes and Gardens,* so I said, "How about Sir Walter Ralegh?" And he said, "Great," and the next thing I knew, I had gotten a contract in the mail to do a book on Sir Walter Ralegh. Well, it goes on from there, because I said to myself that I'd just brush up on my research, but it seems that in the last year or two, massive libraries of Renaissance research had been pouring out. I'd been reading along, but very casually; I hadn't been pursuing it. I'd written some notes about what I'd like to do, but they had to change very quickly. Well, I caught up on the research in about a year, but it took until . . . well, a year ago, Christmas, 1968, before I actually finished writing it. For Meredith. Thereupon, to make a long, happy story even happier, their trade department went out of business, so I had to find myself yet another publisher. Now, I think, Doubleday is supposed to do it in the fall of 1970. [The book was published in September, 1971.] And there *are* little problems, like I have to do a little bit of cutting since I had overwritten on purpose, in a sense, to find my way, a process of trial and error. Meredith liked that. They said, "Don't cut any of it. We'll make it the biggest, thickest book ever published." That was their idea. That was how they were going to run it. I don't like to mess around, so I said let *them* do the book. But Doubleday, a little more wisely, said that that wouldn't necessarily be an advantage, to have it the biggest, heaviest, thickest book ever published. But there was a lot of extraneous stuff I had planned to cut anyway.

INTERVIEWER: How many thousand words is it at the minute?

GARRETT: At the minute, it's about 300,000 words. . . .

INTERVIEWER: Do you think an American publisher is really going to publish a 300,000-word book?

GARRETT: I think maybe they didn't want to read it. And they thought, "Oh boy, it could be heavier than *Hurry Sundown*." It could be five pounds. You could put it in at Christmas time with *Better Homes and Gardens*' chocolate candy sampler and hustle it for a Christmas gift. "Give someone on your list a big heavy book!" You could . . .

INTERVIEWER: Use it at riots.

GARRETT: Use it at riots, knock out windows . . .

INTERVIEWER: For third base, it'd be dandy . . . But you said you overwrote on purpose.

GARRETT: Yeah, and it was strange. I tried every conceivable way that I could think of . . . What finally happened just sort of happened, just grew. Because I tried everything else before I ended up doing it the way I have done it. It's not exactly what I would like it to be, and the real lesson from it, I think, is that I probably shouldn't have done it at all, but I had a lot of fun doing it. It's a very, very difficult narrative problem. It's going to have faults. It has built-in faults. But that's very educational, too, you know. You make choices, and you make more choices, and eventually . . . It's kind of exciting. You realize even as you're doing it that the choices eliminated and the opportunities and the options taken are going to make for certain defects which have to be compensated for. It's like a baseball player who can't hit an inside curve because of his stance, but can't hit a home run unless he stands that certain way. So he just takes that risk. And I hope it's not a complete strikeout, but . . .

INTERVIEWER: What are the built-in faults? Wait, let's back up. Can you run through it, since I've only seen a little of it, and tell me, basically, what's happening?

GARRETT: I'll give you the description I gave one guy. I *bugged* them at Meredith. I said, "To give you a clue as to how it goes, in the first 250 pages, the action may be summarized by saying that three people unbeknownst to each other have difficulty in getting to sleep." What I finally ended up doing was dealing just with the last two days of his life and working through a variety of other characters and through his own mind into the background. Instead of being a biography, it became more and more an exercise of the imagination. And that's what really became interesting to me. It was not just my trying to imagine what it was like and what different people felt like, which I found a great deal more difficult than you might think, but also trying to imagine how they imagined other situations. I think one of the most peculiar things about it, since it's rather an interior book in a strange way, is that some of the more vivid scenes, and I believe that they are *dramatic* scenes, are totally imaginary—and some people may not realize this at first because of the context in which they come across these scenes. For example, I would have Ralegh sitting by the window in the porter's house at Westminster the afternoon he had been sentenced to die the next day, looking at the weather and imagining what different people are doing in the weather and that's very, very vivid.

INTERVIEWER: Why shouldn't he have poetic license? After all Ralegh was a poet.

GARRETT: Agnes Latham said back in '52 when I was reading Ralegh's poetry, "It's a little difficult to believe in Sir Walter Raleigh. There's always been something legendary, something fantastic and not quite credible about him. Even to his contemporaries, he seemed a man of no normal stature." Which in fact, at six feet four, he was not. "So monstrously proud, so dangerously settled, and in the end so horribly wrong. They never viewed him calmly as a fellow creature with flaws and talents like their own. They must either execrate him or laud him, as though whatever he was, was in excess of the common." And here's the part that really kind of caught my attention: "He might have walked out of an Elizabethan play, a figment of the Renaissance imagination, a compact of ordinate vices and virtues destined to strange ends." That's a really magnificent piece of scholarship. It's *The Poems of Sir Walter Ralegh* by Agnes Latham, and it's just fantastic.

The trick on my book was that I decided not to do—I had certain inhibitions and negative rules, all along—and one of them was that I was not going to do the sort of thing that John Barth did with *The Sot-Weed Factor*. Generally speaking, one way for a contemporary novelist to react to bad historical fiction is to hoke it up in another way—and I think Barth does it very successfully

And probably the most successful example of the novel that combines a great deal of truth with enormous absurdity is Thomas Berger's *Little Big Man*. I didn't *want* to do that, though. They've already done that. I just wanted to see if I could do it sort of straight. Not in the technique of telling it, but in my attitude toward it. And I've given myself another little problem, and I don't know what the answer to that will be, and that is, that I wasn't going to be self-consciously relevant.

INTERVIEWER: But isn't it relevant in spite of itself? Here's a man who's executed for political reasons.

GARRETT: That's like . . . Well, I deliberately did not do the Nat Turner kind of thing and relate this novel to immediate concerns . . . . After all, though, somebody *now* is imagining the story, and even if I'm self-consciously trying not to say, "Look, this is like it is today," the things that interest me as a person in the middle of the twentieth century will be relevant in some way. *But*, it seems to me that when we try to artificially convert history to some direct kind of relevancy, we usually do history an injustice. I think that the relevance is built in by your own fascination with the subject. You don't have to prove it. . . . You know, just following the career of Ralegh, his ups and downs, in straight historical scholarship, I found that straight historians have never been able to accept him as anything except an "either / or" character. Either he's just the greatest, most saintly and wronged man that ever lived, or he's a monstrous brute. And I don't think he was either one, really. He's not Sir Thomas More, and he's not Torquemada. He was a very complicated guy, but in fiction I think you do find—and in history as well—that there is, continually, the necessity of defining yourself in terms of events. So that all history is really revisionist, because what's important to us will not be important to our children—certain aspects of it, that is.

INTERVIEWER: Did you find that certain things we know now about Elizabethan times, from court papers, for instance, that Ralegh could not possibly have known about, limited your characters' knowledge of their own times and each other? That even though you have a much better picture of the times, you can't use it because Ralegh didn't know it?

GARRETT: I think that's very much the case, and I think there's another side to it, which entails our own . . . limitations of imagination—and our own ignorance. For example, and you've got to admit this after reading any kind of scholarly or popular book about the Elizabethans, that we have a view, partly as a result of our technological advancement and evolutionary theories and so forth, that they were rather primitive. And this was encouraged, in fact, by eighteenth-century England, which I find to my amazement, the more I delve into it, was probably technologically inferior to Elizabethan England. I think what happened, and this is something else that ought to be mentioned, is that in England, after the Stuarts got kicked out, and they had the Puritan revolution and Cromwell and so forth, they had about twenty years of revolution and counterrevolution, during which most of the stuff, the *things*, of the Elizabethan and early Jacobean period were destroyed. *Very* little survived. The only thing we've got left of their clothing, for instance, is some doll clothes. The beautiful silver stuff was all melted down to make money to fight with. And they had fantastic tools. They had flush toilets—although they didn't like them too much because they thought, as American farmers did at first, that there was something sort of nasty about having a toilet in your house. And they had plumbing and heating. They made do with what they had just splendidly. It's just like Pope and others in the eighteenth century judging Shakespeare's theater and saying, "My goodness, what a sloppy playwright" because it didn't work on *their* stage.

INTERVIEWER: And haven't we also lost any kind of spiritual contact with that pre-Puritan society? We understand the eighteenth century a little better, it seems to me.

GARRETT: The imaginative leap—maybe that's what excited me once I really got going—involves trying to project yourselves into a world where they couldn't have imagined us; and it's *very* difficult to imagine them.

INTERVIEWER: What was the treason Ralegh was accused of?

GARRETT: That a few of them were going to overpower James and put in Arabella Stuart, who also had a claim to the throne. I doubt that very much, although Ralegh did play around a little bit with it. But I think his reasons may have been very complicated.

I think he wanted to win favor with James by exposing the plot. He knew that James was terrified of all sorts of treason because all of his life had been a series of near-assassinations. When he was a little child, he had seen people around him stabbed to death by rebellious Scottish lords. It was so traumatic that he would not permit an unsheathed blade in his presence. And James wore a daggerproof and bulletproof vest beneath his clothing all his life, even though it made him look a little silly. He was terrified of being killed. And here was Ralegh, and one thing James did know about him was that he was not afraid to kill people— because of his war record in the army, and because he was a very fine swordsman. Ralegh's nickname was "The Fox," and that was also one word for a swordsman, because a blade was known as a fox. And Ralegh had a reputation for being Machiavellian.

The contemporary figure I can think of who is closest to James, in my mind at the minute, is Joe Stalin. James was a very clever guy, but he outfoxed himself many times. On this, I think he thought that when he executed Ralegh—to the amazement of Spain; they just didn't believe he would do it, because they understood that Ralegh was very popular at that time—that the Spanish would owe him something, that they'd have to go through with the marriage. But I don't think he conceived of Ralegh's execution having all of its ramifications. The future is precisely what you can't predict in the present. And one of the things biographers love when they write about the execution is that three or four of the primary leaders of the Puritan revolution, unbeknownst to each other—they didn't even know each other at the time, that is—happened to be present at Ralegh's execution and all of them said later that the execution was the biggest event of their lives. The Puritans said that from then on, nothing . . . nothing but the blood of the Stuarts would avenge this deed. And that's very ironic. And it's ironic that Ralegh should become the great hero of the period.

INTERVIEWER: He was not a Puritan, was he?

GARRETT: No, he was not. It would be hard to tie him down, but he certainly was not a Puritan.

INTERVIEWER: Not a reformer?

GARRETT: No, and yet he became their hero.

INTERVIEWER: Why? Because they interpreted some of his poetry to be—?

GARRETT: It's the way images work in history, plus these people being present. He was the last great man, whom they could claim, to have gone down before the Stuart fury, and it was a great injustice, etc. Ralegh's principal concern, among other things, I'm sure, was to try to save what he could, his inheritance, for his wife and son. And usually they wiped them out. Families lost everything and were turned out to beg, practically. Well, James took a lot away from them, but they were fairly comfortable. Ralegh's son became a great friend of Charles. But, nevertheless, when Charles got it, the Puritans returned to Ralegh's son many of his perquisites. Anyway, what happened there was that the son, who was not particularly a Puritan either, Carew Ralegh, the only surviving son, maintained good relations with everyone. The Puritans gave him back some of the money, and he ended up decently well off.

Ralegh's execution was done on Lord Mayor's Day, which was kind of unheard-of, because that's a big holiday. It was done between eight and nine in the morning, in the Old Palace Yard in Westminster, which was some distance from London. So it's been naturally assumed—all the biographies, even the best ones, say that they were trying to keep the crowds away by doing it there instead of at the Tower or somewhere else, and they say what a clever thing it was of James, but look how it backfired, because large crowds came anyway. Now, while I was in England, just fooling around, doing hit and miss research, I discovered that between eight and nine on the morning of Lord Mayor's Day, the Lord Mayor and his entourage come down from London to Westminster to get sworn in. And then they go back. So that the Lord Mayor is getting off his barge just in time to see an execution on that day. That's a nice greeting for him.

It seems to me that the execution was more in the line of a big insult than any clever device, because those that knew about the execution had only a limited amount of time to spread the word, since it was just the afternoon before that they'd announced to anybody that they were going to do it. Those that knew about it mingled with the thousands of people who had showed up to watch the Lord Mayor. And I have a notion, for what it's worth—since he made an unusually long execution speech—that he was stalling in various ways to be sure that they had the full crowd there. And he had a very soft voice, which he used to his advantage. He said, "I have to speak softly," and then everyone would have to listen. A great many of the distinguished guests were up in apartment windows, not down on the ground, and as he began his speech, he apologized to the lords for their not being able to hear him very well, and they said, "Why, in that case, we'll come down." And everything stopped for about twenty minutes while they came through the crowd, came up, and then there were introductions all around. By this time, it's almost amusing, because the poor sheriff was trying to get the show on the road.

INTERVIEWER: Was it his execution speech which impressed the future Puritan leaders?

GARRETT: That, plus his great bravado, and a kind of Protestant faith that delighted these Puritans. He said he had no doubt. He said that he was not afraid because he was going to his just reward. Essex did a great show, too, and other great men who were executed in general gave a kind of fine farewell appearance, but his was especially unusual. James could imagine almost everything, but he couldn't get away from his own terror of violence and he had to imagine that Ralegh would be afraid, and at last exposed in some way as a cowardly man, as *he* might have been. But the one thing Ralegh wasn't afraid of was dying, and hadn't been from about the time he was seventeen on.

INTERVIEWER: Why? Was he a fatalist?

GARRETT: He went as a very young man into one of the worst . . . This really may be the key to his character: I find it terribly significant that at about the time he was sixteen or seventeen, he went as a common soldier into some of the most bloody combat that was taking place in the world at that time, which was the Huguenot revolt. He was in a troop of cavalry from Devon; he'd quit Oxford, run off, to fight on the side of the Huguenots.

There again, *imagination*. You take the sixteen-, seventeen-year-old boy who survives, who becomes a real veteran, not just of the initial shock of combat, but of several years of it, and he *knows.* And this explains why, time and time again in his life he did these apparently fearless things. He has a real veteran's attitude: it's either going to get you or it's not. Years later, when they attacked Cadiz, his ship sailed in first, right under the Spanish fort, a very dangerous situation there on both sides, and the Spanish are blasting away at him, and one would ordinarily be expected to reply, but he wanted to get at their ships. So he steps boldly up on the deck, and he has his trumpeter blow raucous bugle calls back at them, you know, like a Bronx cheer. [*Author illustrates.*] And the crew thinks that's great. And he was this way until he was a very old man. And he *was* a very old man for the time, and full of disease and pain and the aches, so it must not have terrified him too much. He'd had his life. And I notice that in his *History of the World,* in talking about death —and he doesn't believe in ghosts, as do some of his contemporaries—he remarks that the one thing we do know about the dead is that whatever else it's like over there, they don't care about what's happening here.

INTERVIEWER: Let's talk about writing in general. You have had kind of a fantastic publishing history.

GARRETT: Well, I can't even follow it myself. It's a mess. Although I think that's very often the case. It's the exception now when you have a writer like Updike or O'Hara, who go always with the same house. I'll tell you, it's an amazing thing. Back when Hemingway and Fitzgerald and Dos Passos and all the rest were coming along, the way to do things was to stick with one house. You built up your reputation and they kept your work in print.

INTERVIEWER: And good old Max Perkins patted you on the head.

GARRETT: That was the theory. And they just don't believe that anymore. It's not, in their view, economically sound, although I don't see anything economically sound about the publishing business, anyway. The last person I would listen to on the subject of economics would be somebody in publishing. Now, if you look at the records of most of the writers who are around today, the man who stayed in the same house is the exception. How many publishers has Wright Morris had, twelve or thirteen out of fifteen or sixteen books? The situation is that if you're not a top writer or best seller, or you don't hit it real big in what they think of as the prestige market, then the next time around, you've got to go with somebody else. Each time it's a new ball game, and I think this has been true with a great many writers. And now, to the dismay of the publishers, even their more successful ones want a better price. A former student of mine is an editor now at Atheneum. He had a little story in *The Girl in the Black Raincoat* anthology. We got a correspondence going for a while about publishing. I gave him the writer's point of view: "Why don't you guys bet on an individual right at the beginning, build on it, and build a *loyal feeling*?" And I got the standard answer back from him, which is what they all believe: "What good does it do? You bet on them and as soon as they get to be successful, they immediately go to a better house, where they get more money." I don't think it's true; I think *they* have created this situation.

INTERVIEWER: You say the publishers created it?

GARRETT: Yes. In other words, a fellow feels no obligation to them, morally or otherwise. And once they have treated him like dirt long enough, if he gets a better offer, of course he'll go. I think they don't understand that young writers today would be singularly loyal if they got a little support when they needed it.

INTERVIEWER: It would overcome their paranoia anyway.

GARRETT: I think that writers are apt to be overly loyal.

INTERVIEWER: Don't you think that writers respond to anybody, whether to an editor or an agent or the guy next door who puts in plumbing, who's interested in them? It's a solitary craft, as has often been remarked, I suppose, but about the only contact I have with people interested in my writing is when I make an occasional visit to my agent and or sit down to talk with you and Fred [Chappell] and some others.

GARRETT: Absolutely. What my editor friend said is exactly what I've always heard from the producers in Hollywood. They talk about "Those crummy actors, as soon as they get to be big shots like Liz Taylor or somebody, they come in with a 100-page contract and demand four cases of Coca-Cola every day on the set and all this stuff." They say, "*See*, no loyalty at all." I was rooming with an actor when I heard all this, and I saw how badly treated this guy was at that time. He was just a character actor at the time, but since then, he's come along to be a star, and every time he gets them over a barrel, he's going to get everything he can out of them because they have kicked him in the teeth every day out there. And of course this is the same thing that has happened to the stars they bitch about. The stars have been kicked and kicked and kicked and when they finally get to be stars, why not stick it to the producers?

INTERVIEWER: Tell me the story about *Do, Lord, Remember Me*. About when you got a call that they were definitely going to take it.

GARRETT: Oh, that one. When I called up my editor, it became apparent that he had not examined this book very closely, and then finally it became clear that he had never read it at all. And here they were already in production with the book. And so I said, not in a malicious way, just very quietly, I said, "Well, that's very interesting that you'd publish a book that you haven't even read." And he said, "Well, I'd been getting nervous because I hadn't gotten any manuscripts from Candy Donadio"—and she was a very status agent at the time, and, I imagine, still is—and he said, "So I just told myself I'd take the first thing that came in from her office, and I did." After the book came out, he read it and said, "Not bad."

INTERVIEWER: That must have made you feel good, having your editor read it in a bookstore.

GARRETT: Well, it was being published and dumped, so to speak. I didn't realize that at the time, but they explained to me later that they had needed a tax loss and had just decided to publish anything that was at least half good. Another thing which is wild about publishing is the basic economics of it. They've got these poor little editors scared to death because they give a fellow, as I understand it—and the whole thing isn't very clear to me—but ostensibly, a man is given, say, $500,000 to play with it. You can do what you want to pretty much, they all vote on it, but if you say you want to do it, it's your responsibility. At the end of the year, the accountants come in, and they say, "Boy, you sure blew that $500,000 and you haven't got anything to show for it." They *do* have to turn a profit. So they end up running scared most of the time. They're part of the corporate rat race, and yet these corporations are so poorly run. Oh, there's big money in it, but not—

INTERVIEWER: Capitalism on that scale is basically inefficient.

GARRETT: Well, this aspect of it is capitalism at its worst. There are aspects of capitalism . . . There is a great deal of a certain kind of integrity in some of it, because their sole aim is to make profit. But in publishing, it's mixed up with "advancing letters." If they really wanted to make a profit, they would then support the books that they publish. Can you imagine a maker of toothpaste just dumping a new toothpaste on the market and then saying, "Well, it's going to be a tax loss, anyway"? I think one of the reasons why novels are not read as much now as they were twenty years ago is *not* that there has been a deterioration of the reading habits of the public, but because publishers do not merchandise their product.

INTERVIEWER: That's a good point. I have a class of people at UNC-C who want to write, and their big deal is just to get something published. And it's rather hard to tell them that's only the first lick in a big fight.

GARRETT: Well, it's terribly important to a young writer, though, you know. And one of the things I keep trying to tell publishers is that if they were smart and wanted to get these young writers into their establishments, they would publish their short stories and poems. They don't want to publish short stories and poems—I'm talking now about collections of short stories and / or poems— if they can help it. *Anything* to avoid publishing short stories and poems. They want a novel, at best, or a nonfiction book; you can even get an advance on a nonfiction book. But what do young writers do when they're in college? Usually, poems and short stories. One of the things I've been after publishers to do for years is to help subsidize the university presses. It costs very little money. University presses don't have to turn out a profit, and something like a $1,000 subsidy from a publisher would guarantee publication of a young writer's short stories and poems. The publisher could then take an option on him and the publisher would have given this young writer a beginning, which is crucial, and would have themselves a writer at one-tenth of the expense—but they're all running away from it. In a way, because the whole thing is so complicated, and so much out of your hands, maybe it's not a bad time for a writer. Because there's no point in worrying about it. You can figure that they're not going to handle it right, 99 percent of the time, so all you've got to do is write the book. There isn't anything else you *can* do. They're going to goof it, given half a chance, in every conceivable way and . . . unless it is being handled as a piece of Brand X merchandise from the beginning, which is probably not the book that your good young writer is going to do anyway.

INTERVIEWER: When you and Bill Harrison and Fred Chappell were visiting my and Bertha Harris' classes at Charlotte, Bill Harrison maintained that all the good writers are known.

GARRETT: That's a phase I think people go through when they're having a bit of success. I think that at the moment of success you *have* to feel that virtue is rewarded. I would say that his statement is not only incorrect, it's just wildly erroneous. My guess is—and I have some substantiation for this—that the finest poets and novelists of our time are completely unknown and probably a lot of them are unpublished. Period. *That* they would find very difficult to believe because they claim they're out looking for things all the time. I know some people . . . I have one crazy friend who has written three or four really fine novels. I enjoyed them thoroughly, and I don't *think* I'm so out of it. He's a guy named Hugh Akerman, and he has gone on and had a career and never published anything. It never bothered him particularly, and there are a great many poets and story writers I know who've had terrible luck. Now a man that has good luck . . . Luck is such a factor. A man has got to attribute it to cause and effect. "My good work was recognized." I don't think that's the case at all.

INTERVIEWER: You know, considering that luck is such a factor, aren't you pretty dumb to start writing at this time in the history of American letters?

GARRETT: Well, there are a lot of different ways of looking at it. It is certainly an irrational thing to do if you want either of the usual rewards of fame and riches. Of course, they're there, but no self-respecting gambler would get into this game at all. Not even a wild one. Nick the Greek would faint at the odds against the writer. And here's an interesting fact that a lot of people haven't thought about. Maybe they have. I come slow to all these ideas. Have you ever stopped to think that for the first time, there have been no rational rewards for writing in the way that there were in the past? Much earlier, if you had a patron, that was why you wrote. Obviously, a different type of man is writing books today than was even in the nineteenth century, because when Dickens wrote there was a very definite cause-and-effect relationship. If he wrote the book and it was good and it was published, then he made a lot of money and improved his situation and was highly regarded. And if Shakespeare's plays did well, as they did, and he was a stockholder in his company, it was a rational enterprise. Nowadays, it's about as rational as saying, "What do you do for a living?" "Well, I'm a kite-flyer." I mean, there's not a great demand for kite-flyers around. There may be a few who draw a little money. Therefore, today, writing appeals to a different mentality. A Shakespeare today might be doing something else that's more rational. Now the other thing is that because this is true, fundamentally writing doesn't matter in the world of commerce. It has a certain kind of—I wouldn't say *purity*, but *freedom* that it never had. My little story about "I never read it, it was a tax loss" is a truly metaphorical situation. Wild. That little story indicates one thing: that, in fact, since it was unread, I had been free to write anything I pleased. The copy editor picked up a couple of little things, but the editor himself didn't bother with it at all. Why should he? So I was free. I really had more freedom than Dickens or Shakespeare in that sense, in that nothing was riding on this. You know, for 99.9 percent of the people who are writing, there is neither prestige nor direct pecuniary reward—we get it indirectly: you're doing a little teaching, I'm doing a little teaching, and we may not always be, but we earn our bread that way. Because that's so, we have, in a sense, a greater freedom to write what we please, since it doesn't matter anyway, than any writers in hundreds and hundreds of years, maybe ever. And as long as luck's involved in it, you don't have to worry too much about that, either. You can't worry about luck. You really can't. That's absolutely ridiculous.

INTERVIEWER: Did you ever wonder if writers write about and around the existentialist concept of the absurd because the craft which they practice is a little absurd?

GARRETT: How would you like to own the last celluloid collar factory in the world? Yes, it's an absurd craft. However, it's a little different in the United States than in Europe. There's still the prestige of being a writer in Europe. They don't have any common folks writing novels over there. About the nearest thing to it would be somebody like Silone, who for years offended them because he didn't write like a university graduate.

INTERVIEWER: Or Sillitoe in England.

GARRETT: Yeah, and that's a very new thing in England. But we've always had that over here. Anybody with a typewriter and a piece of paper can be a writer and set up in business, and even if we go to the universities, so far—although they've been trying to standardize it—we don't all learn the same things. So that there's a wonderful variety in American writing.

INTERVIEWER: Let's talk about the South and our different attitudes towards it.

GARRETT: You used to be a member of the Weathermen, didn't you?

INTERVIEWER: No, I'm a member of RYM (Revolutionary Youth Movement), one of the groups left after PLP was thrown out of SDS this summer. Weathermen split then from RYM and for a while, we were known as RYM II and they as RYM. Now we're RYM-SDS and PL is PLP-SDS and Mark Rudd and the group are in hiding. Is this about the South, George?

GARRETT: I just think it's interesting.

INTERVIEWER: Oh.

GARRETT: I had a great-grandfather that lived, of all places, in Florida, north Florida, around Apalachicola. He was an ardent abolitionist. But a different kind than most people would think of if you just threw the word out at them. His whole plan, and that of the group he belonged to, I gather, would have ended it by, say, 1900. They had it all planned out. They were going to free all but one of the children born in the present generation—this was about 1850—then the next generation would be free, and there'd be no more slavery, and then there'd be no economic loss, either. But then, like everybody else, he ended up fighting rather strenuously on the Southern side.

INTERVIEWER: Proving that when there comes a showdown, the half-measure boys are really the enemy, too.

GARRETT: It's a very curious thing, though. He saw the handwriting on the wall. He was captured, finally, and put on Governor's Island, and when the war was over, the Union men at the prison did a crazy thing: they walked in one day and said, "Okay boys, the war's over," and gave them money for the ferry rides to Manhattan and that was that. They had to get home the best way they could. Well, a lot of Southerners apparently didn't see that it was all over and staggered along home and tried to reinstitute the whole culture in a new form, and the culture was dying anyway. But my great-grandfather went over to Wall Street in his raggedy clothes and moved into the business world. He just stopped long enough to sell off some land before they even got a chance to tax it, and then he took what money he had and took his woods, he owned a lot of woods, and went into the naval stores business, handing over the farm land to his freed slaves. And there they are today, and they all have his name. So he came out of the war all right.

INTERVIEWER: I think the thing about Southern culture which only a few historians realize is that it would have died anyway, because it was a seigneurial, Hellenistic, anticapitalist culture appendaged to a society which opposed it in all those areas, and especially in the areas of social mores and culture. There was no way for it to survive inside a nation that was becoming more and more capitalist and bourgeois all the time. To say nothing of the evangelical streak that came out in the *real* fire-breathers. I think I'd like to suggest that the South would have fallen anyway, but a recent book by a man named Starobin called *Industrial Slavery in the Old South* is blood-curdling, because it points out that the Bourbons were about to create an industrial proletariat out of slave labor.

GARRETT: Well, what all this has to do with literature, I don't know, except that we are the only people in the United States who know one great truth that other people are just beginning to find out:

that we can be whipped. And that's something of value. The notion that you can really be defeated has never soaked into the U. S.

INTERVIEWER: As witness Nixon's remark that he was not going to be the first President to lead this country to military defeat.

GARRETT: There were only a handful of Southern writers or politicians who did not immediately accept the full consequences of the defeat. There were a couple of crazies who committed suicide, and some few ran off to Brazil or Mexico, to make endless grist for television stories, but the great majority said, "Okay, that's it, we've lost," and even before Reconstruction moved towards reunification. One of the best examples of this is another distant relative of mine, who wrote a book much misunderstood in many ways. It's one of the all-time best sellers: *Aeneas Africanus* by Harry Stillwell Everett, who was a Georgia writer. One of the reasons it's misunderstood, I guess, is because of the racist jokes, but the hero of the book finally and after all is the indomitable Aeneas. It's the only picture I know of the society at that time done by a writer who was alive at the time—and they're all thinking about the future now. They're not thinking back, there's no sense of recrimination. Instead, there's a sense of maturity.

INTERVIEWER: Have you ever thought about doing the Civil War?

GARRETT: One of the first short stories I ever wrote was "The Pianist." It was a wild and woolly Civil War story. I was six or seven.

INTERVIEWER: Have you been writing that long?

GARRETT: Before I could read and write, I decided to be a writer. Before I ever read a book. There were people around, you know, and I'd heard about writing and decided that's what I'd do. I can't understand the patience of my father, who let me dictate to him in the evening when he came home, and I wrote when I must have been about four a long epic about Richard the Lion-Hearted. It was really adventurous, jet planes and everything. Fortunately, it's lost somewhere. Probably it's the best thing I ever did.

INTERVIEWER: Which brings up a not esoteric point. It seems to me that one of the things that distinguishes the modern novel is that it's the novel of artifice.

GARRETT: Yeah, the very recent novels. The perfect novel that was described—but not written—by James, and is maintained by Tate and Gordon in *The House of Fiction,* is a movie. The qualities of fiction, it seems to me, offer a great deal more opportunities than that of writing the dramatically presented situation. And the obvious artifice can be a lot of fun. I could never do . . . I love *Dagon,* but I could never do a thing like that, nor could I think, I wouldn't be able to say, that is—maybe it's been a great defect—"This is a satire on Puritanism." Because I'm not an intellectual writer, really. I'd like to be. I'd like to be able to say, "Yes, that's a really great satire on disestablishmentarianism," but I end up with images. You know, my feelings about Ralegh are so ambiguous that I suppose the whole thing will be ambiguous.

INTERVIEWER: Do you think that's good writing?

GARRETT: I don't know. It's the only way I can do it. I'm getting more and more the quality—I guess maybe it's just old age—of mixed feelings about things, and I think my job is to be true to that . . . Being true to your own mixed feeling about things. I do know that when I feel absolutely sure about something, that this guy is good or that guy is bad, I like to go back into an advocacy situation and make my villain have everything that I can think of going for him.

INTERVIEWER: It's good spiritual exercise, anyway.

GARRETT: It may make for a great deal of confusion, though. Take a book like *Do, Lord.* Those few people who've read it say they don't understand the first thing about it, that is, what it's about. They'll say it's nicely written, but they don't understand it. And there's a great deal of ambiguity there, by the nature of its organization, many characters looking at different things. My favorite's always been the num-num, the guy—was it Cartwright? —who was giving away all the money. He rushes upon stage and says, "Won't you all join me?" and he can't think of a hymn, so he starts singing "Love Me Tender."

INTERVIEWER: Which reminds me, for some reason, that we sat up last night and watched Tiny Tim's wedding. Nobody else would have anything to do with us, and I notice they're looking at us strangely today. But I guess writers are entertainers too in a very gross—or is it a very subtle?—sense.

GARRETT: I suppose the only big difference is that we are working with an audience of one. There is a dialogue—wait, I don't want to use that nasty word *dialogue*—there is a *conversation* that goes on in an unbroken way between the reader and the writer. If the book is any good, and he's hooked on it, he's bringing something in. And there's a question . . . maybe this goes back to your thing about artifice. There's a question of people recognizing that this is so and so working hard to bring the reader into it and to get a real copulative spirit going in the reading experience. I remember a guy, one of my num-num editors of the past, who used to worry about epigraphs in a book. He said, "Epigraphs remind people that they're reading a book," and I thought, "Well, they are." There are books that can engage you so that you don't want to go to work or something, that's true, but you know you're reading a *book*. Readers are not *that* stupid and unimaginative, and there is no prose that transparent, and even in a movie, you know that you're watching *a movie*.

The important thing is that something happens to the imagination. We live by . . . People out there in the streets are living and dying for *abstractions*. And I don't think anybody would shoot a gun at anybody else, no matter what side they're on, if they could imagine vividly what a bullet does. I think they'd throw the gun away. Look at our situation right this minute with Hanoi. We don't imaginatively understand them, and they don't understand us. They really believe—and it shows a *certain* amount of imagination—they really believe that we're teetering on the edge of some sort of coup, because if the same thing were happening in Hanoi, it would be the end of the world for them. O.K., they can hardly be blamed for this. Perhaps the only way we as writers are able to do any good is through the development of the human imagination. The aesthetic experience of any kind cultivates the imagination, which has been stultified by abstractions. People will go out and *die* over whether the Cincinnati Reds are better than the Baltimore Orioles—on the *street*.

INTERVIEWER: Right. Let's amplify this discussion a bit. I went to Columbia recently and happened to sit in on a film class conducted by Andrew Sarris. During a discussion of some Chaplin movies, he said that it might be that the best minds of today, the ones with imagination, are going into science.

GARRETT: The only hot-shot scientists I ever talked to—I never did very well in science in high school because I was so literal-minded about it—the only ones I've ever talked to end up describing what they're doing the same way as a writer does. It's all metaphorical. Who has ever seen an atom? It's a metaphor. When you get right down to it, the stock market is playing with metaphors. I watched them one day and I didn't get the feeling Antonioni wanted me to get in one of his movies, that "Oh Lord, look at these horrible beasts" feeling. Somebody said, "This looks like a football game. They're playing for points." They were running back and forth and so on, and I don't even think they cared about the money. They cared about the *score*; it was an aesthetic experience; it was a *game*.

INTERVIEWER: What's your next step? What do you plan to do?

GARRETT: Well, I have a whole stack of things backed up here. I don't know what will come of them. Some of them are going to be radically different from the Ralegh book. . . . Maybe I'm going to be schizophrenic and do two separate things. I'll have to wait and see. I've got another great big long novel I'm working on.

INTERVIEWER: What is it?

GARRETT: It's called *Life with Kim Novak Is Hell*. I have a great many things I want to do. Some of them may be, in a sense, too late to do. I just don't know.

INTERVIEWER: Isn't that a point some of us miss sometimes, that even in the writing of novels, it may be true that there is no immortal subject matter?

GARRETT: Oh yeah. As a matter of fact, I don't even know what originality is. The more I know about literature, the more I can find you a precedent for anything anybody thinks.

INTERVIEWER: As much as people despise journalism as being ephemeral, or, as Gide said, that which will be less interesting tomorrow than today, don't some novels, too, have to be released at just the right time?

GARRETT: I'm sure that's so. And the more I think about it, the more I'm beginning to think all these distinctions, which are relatively new, between, say, Tom Wolfe's *Electric Kool-Aid Acid Test* and a novel, are absolutely artificial distinctions. Much journalism, so-called, or reportage, such as *In Cold Blood*, involves the kind of selection that takes place when you're writing a novel except that the story is quote, "true." Much that is fictional has as much "truth," unquote, as anything else that claims to be nonfiction has. I think that the distinction between fiction and nonfiction has for a long time been invalid, just as it seems crazy to me that in our time we've made the distinction between prose and poetry, whereas for thousands of years there was prose and verse, two ways of writing lines. An historical book could be poetry. We say so-and-so is poetry, when we are really admiring a work of non-fiction. The great Faulkner novels are the great epic poems of our time. That's the only way to conceive of them. Because they're not in verse doesn't mean they're not poetry.

INTERVIEWER: Don't you feel that there is a great coming-together of the allegedly different areas of writing?

GARRETT: That's part of a lot of things that are happening right now. All sorts of artificial distinctions that were imposed in the past are at last being questioned and are breaking down. It's just *happening*. We don't know enough. It's not purely the imagination. But, in the education of our children, from the beginning we fail to permit them to cultivate their imaginations and to keep their imaginations alive. It's an interesting thing. I had a student once who was a very imaginative, creative boy who had done all the trips before they even came in. He'd been on a merchant freighter and taken every drug known. And he found ultimately that be-cause he already had a full and rich imaginative life, that this didn't add to it, but he saw people whose imaginations had been so crippled that only the drugs enabled them to do things imaginatively. They would dance, for instance, and this was an imaginative act on their part, but for him it was an ordinary thing. In a sense, freaking out is pathetic, because it just demonstrates that society, the system has crippled these kids' imaginations so much that they have to rediscover basic things. Another of the pathetic aspects of the youth culture is that it is antitechnological, and yet it is within the realm of technology to depollute, for instance, Lake Erie. They say it is going to take 500 years for it to return to normal. You put a really imaginative chemist, who is now making bombs, to work on that and say, "Can you figure out how to unpollute it in a year?" and he'll do it. Let's not pretend that technology doesn't exist and go out and drink water out of a well with typhoid germs in it. And after all, our parents can't be blamed. We just discovered some of the effects of the things we've been doing. They didn't go out and deliberately wreck the world.

INTERVIEWER: They did a good job, anyway.

GARRETT: Yeah, a fine job. My only optimism is that the very destructive technology they've developed can, if imaginatively applied, answer any of these problems. Any of them.

INTERVIEWER: Given the imagination?

GARRETT: Given the imagination.

The Making of Fables:
❧ JESSE HILL FORD

Interviewed by JAMES SEAY

Jesse Hill Ford quit a public relations job with the American Medical Association in 1957 and went to Humboldt, Tennessee, determined to do nothing but write. Somehow, he made it (and talks about his survival in the interview below) and out of that dropping out have come three novels, a book of stories, and stage, television, and film scripts. His first novel, Mountains of Gilead *was published in 1961. Then came* The Conversion of Buster Drumwright: The Television and Stage Scripts *in 1964.* The Liberation of Lord Byron Jones *was published in 1965, and was later made into a movie,* The Liberation of L. B. Jones, *released in 1970. Ford was co-author, with Stirling Silliphant, of the screenplay.* Fishes, Birds, and Sons of Men, *a book of stories, was published in 1967 and was followed by* The Feast of Saint Barnabas *in 1969.*

Ford was interviewed at his home in Humboldt in the early fall of 1969.

INTERVIEWER: Do you think there's any validity to our talking about a Southern writer?

FORD: Of course the term is used by *some* critics and reviewers as an opprobrium, but we are a nation of regions, and to say the truth of the matter, I believe that Southerners who write trade on backgrounds. No reason why they shouldn't. People reared in New York or Connecticut or California or the Midwest or wherever attempt to trade on their origins, but they never—to me at least —seem quite so successful with it as the Southerners. My God, the University of North Dakota is having a Southern Writers Conference! We talk about Southern writers because Southern writers have talked at great length about themselves as being Southern, and as being different. I know we are different. I know that the South is different. But if the South has problems—and it has them—then they are American problems. If the South has qualities we admire, I think we have to say that these are American qualities. America can take credit for the South, and America also must take responsibility for the South. For a long time, I think in that generation of Americans just before my own, there was a feeling of "us and them." The South's response was in kind. *We* were the South. *They* were the North. *We* did not like or respect *them*.

INTERVIEWER: When did you notice this?

FORD: From early childhood I noticed, but then in the people that I studied under and associated with in, let's say, the late 40's and early 50's. I recognized the trait in my tutelaries.

INTERVIEWER: Donald Davidson and Andrew Lytle?

FORD: Davidson and Lytle and many, many others. I found that streak of . . . well, it was "us and them." They felt that we were God's chosen. It is a very exclusive feeling. We were aristocrats and we were genteel and our sense of historicity set us apart. Though a conquered people, we were proud. If there was a field on which we could continue the struggle against the wicked North, it was in the realm of the imagination—most especially in poetry and fiction. So we were Southerners and there was the rest of the world. The impression I got in school, in writing classes and in writing groups, was that editors by and large are stupid because they're mostly Yankees. They can't have any sense. That before we let a manuscript leave this region, we all read it and be sure it is what "we" really want to say.

INTERVIEWER: Because they're not going to know up there?

FORD: Because they don't have any idea what's going on up there, you know. They're just idiots. I found to my surprise that my editors and publishers in Boston were very nice gentlemen, and they taught me a lot. I have never felt since I began to publish in a professional way any sort of animosity toward people outside the South. Beyond telling the truth about the South, I've never felt that I owed anything in particular to people in the South. Certainly there is a negative obligation. I owe it to them not to lie on their behalf. I owe it to them not to back them when they are wrong-minded and wrong-headed. Let me say, though, that although educated in Tennessee and reared in Tennessee, I am a native of Alabama; both my parents were born in Alabama. My great-great grandparents are from Alabama. My forebears were first settlers in the Alabama territory, coming there from Virginia. Most of my kin—and I have a great many kinsmen—still live in Alabama. And Alabama people do not think like Tennesseans nor like Mississippians or Georgians or Kentuckians. We who are Alabamians have a rather special view of the world. We are not hothouse plants. We tend by and large to travel well. We are in general well spoken, voluble, and gregarious. We don't have to ponder about being aristocratic or artistic or right-minded. We don't tend to brood. Tennesseans are like Swedes—they *like* to brood. They *hate* to feel *well*. They always like to be just a mite porely. Georgians also have this dark-mindedness. Evil is taking over the world. There is a devil behind every bush. Mississippians are hothouse plants. They need a certain soil and climate found only in darkest Mississippi or they perish or go mad or drink too much. Your Arkansans are so uncivilized they don't bear mentioning—they are the South's Okies. And we could talk all day about Texans. They are mostly transplanted Tennesseans to begin, but there is a saving strain of Alabama blood in Texas. The greatest trouble with Texans is that they are rather loud, but they do travel well and they take friendship very seriously. Yet they tend to become converts to the first new idea they encounter, and they go on and go through life being converts and trying to convert everybody else around them. They want you to be like them.

But getting back to my education in Tennessee, I got the impression that the North had started the war and the South had won it. We in the South inhabited an oppressed region through no fault and through no choice of our own. I have recently begun to read that history for myself. The referendums were very close, whether to secede or not.

INTERVIEWER: In the Deep South?

FORD: Of course in the Deep South. Good sense was not confined to the border-state Southerners. Good sense had strongholds in the Deep South. The Deep South by and large knew what it had to lose. Seccesh sentiment, however, spread like influenza. The older and wiser voices of moderation were silenced. Put it another way. The South, once committed, was solidly behind the fight, although not solidly behind the war. Once the sword was drawn the scabbard was thrown away. But 60 percent, by and large, cautioned against drawing the sword to begin with. That war was another case of the defeat of the Silent Majority. It was rhetoric that got us into the war and it was rhetoric afterwards that tried to make us glad over the mess and rhetoric again that taught us that we ought to hate the North for winning—or that tried to teach us. Some of us never got glad about that war. I happen to be one who is sorry it was ever fought. That war and the aftermath created the region we know now as the South.

INTERVIEWER: Do you think that it created the concept of a region that had not existed before that time?

FORD: A concept was always there by virtue of soil, climate, and geography. The South of course felt that it was separate, and it *was* separate. So that there was regional identification from the first. The South always preferred to trade with England because English goods were better and cheaper. Northern colonies and states were anxious for trade restrictions and tariffs. They wanted that great market—the South—for themselves. Why shouldn't they want it? It was *there*. I'm just saying that the real creation of the South as a region as it *now* exists came on us by virtue of a whirlwind of events which many but not nearly enough could understand and finally realize. Andrew Jackson knew and realized the situation. He saw the danger and he put his finger on it, but then he had the *true* lesson of New Orleans and the *true* lesson of the American Revolution to shape the character of his intellect and that of his generation. By the 1850's too many of Jackson's generation had died; too few Southerners held to his verities and to his vision. The Jacksonian conviction "the Union, it must and shall be preserved" had been fatally diluted. The industrial revolution, the abolitionists, the terrible, misbegotten war, and last of all, the Reconstruction—a cataclysmic whirlwind. The South was transformed to a dark and bloody ground and its people were envenomed and so they remain, a great many do. The misery and the bitterness is exported now, into the North, to the East, and to the West.

Much of the silliness, the writing about the Negro not being a human being and not having a soul, that walking erect was his only human identification, came on during the Reconstruction. There was some of this, but not a terrible amount of it, before the Reconstruction. During the Civil War slaves, interestingly enough, went with their young Confederate masters (they were called servants) into the trenches and on several occasions begged for arms, fought in hot situations, and shot Yankees. And a good many Southerners, when Lee called for more troops, favored putting slaves into uniform. It was suggested they be given their freedom and armed and used in the Southern armies. And if the South had enough confidence in the slaves to arm them and give them their freedom, you *know* whose side the majority of slaves were on. They felt that the North was an invading army, and they felt threatened like their masters.

INTERVIEWER: Of course, there's a great deal of myth in any of this, and you're looking more closely at the record now than I've done, and so a part of my concept would be molded by myth also. But do you think that kind of fidelity you're speaking of in the slaves was—and when I say this I'm not suggesting anything about the quality of mind—but do you think it was more like an unquestioning child following its father, that kind of fidelity? Or was there some tie with the land and the people that would compel them to do that—the slaves to respond in that way?

FORD: Well, there was *some* tie with the land and the people. The horrors of slavery had been largely relieved except in the one area of education. Southern officialdom was afraid to have literate slaves because they feared they would write their own passes and get fancy ideas, and so they would have. But there *was* affection between master and servant, undeniably. It was much the same sort of thing that you found in Tolstoi's Russia. It was closer to *that* than what the abolitionist writers would have had the world believe. And the proof is in the simple fact that the white men left and went to war, and the white women stayed home and ran the plantations. And the slaves did not rise, they did not bolt, and slaves did defend and protect the life and the property of their masters. So the slaves identified with the South. Now this old piddling fact is unpopular as hell among a lot of black people.

Yet that *was* the *general* attitude. Otherwise the South would not
have been able to field the vast armies that it did. The Confederacy would have to have had thousands of troops on the
farms keeping these black people down. Then there was that ante-
bellum commission founded by a resolution of the Virginia legislature and subsequently funded by private individuals long before
the war to repatriate the slaves. These Southern philanthropists
were going to Congress to ask for an appropriation of a quarter
of a million dollars a year and that, with private funds, they
figured would have all of the black people in America at that
time (during the 1820's) back in Africa by 1856. That was the
long-range plan. But where the plan backfired was that no black
slaves wanted to go back. They didn't want to *leave* this country,
and one of the common threats . . . children, for example, would
tease a black servant by saying, "I just heard my daddy say that he
was going to free you and send you to Liberia." Well, it would
just scare the poor Negro to death. It would terrify them, because
they were *Americans*. They *felt* themselves to be Americans. And
the other thing is that when you talk to . . . I have talked to
former slaves, and I have talked to people whose people were
slaves. And I have said, "Wasn't it *terrible*, you know, coming to
this country, being put in chains and brought on over here in a
ship and everything?" And the invariable answer, which always
bowled me over was, "Oh, no. We were glad to get here." "Why?"
"Well, my gosh, it's so much better *here*." "Why?" "Well, my goodness, you know, we were being captured and slaughtered and
rustled around. The people on the ship were not nice, but man,
when we got *here*, we were *happy* to see this land." So they
didn't, for the most, come in as surly individuals. And most learned
willingly and most did their jobs willingly. And, of course, the
force of law was there at all times, American law, not mere
Southern law. We were not occupied by armies in order to maintain this labor source. If I should be so misunderstood as to sound
like a segregationist or a racist, I'm sorry, but I'm looking at the
facts, speaking as a historian now, and that's what the historical
facts show me.

INTERVIEWER: Well, I think anybody who's read *Liberation of Lord*

Byron Jones or some of your short stories or *The Feast of Saint Barnabas* would of course sense that you're no bigot. In fact, it's very clear that you've been deeply concerned about the ramifications of slavery and the racial difficulties that we've had in all this. And it's interesting to note how we began talking about you as a Southern writer and then drifted to where we are now . . . It's obviously something that you're really close to and involved in. You've evidently been reading a lot lately trying to get into the roots of all this. My next question had to do with . . . but it's clear to me now. . . . The question is answered that you've never had any qualms about being called a Southern writer? I mean, that's never bothered you?

FORD: No. And I have held to my Southern speech and accent.

INTERVIEWER: Going back to the way you revealed your concern for the racial problem in the South and the problem of the native Southerner, do you plan to continue with this? In the end of *Liberation of Lord Byron Jones,* Victor X is in the car with his mother, Emma, and that's pretty well where it ends, with the cold look in his eye. Do you plan to continue this on into Victor X's generation, or will it take a few years for you to see which way things are going?

FORD: Well, very possibly I will. As you know, Lord Byron Jones appeared as a character in *Mountains of Gilead,* my first novel.

INTERVIEWER: His funeral parlor, that's where Bojack Markham is taken when he dies. And Gratt comes to see him . . .

FORD: Right. Gratt comes to see him. And one of the last people we see in the novel is Lord Byron Jones. And then there's a story in which he is concerned.

INTERVIEWER: Yes, in the short story collection. I know that there're at least one or two stories in which he figures.

FORD: Yes.

INTERVIEWER: Peripherally.

FORD: Yes. Just as being there. And of course *Liberation* is not only his story. It's also Hedgepath's story, and so very possibly I'll do something with Victor X, but he must have some years in which to grow up. And we'll see what kind of man he is. I can only say that if I find a character interesting, then I will use that character in a story, and I never know what will be interesting. I had no idea that Lord Byron Jones would figure in a novel like he did, but it turned out so.

INTERVIEWER: When you were writing *Mountains of Gilead,* you didn't have that idea?

FORD: No. No, I didn't. I knew of the incidents in West Tennessee. I knew the gist of the story, but I was not fascinated with it at first. It was only after I had been out of this country for a year that I discovered more about the story and became interested in it and wrote it. What I'm doing now is going back. I'm writing the story of my fathers and how they settled this land.

INTERVIEWER: *Elias?*

FORD: Yes. *Elias.* And that will go from 1800 to 1865, to the end of the war. And so some of the same families that appear in *Mountains of Gilead* and then in *Liberation* will be reflected in terms of their ancestors. And you remember Tom McCutcheon in *Mountains of Gilead.* He's Patsy Jo's father and shoots Gratt's bride, Eleanor Fite. The protagonist of the novel, *Elias,* that I'm writing now is Elias McCutcheon, forefather of these McCutcheons who settled what came to be West Tennessee. The story is a story of the settlement of the land, the Indian Wars, and the plagues, floods, famines, all the things that happened, the dire events that swept over this land while it was being settled. *Elias* is a saga novel. Not a historical novel. That's a narrow term. This is primarily a novel, and a saga novel because it is concerned with the history of people as people, as personalities. I'm writing the people, not events. There will be no identifiable historical personage in *Elias.* It's turning out to be a long book, a *very* long book.

INTERVIEWER: Longer than *Liberation?*

FORD: Yes. Two or three times that long. A long story. *Liberation* is rather short.

INTERVIEWER: And you're going to do it in one novel, I mean in one volume?

FORD: Yes, that decision has been made. It's been decided by my publishers that *Elias* will be published probably in 1972 as one volume.

INTERVIEWER: Let me backtrack a little. You mentioned that one of your main interests in *The Liberation of Lord Byron Jones* was in Oman Hedgepath. I'm interested in your feelings about that man, and I want to preface my question a bit. Sinclair Lewis, however satirical he was with Babbitt, had a place in his heart for Babbitt, certainly. And Faulkner was the same way, I think, with Jason Compson. He couldn't help but delight in Jason's wit. Let's see, I'm trying to think of some others . . . Well, those are only two; what about your experience in this sort of author-character relationship? It would be hard to be all for Oman Hedgepath, but he had a place in your heart, didn't he?

FORD: Yes. I've known Oman in many guises. I wished to portray a Southerner who was educated, cultured, charming, witty, the kind of man you would like if you met him. Any American, any person anywhere in the world who met Oman Hedgepath would immediately like him. He would soon have them laughing.

INTERVIEWER: He would tell stories?

FORD: Stories, jokes. He would make it his bounden purpose to make those people enjoy themselves. And that's how he attracts industry into the South. That's how he makes the South run. He runs the South and makes it his kind. The slack-jawed, tobacco-spitting, rifle-toting Southerners and the sheriff, you know, who whips up on niggers and all that kind of thing is not the man who runs this neck of the woods. The South is run by charming, intelligent, and well-educated people, some of whom are bigots. That's Oman Hedgepath. He's a charming bigot, and makes no bones about it. He doesn't apologize for his bigotry, and he's not really prejudiced because he's *thought* about it. He's made no *prejudgment*. He's thought about it and he knows *exactly* how he feels. He's even willing to give up his religion. He's willing to give up life after death. Christianity? Forget it! He simply means to go where his fathers have gone because he believes like they believed. There has never to my knowledge been a character like that in American fiction. And why? He exists. Part of him is in my father. Part of him is me and my grandfather and your father, all the gentlemen we know who just *believe* that way. And they're not on the defensive about it at all. Hell, no. That's what fascinates me about Oman.

INTERVIEWER: Do you think he's a vanishing breed?

FORD: Yes, and *he* knows he is. "Omanism," to coin a word, has to do with a life style and a way of speech too.

INTERVIEWER: Oman operates on rhetoric a great deal, doesn't he? And the narrative impulse?

FORD: Yes, and he has . . . He is a master of misguided and misleading rhetoric. You can't get around him, you see, on his arguments. Never, for Oman has bolstered his opinion with facts, and he can talk you down on just any subject about his beliefs. He's well founded in that way. He's certainly no dummy. And what he does not accomplish with sheer rhetoric he will gain with charm and wit and a really smashingly cynical comedy. Yes, that is "Omanism." Yet the very name is a plaintive cry: "O man; oh, mankind." With all the devious ways of a path leading through hedges, in the midst of hedges—Hedgepath. "Omanism" is not confined to the American South.

INTERVIEWER: This leads me to an important part of the interview, about your experience with the making of a film out of a novel, especially the problems that were encountered with *The Liberation of Lord Byron Jones.*

FORD: There were problems, but none were even in a category with the troubles I had writing the novel itself. By the time the screenplay came along, the major problems, insofar as I was concerned, had been resolved in a little soundproof windowless room—hot in summer, cold in winter—where I spent ten hours and more a day for two years writing *The Liberation of Lord Byron Jones.* My children were farmed out during the day with their grandmother, my wife was teaching school to help feed us, and for company I had a Saint Bernard named Captain. He was the family pet and we roasted and froze together in that room on South Seventeenth in Humboldt, Tennessee, that dog and I did, and he had about as much idea as I did about whether the book would even be published or not. I had no advance from my publishers and no hope of any help from any direction. All the people and the foundations and the "help" that seems forthcoming now, well, all that was in the future then. All I had was an old typewriter and cheap paper and desperation—sheer and utter desperation—and somehow the book got written. Ted Weeks was editor of the *Atlantic* back then and he bought short stories from me and wrote me encouraging letters and Peter Davison was, like Ted, my book editor, then as now, for the Atlantic Monthly Press, and Peter wrote encouraging letters—but there was no money to be had. So I just rode it out and of course I was miserable and happy as only you can be when you have nothing but a vague hope, when the kids are sick and the pipes under the old house freeze and there's no water running and you warm your fingers using an unvented gas heater in that room because you can't afford to have it vented, wondering all the time if carbon monoxide is going to overcome you and kill you. Well, after the dog and I went through that we weren't much concerned with problems with the screenplay. The screenplay was a breeze from the ocean compared to what we had endured before, between 1962 and 1964 when nobody but Ted and Peter and the dog (who didn't know and never knew any better) would have given a nickel for my chances. Maybe all that didn't *hurt* me, but I am not one of those pious jackasses who can find a lot of damned *virtue* in suffering and deprivation on *that* order, either. And if you go back to 1957 when I first went to Humboldt and underwent the transformation from a well fed and well paid and well drunk PR man on the Chicago staff of the American Medical Association to what a former AMA colleague called me to my face, "a Humboldt bum," when he dropped down South to try to talk me out of my madness and found me wearing wash pants in January, well, the screenplay posed *very* damned few problems that I could not face with a certain calm and balance and bravery and fortitude. There is a lot of difference between a thousand a week and a thousand a *year*. And I am sorry for anybody who has to experience the difference firsthand to appreciate it.

INTERVIEWER: Getting back to making a film out of a novel . . . I want to talk about problems that a writer might encounter if he possibly has one eye cocked on the possibilities of a film script when he's writing a novel—if that poses any problems. Why don't you just start with your experiences, good or bad, with this film script? You helped write it, didn't you—*The Liberation of L. B. Jones?*

FORD: Yes. I was co-author of the script with Stirling Silliphant. When Ron Lubin bought the screen rights, when he optioned the screen rights to *Liberation,* he got Stirling interested and then he got me interested, and Stirling felt that the way to get the picture made was to write a Broadway play and put it on Broadway and then have it filmed. I was in favor of it, and we went to Colorado Springs in the winter of 1965—no, it was the spring of '66. Silliphant, Lubin, and I all went to Colorado Springs. And Silliphant and I there blocked out the play, and we agreed that I would go to Tennessee and write certain segments, and he would go to California and write certain segments, and then he and I would get together and rewrite the play, and then we would go to Broadway. Well, complications ensued when Stirling's options were all suddenly taken up. He had written a picture called *The Slender Thread* with Sidney Poitier. He had several projects with his agent, and he had been waiting for years for this to come along, and it *came* along. Suddenly everybody wanted Stirling. He wrote *In the Heat of the Night* at that time. The result was that I wrote my half of the stage play. I didn't want to do the rest of the play. I just felt I had spent enough time. Besides, I was writing other things.

INTERVIEWER: As you look back, do you think it would lend itself very well to the stage?

FORD: Very well. That's one thing William Wyler said. Willie said, "I don't understand why this hasn't been a stage play." Willie read my portions of the stage play, and thought it very good. Much of it was used in the film script.

INTERVIEWER: I can see it cinematically, but I can't see it on the stage.

FORD: The nice thing about the stage play is that it can do things a picture *can't* do. In other words, Oman's character would be dominant onstage as it cannot be on the screen. Onstage his rhetoric will play. It's just a different form. One thing I did from the outset was to reserve the rights to stage production. Those are mine. I told Lubin he could make a film, but he could not have stage rights, and he agreed to it. And then he decided he wanted to go to the stage, and that was when Stirling came into the picture, for I had said that if Ron could find somebody that I respected, an experienced dramatist, that I would then co-author a stage play. I've still retained those rights.

INTERVIEWER: So that's in the balance right now?

FORD: That all depends on how Willie's picture is received. It depends on how strong I feel the material is. I have seen one reading of the play . . . of the novel as a play at the University of Missouri, and the theater was so packed, people were lying down in the aisles to see it. It was fabulously received. And depending on how the picture does and how the times are, I may or may not do it as a stage play. But I feel really that as time goes on . . . I'm so interested in my new novel. I have other stories I've got to write, and I think one screenplay is enough for anybody. And there is plenty of time. I don't have to be trigger-happy about the stage because either this material will hold up or it won't. If it holds up, I have a stage play. If it doesn't, if it gets where people aren't interested in it, I don't. If Willie's movie vitiates the possibility, I'll know that too. So there's no need to be concerned about it right now.

INTERVIEWER: This was your first venture into actual film script, wasn't it? Did you go into it with fear and trembling?

FORD: To the contrary, I went into it with a great confidence because I was associated with a man that I consider the *Shakespeare* of film writers. Stirling Silliphant is a man who works at top speed and turns out excellent plays. That's what Shakespeare did. Shakespeare *really* knew his craft. Stirling *really* knows what *he* is doing. Because I was working with a pro, I didn't *have* to worry. I was very relaxed, and I enjoyed every moment of it. It's the only collaboration that Stirling has ever entered into and the only collaboration that I ever entered into, and neither of us ever intend to collaborate again. We're essentially loners, but we happened to hit it off, and we are fast friends and quite proud of our screenplay.

INTERVIEWER: We've been talking about your experiences with the film script, the aspect of turning a novel into a film by way of a film script. Can you comment now on any particular problems you might have encountered in this, specifically or in general?

FORD: It was not a difficult adaptation because we had more material than we could use, a great deal more, because it was a hefty novel. It was an embarrassment of riches in that respect. We had to be selective and decide what would be most interesting, scene by scene. Stirling took my half of the stage play and wrote a screenplay, and that's what we came to call "red script." Had a red cover. That was the first screenplay. Then I went to California and sat down with Stirling and we rewrote red script to get blue script (blue cover) which I still think is perhaps the best version we wrote. Then Stirling and I got out of the project and left Ron Lubin with it because we'd given all we could. Ron was having no luck with the studios. He just couldn't get a studio to take it on. He couldn't get a major director. He couldn't get a major star. He had lots of nibbles. That sort of thing goes on. *Liberation* was one that the studios were deathly afraid of. But *In the Heat of the Night* came out and was well received. *Guess Who's Coming to Dinner?* appeared. It did all right. So George Cukor, who directed *My Fair Lady* and forty more pictures as good or better (George has been a friend of mine for a long time), called me one day in response to the letter that I had written about Spencer Tracy's death and he said, "I think that your picture is going to be made because Katharine Hepburn's niece was in *Guess Who's Coming to Dinner?*" George had just seen *Guess Who's Coming to Dinner?* and he was impressed with it, and he said, "That and other pictures that are now being made make it possible for your picture to be made, and I just want to tell you that I think it *will* be made." Well, months passed, and Ron said, "William Wyler wants to direct *Liberation*, and we have a deal at Columbia." And he said, "There's just one problem. The screenplay has got to be rewritten for Wyler." Inwardly I groaned at that thought, but I had just come from Boston, having finished *The Feast of Saint Barnabas*, so my new novel was in the bag, and I went on out to California in late August of that year, 1968, went to Malibu, and there I met William Wyler. Willie and I became friends. Stirling and I set out to rewrite the script for Willie, and we rewrote it together I would say maybe six times. And then Stirling's son was so tragically killed, and his house burned down. Those two calamities served to sever Stirling from the project because he was away in terms of grief and shock and distraction for a length of time such that Willie and I began to work on the script together. Stirling never really came back in on the script. He went on to other projects. But his scenes stood virtually unchanged. I think he was happy to get away. There were other things that he wanted to write and he needed to work out his grief in his own way. Stirling is in the vanguard of those writers who came from television into pictures and changed movies and brought in new techniques.

INTERVIEWER: What about the matter I mentioned earlier? Do you see any danger in your own writing or in that of other writers in working on a novel while keeping one eye open for the possibilities of a film sale? Will that limit or harm a novel in any way, do you think?

FORD: It can.

INTERVIEWER: Aren't a good many writers doing this now?

FORD: I shouldn't be surprised, because when you look at the money that can be made from a film, especially now when the writer and the director are as important as they are in the picture industry, it isn't surprising that someone would write a book that would be easily adaptable to films. But I think that's wrong. I think you should write the book so that it's the best book that you can make. *I* would not slant a book or write a book so that it would be easy to adapt. I'm working on a book right now, 1800–1865. The obvious thing for me to do is to narrow *Elias* down and to make the action of this novel play itself out in six months in 1864, and then I've got a Civil War novel which will get a movie sale, and I can write that kind of novel in eight months. But I'm *not* doing that because what I'm writing is a saga novel. And *Elias* is going to be *difficult* to adapt to the films.

INTERVIEWER: Do you think it has possibilities as a film?

FORD: I'm certain it *will* be filmed. I have no doubt about it, but I don't think about that. *Elias* is going to be an Edna Ferber problem for the movies. It's going to be like *Giant*, where people are young and then they get old and other generations come along.

INTERVIEWER: Like *The Forsyte Saga?*

FORD: Yes, it's that sort of problem where a film is concerned. *Elias* is a *long* story. But I'm not concerned with that. I'm not going to throw in unities of time, place, or action for the sake of a movie. *Elias* is a fascinating story; I'm writing it as it must be, that's all.

INTERVIEWER: If a writer were trying to increase his chances of getting a novel accepted for a film script, what would be the limits in technique as far as the novel itself? For a film, do you think that something scenic and episodic would lend itself well? And then you'd be limited by something like stream of consciousness, wouldn't you?

FORD: Well, you see, all sorts of stories, true stories, stories that are fictional, novels, even *Life* magazine articles lend themselves to adaptation to screenplays, so there's no limit on raw material. I contend that if a writer were looking toward a film sale, the best thing he could do would be make his novel the best *story* he could so that it would have interest all the way . . . proper suspense . . . and to be so well constructed that it could not be picked apart. Because when a producer looks to buy a property, he looks for story and for characterization, and he takes a very close look at motivation. It's strange, the image that we have of the Hollywood producer—and some *are* dumb as mud, that's true—but *all* of them, if they *succeed*, have this in common: if there is a fault in a story, they will find it. They have people who work for them who look for this. All the threads should be tied up. It should be a well-contained story whether it's a short story or a novel. Either can make a film if it's a good story. That's the first thing. Now if you do cover a long period of time, if your story does jump around in terms of location, if it does any of those things that would violate the idea of drama as envisioned by the Greeks, it's going to be more difficult, and those things are going to hurt. But what they look for is a work that succeeds on its own. If it's a novel that succeeds on its own, if it's a story that does, if it's much talked about, then they want it. I should say the same things that make a good stage play, if those same things are in a novel, then it's sure to be bought.

INTERVIEWER: Were any things left out of the film of *Liberation of Lord Byron Jones* that disappointed you, things that should have been in that they felt could not be handled?

FORD: No. Nothing. I like the film very much.

INTERVIEWER: Do you think Oman's is a view shared by a majority of Southerners today, or better yet, has life changed radically in the South since the time when Oman's views would have gone virtually unchallenged? And if it's changed, does the change have anything much to do with that contest C. Vann Woodward writes of—the race between the bulldozer and the magnolia, in which the magnolia is losing out?

FORD: Novelists are best off when they stay out of the arena with the historians and the sociologists. Facts and data come to the rescue of the historian and the sociologist both in a way they can never help or rescue the novelist. The novelist is searching for truth, searching for a way to make truth felt and realized rather than simply known. I find all the time that people know things they don't realize and that they realize things they don't know, and in fiction, in good fiction, there is a bridge and a synthesis between knowing and realizing and this amounts to the communication of truth and the beauty of truth through the eyes of a reader into his brain and into his soul and his spirit. Good fiction becomes part of the reader's experience, and becomes a part of his life.

Now I really have no way to know whether or not Oman's view is shared by a majority of Southerners. I don't have the machinery for taking such a poll, even if such a poll were possible. Of course life in this South has changed since that time when Oman's views would have gone unchallenged. Oman's views are essentially his father's and his father's father's views, and these have been challenged for better than a century. And none of this, it seems to me, has the least thing to do with the race or the contest between the bulldozer and the magnolia in which the magnolia is *losing?*

Once in Gainesville, Florida, when I was freezing—when I was a student with two baby boys and my wife was pregnant and we didn't have any firewood, I tried to cut up a magnolia log with an ax and that's when I found out that next to a dozer blade a magnolia is probably the hardest damned thing in the world. I gained a certain respect for even a *felled* magnolia, a *dead* magnolia. Oman wouldn't be above operating a bulldozer himself if he couldn't find someone to run it for him. Oman is not the New South and he is not the Old South. He is the South, the Now South. I'm sorry he's a bigot, in a way, but why should *he* be so different from everybody else in the world and in this bigoted country? Just because he is Southern and descended from slave-owners and thinks a certain way, must we expect that he will go his whole life repenting and apologizing? I think he won't act that way. He's a vanishing race and so is the human race, in general, about to vanish, if all of us don't watch out.

Dealing with the Grotesque:
❦ FRED CHAPPELL

Interviewed by JOHN SOPKO and JOHN CARR

Fred Chappell looks like a guy who goes around sticking up service stations for fun and profit. He is also somewhat absent-minded. When he wheeled onto the campus of the University of North Carolina at Charlotte in the fall of 1969 (he was to do a public reading that night), he smiled at the welcoming committee and then recollected he had left his wife Sue standing in front of the bank in Greensboro waiting for him. But he had remembered to bring her bags and the tie she had tied for him.

When not going on out-of-town trips (including Grand Forks, North Dakota, for the Southern writing conference, where he nearly had to stay until the July thaw after he lost his plane ticket at a party) he lives in Greensboro, where he teaches English at University of North Carolina at Greensboro. He and Sue have one child, son Heath, who is fast becoming an expert rock-and-roll drummer.

Fred was born in Canton, North Carolina, and his first two novels, It Is Time, Lord *(1963) and* The Inkling *(1965) are set in the mountain country. His next novel,* Dagon *(1968), takes place in the mountain country, but it is a weird, allegorical work that owes as much to Poe and H. P. Lovecraft as to any regional tradition. His first collection of verse,* The World Between the Eyes, *was published in 1971, and his fourth novel,* The Gaudy Place, *in 1972. His verse has appeared in these periodicals and anthologies:* Above Ground Review, Aim, American Scholar, Brown Bag, Contempora, Dragonfly, Fly by Night, Mill Mountain Review, Paris Review, Southern Poetry Review, Wasatch Front, A Decade of Poems, A Duke Miscellany, *and* Under Twenty-Five. *He was also one of the editors (along with Ann Lloyd and Ed Middleton) of* Fly by Night, *a giant ad hoc underground magazine that began and ended with one issue. But in that one*

216

issue . . . stories and poems by May Swenson, William Pitt Root, Fred himself, Kent Anderson, Richard Dillard, Anthony Burgess, George Garrett, and others.

The first of these interviews was a question and answer session in my early (8 A.M.) English 102 class at the University of North Carolina at Charlotte. Both of my 102 sections and visitors from the faculty jammed into the room and Fred just took questions as they were thrown at him. Later that day, there was a party and John Sopko and Fred went upstairs and talked about projects past and future.

I

CARR: Everybody in here has read your novel, except some of the visitors, and I told them the floor would be open, whether for questions about *Dagon* or questions about American novels in general.

STUDENT: Have you had any experience with insanity?

CHAPPELL: No. Insanity, in most novels, is not medically straight. It's a literary convention. You say all the crazy things you want to and give somebody else the blame for it. It's not real insanity. If you think of Faulkner's crazy people, for example, they're much smarter than you and me. They see things. They just don't think in the same way. It's the same literary convention as in Chaucer's dreams. You say: "They're just dreams. O.K., now I'm going to take off."

STUDENT: Mr. Chappell, your book seems to be a religious journey.

CHAPPELL: Well, first of all, we're talking about a book I don't remember all that well. But that's an interesting notion. I never thought of it that way. It is a religious book—if only because you and I don't grow up here in the South without being religious one way or another. I had Puritanism on my mind when I was writing it. But everybody told me, "No, it ain't that. It's something else." A great deal of the book—this isn't too important—but a great deal of the book is a parody of books written about Puritanism. Some sections parody Hawthorne's *Scarlet Letter* and there are sections which parody *Moby Dick*. Which are books that are also about Puritanism. When I wrote it I had this wonderful science fiction, like *2001*, notion: "Puritanism is true. Maybe all that stuff they've taught you is true. Then what? What if you die and go to hell?" So that's what makes it so weird. But it's no more weird than when you . . . Did you ever turn on your car radio and hear a preacher, from Spartanburg, South Carolina, say, get started with the "thees" and "thous"? It's no more weird than one of those sermons.

STUDENT: The last chapter isn't about Puritanism, is it?

CHAPPELL: No. The last chapter is a parody of something else entirely. There's a long poem of Chaucer's called *Troilus and Criseyde*. The last chapter, if you've ever read Chaucer's poems, is just a long love affair between Troilus and Criseyde and you spend pages and pages with this wonderful rhyme. The story goes back and forth with these intense agonies. At the end, Troilus dies. And then he looks down from heaven upon this little spot of earth and says, "What a silly thing, this little love affair, and I thought it was so important." I wanted to get an entirely new perspective into this novel. Somebody told me I should just cut the last chapter. I couldn't, because it leaves the end of the book so "ech," you know? And I wanted to have a little happier perspective on the whole story. Get some fresh air in there, you know. Also, I did it to relieve myself. I was bored with the book.

STUDENT: Did you have any special thing in mind about the letters he found in the book?

CARR: Yeah. We were going to ask you about that. What do those words mean in the epigraph? Some, I can't even pronounce.

CHAPPELL: Oh, listen now. There was a pulp writer in the 1920's called H. P. Lovecraft who wrote for *Weird Tales*, a pulp magazine, and he invented a mythology. This mythology was that the earth had been inhabited by all kinds of races before man came along. One of them was some kind of fungus with long tentacles. It was driven out by some other race, which looked even worse, and as soon as man destroys himself by atomic fusion and black magic, they will take over the earth again. The little epigraph there means: "In his house at R'lgeh"—which was in an undersea city, in Lovecraft's mythology—"dead Chthulhu lies sleeping." It's absolute nonsense. That's why it's there in front of the book. Just to fake people out. Just to hassle my publisher, more than anything else.

It's a curious book. I can explain it in personal terms better than in any other way. The purpose in my mind was—I wanted the protagonist to become passive. He's not really an active sort of person throughout the novel. Not a person, but an object, like paper. Becomes more and more passive. Finally he becomes so completely a victim that he's not even human anymore. And I wanted to make him a part of nature. I hope this came through. That tattoo scene is a parody from *Moby Dick*, by the way. And the symbols on his body all have a religious significance. And at the end, he flows into the universe.

STUDENT: What type of research did you do on *Dagon*—on the worship of Dagon? Like with the practice of it today, if it is practiced?

CHAPPELL: As far as I know, it's not practiced today. There were a lot of fake passages, a lot of fake scholarship, in the book to see if I could do it and get away with it, to see if anybody would notice it. But the passage from William Bradford's journal about the worship of Dagon is really true. At one time there was a cult. I don't think it survived. I hope not. But it was there. You have this America we all know about, but you also have this anti-America, too, made up of the criminals, who want to get back at the Puritan people who had exiled and outlawed them. Edward Morton, I think, struck Merrymount.

STUDENT: Thomas Morton?

CHAPPELL: Yeah. Thomas Morton. Hawthorne has this story, *Maypole of Merrymount*. It's worth looking up. Dagonism was a real worship. I think it did survive among the Indians for a while. We have some indications that it did. Mostly in fertility rituals and so on. Indian religion was not like ours. It had no books or anything, so it was plastic. It was a very malleable religion which changed constantly. For example, Indians worshiped Pocahontas for awhile, not the Indians out West, but the Indians who had heard about her. They called her a goddess, said she was twelve feet tall. Wherever she stepped, corn would grow. They had all kinds of things going, because their religion allowed for historical circumstances.

STUDENT: Has it been practiced recently within the last few hundred years anywhere else in the world?

CHAPPELL: The worship of Dagon or the worship of a fish deity? The worship of the fish deity is still practiced in South Sea Islands. And it was practiced among the Indians much longer than you'd think. If you remember, the Indians had a practice of planting fish along with their corn. You hear, even now, a lot about fertilizer and all that. Hell, they didn't know nothing about fertilizer. It was for religious reasons that they planted the fish. It did have fertilizer value, but the fish was a symbol of fertility for them and the burial of the fish with the corn was just to insure that the seeds would come up.

STUDENT: I got the feeling that Peter, when he was a child, had visited his grandparents, and was influenced by the Dagonist idea. When he returned to the house he seemed drawn to it by some supernatural force.

CHAPPELL: Yeah, I wanted to get a haunted house without saying "this is a haunted house" with three big eyes and one big tooth, but I didn't know how to do it, so I just let it hang in the background and didn't do much about it. There is the inference in there that he inherits this worship—or was drawn to the religion —because of his father. You have this little flashback in there. It's so very confused because I didn't know how to do it. He remembers his father, or imagines his father, being tortured and beaten and I'm not sure it came off.

STUDENT: How long did it take you to write that novel? And how many have you written?

CHAPPELL: I've got a novel at home, which I got to finish. That will make four. Then I'm going to get out of the racket for a while. I'm tired of writing novels. I want to write verse. The first two novels took me five weeks apiece to write. I just sat down and wrote. *Dagon* took me three years, agony every step of the way. I had nightmares, woke up sweating and crying at night. It was a real tough book. I thought my wife would climb the walls. But if it's hanging on to you, you got to do it, so I finally did something with it.

STUDENT: What inspired you to write the novel?

CHAPPELL: I don't know. When I was a little boy I didn't see my parents very much. They were both schoolteachers and my father was a farmer. They taught away from me. I lived with my grandparents in an old house—well, it's the house in the book—and I think that's what was on my mind the whole time. My grandmother is a very religious person. She's ninety-four now, ninety-five. Every time I see her, she gives me a quiz on the Bible: "How many flocks did Samson set on fire?" "I don't know, Grammaw." In a way, that novel is my whole life.

STUDENT: A lot of writers go into seclusion to write. Do you write in your own home?

CHAPPELL: Now I have a house with a little room for myself; but before, I'd just sit at a card table set up in the living room. When we were broke, my wife was working and I was baby sitting with my little boy. I'd turn on "I Love Lucy." He'd watch and I'd write a novel. That's when I was in graduate school. If you go to school when you get married, you'll do the same thing.

CARR: It's kind of an illusion that people go to the mountains to do these things.

CHAPPELL: Oh, they'd just say: "Well, here I am on the mountain top. I'm not going to write that old book." You can't do that . . . If you don't have the give and take, the push and pull, yaw and pitch of everyday reality to fight against—whatever everyday reality means—it's too easy. You got to have something to shove your muscle against. Oh, it'd be nice to live like Proust, but very few Americans can. We are too gregarious a people. Literature is not all that important. It's not even important to a writer, so you know it's not important to anybody else. Everything's part of everything else—he said wisely.

CARR: Somebody has said that one of the characteristics of modern literature, is the use of artifice. Where's it leading? Is there any more nitty-gritty to write about or are we always parodying our own stuff?

CHAPPELL: Oh, I think there's a whole lot of horrible reality out there, and there are a whole lot of writers who are not artificial in this sense—in the literary sense. Writers like James T. Farrell, who's still going, who's still writing novels. You know—Chicago, the way it is. The trouble is that we've begun to see the end of the novel as reporting. In the first place, you can't do it as well as people who just go out and report. There's a wonderful reporter named Michael Herr, who has a book coming out about Vietnam, and—

CARR: The latest installment, in *Esquire*, is called "Spooky at Khesanh."

CHAPPELL: Terrific book. A novel would never be that good. A novel has to have a plot and all that stuff, that out there, there ain't none of. Once you realize that, you can't go back to straight reporting. You just can't. You write about Jane: "Down the street, it was a hot day. Yes sir. She was eating ice cream." You get tired of it, you can't do it—you just don't believe it anymore. You believe that's Jane, or you know that's ice cream all right, but it's something else: it's Jane's liking for cold things. Those *things* are an invention, and if you get hung up on the idea, that in the novel the writer tells you straight, then you're dead. Somebody can tell you all that better. A guy who makes $40 a week on a newspaper can tell you better. Simply because that's what he's doing and you're not.

CARR: Don't you think journalism is taking over many of the fine things that have always been in novels? . . . Well, like Mailer writes *Armies of the Night* and refers to himself as Mailer all the way through. It's almost like a novel. Or he'd have us believe that it is.

CHAPPELL: In journalism today, we're getting real high class. Of course, novels are getting low class, which really ought to happen. But then the novel started as somebody putting you on, somebody saying "This is the true story about Moll Flanders. Do you want to hear the true dirt about her?" You realize very quickly that that's not really reporting. I think people in journalism now are just writing a lot better than they used to. We're getting a new class of people in journalism, young activists, politically active. Everything's much more urgent, much more real, than it used to be to the guy who said, "I'll take what was said yesterday." Reporting now becomes a political document, a way to get things done. A novel, if you wanted to make some fancy classifications—I guess you could divide up writing into writing of the *will*, where you want to make a difference in behavior or make some historical difference, eventual difference, and writing of the *psyche*, where you really don't care to make any difference, where what you want is a whole, a work of art. Reporting *could* be writing of the will, and the novel could be writing of the psyche, if you wanted to make some fancy classifications.

CARR: When you read *Dagon*, it starts out conventionally enough, then it moves to some very unreal things—

CHAPPELL: I've always had this recurrent nightmare: We start out driving. We're going along and it's a nice ordinary landscape, with road signs and trees. Then it sort of turns pink and purple and there're big spiders and things like that. What's so horrible is not anything that's going to get you out there, but the fact that it has changed very *gradually*. You didn't notice for a long time, until you were *there*. You couldn't get away from it. And that's the feeling I wanted to get in a novel. Peter Taylor told me once that if you ever got a house right, you'd get all the characters right. So I tried that as best I could and wrote a sort of description and then let it gradually get so crazy that you couldn't believe it, but never so crazy that anyone would lose their belief in it. That's why the novel took so long and was such a pain to write. I had to test every sentence to see if I had a transition into the crazy stuff too quickly or if you had been led along little by little. You know. This is a technique ordinary writers have to master, so it's not as hard as it sounds. I'm just trying to make myself look good. But it's not easy either. It just takes a lot of work.

CARR: People think you just write a novel, but it's a process of taking it word by word, isn't it?

CHAPPELL: You get an idea for a book and you think you're going to get a Nobel Prize and $2 million. Then when you start out, you gotta start with "the." You realize you gotta put it all down word by word, comma by comma.

STUDENT: You say it took you three years to write *Dagon*. It seems to be divided into three sections. Do they each represent a unit of writing time?

CHAPPELL: No, I didn't write this novel straightforwardly. At the beginning I wrote one scene which is near the end, when Peter Leland woke up after drinking a long time. I know a guy that used to do this for a living. He ate raw chickens, too. They're called geeks. They're alcoholics who go to work in a carnival and are billed as the "Wild Man of Borneo" or something. Because that's all they can do. That's the end of the road. That's how they get their alcohol. I used to know a guy who did this out in Cherokee. He was all used up. Finished.

I wrote that and didn't know what it meant. I had to aim at it. And halfway through the novel I had to stop to write the last chapter because I knew what I was getting into and I wanted to extend it somehow. I wasn't satisfied with that last chapter. It looks a little tacked on. So the writing of it wasn't straightforward. The whole thing came to me from that one image or character.

STUDENT: When you started with the end in sight, did you know exactly where you wanted to go or did you just have an idea and then write about it, and then gradually build more and more as you went along?

CHAPPELL: The second way. I didn't have the whole thing in mind when I started. I had this thing that was preying on me which I wanted to exorcise—or to understand. Once I got into it, then I could dig into it, go and find out and build. Other novels are written the way you think: Suddenly, you imagine the whole thing, every word of it, and then it's a question of physical labor, as if somebody were dictating to you. But *Dagon* isn't a novel like that. It was a novel I had to search out every step of the way.

STUDENT: When you wrote *Dagon* did you have anything that you wanted to communicate to readers?

CHAPPELL: Yeah. Once I was into it, once I understood some of the images, I had very definite ideas . . . It's a preachy book in a lot of ways. I had some notions about Puritanism, you know. I wanted to say that Puritanism is horrible, that it injures people sexually and every other way. And yet it's a most powerful force in your life.

But once you're aware of it, you can evade it—and it's not altogether bad. It's a pretty good ethic. If we didn't have Puritanism, for all its torture, for all the havoc it wreaks on our psyches, we also wouldn't have man's first disobedience, the fruit of that forbidden tree, etc. We wouldn't have Milton. That whole wonderful . . . well, we wouldn't have America if we didn't have Puritanism. That's why they came over here, right?

I just wanted to say that. I had other things I wanted to say, but there was no room for them in the book. I also wanted to write about Puritanism and money. Money and religion are not only indissolubly linked, but I think money in our way of life may have become a positive good to us, like virtue was to Plato. I don't know. But I didn't have room. The novel had coalesced so much that it was do one thing or another.

CARR: You said that there wasn't room in *Dagon*, yet that was a very short novel.

CHAPPELL: Well, I try to keep my novels short. I don't know if anybody ever did it, but my ideal is to keep a novel short enough to be read in one sitting. It's just a private, personal belief. The kind of novel I like to write aims at one effect, one emotion. As a matter of fact, I've made a practice of writing one novel on the back of one I've written before. This is a form of discipline. It can't be any longer than the one you wrote before or you run out of paper. That's for me, of course. I wouldn't dictate to anyone else. One of my favorite novels is one of Dreiser's and those are big books. . . . Is he going to drown her? Well, on page 900 he finally does. But it's so beautifully done, it just entrances me. And Tolstoi. But for me, being very Southern or whatever I am . . . Poe, Flannery O'Connor, it seems to me, get the most out of the form I like. They have the kind of perfection I'd like to achieve. That's one of the reasons my books go in France. My novels aren't very American novels. Poe is not a very American writer. But this is not the best kind of form at all. It's not—I admire other things—but this is what I got to do. If I try anything different, I'll violate myself. I do that enough without doing it while I'm writing a book.

CARR: Did you ever think of writing a book that would go against every kind of aesthetic principle you believe in?

CHAPPELL: Yeah, matter of fact I sold one like that and I can't finish it. I'll never write it. Just to clear myself out, I wanted to write a long, comic novel, a picaresque novel. I wanted to write about a guy hitchhiking around the South. It was about 300 pages when I finally gave it up.

When I was younger, Sue and I were involved in civil rights. We tried to be idealistic, which we were. We were very young.

Well, this Durham, North Carolina, chapter of CORE *had*

to be corrupt politically, one end to the other. It wasn't a good organization. Guess that's why it's not around anymore, now that I think of it.

I wrote a long parody of the civil rights movement and when I was writing it—while I was in Italy—Dr. King was killed. I felt so guilty, I went and tore it all up. Even though that chapter of CORE *had* to be corrupt, it was not the time to be writing parodies of the civil rights movement.

His death was a strange event for us. We were in Italy and we had no access to American papers or American radios. All we knew was what the Italian papers told us. When Dr. King was killed, there were pictures of America burning down. We thought we didn't have a place to come back to when King was killed. And then Kennedy was killed, and there America was, burning again. And when we came back, of course everything was just the same. I never felt so relieved to hear a New York cab driver cuss me out. I knew I was home again.

CARR: Have you written short stories?

CHAPPELL: I've written them, but I've never written a very good one, I don't think. The hardest literary form to do . . . I don't know why. My novels are really short stories. They're just elongated short stories. But to get it all in those few pages . . . I just can't do it. John has written some good ones. I just never get it off the ground.

CARR: The reason I ask . . . Max Steele is one of the past masters of the short story form. He has the kind of ideas, the kind of imagination for short stories. . . . Somebody said a poem is for the moment and a short story is for two or three moments, a long moment, and a novel is trying to capture a section of a life.

CHAPPELL: I can recommend a Max Steele novel. It's called *The Goblins Must Go Barefoot* [formerly *Debby*]. It's a wonderful story. And I read a little short story by Max a while ago. I swear it wasn't 1,000 words long. You can take that little story and read it any way you want to. It's just a story about a football player with a little dainty cigarette box. That's all. Shows how he acts in a room at a party. It's out of sight. I can't do that. Wish I could.

STUDENT: Have you ever thought of writing anything that might be strictly classified as science fiction?

CHAPPELL: I used to make my living doing science fiction when I was in high school. You couldn't make a living off writing science fiction in those days if you were Jesus Christ, but I did. What I did, I was buying girls bracelets and things with the money. But I did it for a long time.

It's too bad, in a way, that commercial writing has disappeared. There aren't any more pulp magazines, not the *Saturday Evening Post* or anything else like that. Those were the training grounds for lots and lots of writers.

The best criticism I ever got was from the editor of one of those pulp magazines. "Don't send me a story like that again. The pace is so wrong. It's like a Boy Scout hike, half trotting and half poking along." I learned so much about the pace of a story from those sentences. Just one vicious little note. That's good. I wish I could get stuff half that critical now.

CARR: You can have a short story published in the *Shenandoah Review* or the *Sewanee Review*. But, you know, there're about six places in America now that'll buy a story for $1,500. Places like *Esquire*. And there are fifty publishing houses. It's easier now to get a novel published.

CHAPPELL: Oh, there're people writing short stories. They're all over the land. And they're turning out rotten short stories. And nobody cares how they're written. And you can sell it to television or the idea to television. And some guy out in Hollywood with two or three Cadillacs, running three or four whorehouses, can take the idea and make a television script out of it. It doesn't even matter whether the story is any good, or if it's written in the worst language possible. He can make something salable of it. It becomes a product like Luck's canned beans.

II

SOPKO: Do you head the program, the writing program, at UNC-G?

CHAPPELL: No. I don't even know who the head is. I don't think we have a formal head. Everybody pitches in and does some work. Bob Watson is senior there, knows more about it than anybody else. Tom Kirby-Smith, a poet, does most of the administration work now, and Jim Applewhite, another fine poet, just pitches in and does what he can. Of course, now we have Dr. William Blackburn there, teaching a course. He once taught Styron and Reynolds Price [and Fred Chappell].

Sopko: You're thirty-three. You've been writing how long?

Chappell: Well, I've been writing seriously since about 1954.

Sopko: Here's a question that sometimes comes up, and I don't know whether it's interesting or not. When someone decides to be something, why do they decide to be a writer?

Chappell: Well, I decided to be a writer when I was thirteen years old because I had in my mind the idea that what a writer did was live on a million dollars a year in some Fifth Avenue penthouse and date movie stars. And even after I learned the bitter facts, well, I just liked the challenge of it, I guess. It's a big challenge.

Sopko: Last night you were talking a lot about being in the hills, in the hill country; I know nothing about the hill country. Tell me about it.

Chappell: Well, it's just about like it's described on those television documentaries about poverty. That's where I'm from, down at the lint end of the poverty pocket. What to say? . . . Almost completely farming, of course. There are a few industries, not very pleasant ones, like paper mills, things like that, rayon mills, nylon factories. The people are mostly of Scotch-Irish descent, poor, bitter, Puritan; of course, very fine, very honest. Very hard, tough people because they have to be. Almost no black population in that part of the country whatsoever.

Sopko: Geographically, when you talk about the hill country, what do you mean?

Chappell: I would say what I think of the hill country is from about Morganton, North Carolina, on over through East Tennessee. A lot of sparsely settled counties. Most of the people leave to go to Detroit or places like that.

Sopko: Obviously, it's affected a lot of your work.

Chappell: For some reason all four of my novels—that's counting the new one; it's not finished yet—are concerned with where I grew up rather than where I've lived since about 1954. I don't know why. I still go back summers, holidays. My family is there. I seem to know that territory, even though some of my stories don't necessarily have to be placed there or anywhere else. *The Inkling* and *Dagon* don't really have to be placed—

Sopko: No, they seem to be out of place anyway.

Chappell: I just use that country because I'm more familiar with the geography. I feel more at home writing about it.

SOPKO: Do you like it?

CHAPPELL: I like it. Yes, I hate it. I feel about it as everyone feels about his home place.

SOPKO: That's a point.

CHAPPELL: It's your fatherland and it's your enemy too.

SOPKO: Here's a question that has bothered me ever since Harrison came to Hollins, and it might be interesting to ask you, because it seems to be a question of craft to some extent, and that is: Where do you begin with a novel?

CHAPPELL: That depends on the novel. Some of my novels have sprung from a central idea, a philosophic notion. Some have sprung simply from a visual image, some just from a memory of a character, some from—hell, I'm talking about *them* like there were millions of them—from a personal experience.

SOPKO: Harrison seems to feel that ideas, what you have called philosophical notions, are at odds with the purpose of a novel, at odds with the purpose of art and poetry or anything like that.

CHAPPELL: I think that as far as the actual writing goes, that's absolutely true, although at least two of my novels started from a philosophical notion. Still, I've tried to make absolutely certain that the idea is not explicit in the book and is behind it as a structure rather than something being talked about or discussed inside the book.

SOPKO: Is what happened in *Dagon* dependent on a philosophical superstructure?

CHAPPELL: I'm afraid it is. That's the . . . *Dagon* breaks down in this respect because the notion I had was so curious and required so much exposition that I just had—and it's a structural fault in the book—I just had to stop the book at one point and put a sermon in it. There's a sermon right in the third chapter, which sort of explains what the book is about. If you happened to skip the sermon, the book would make absolutely no sense whatsoever. Whatever sense it makes, it makes because of that chapter. And that's a technical fault, but I just couldn't find any other way in the world out of it.

SOPKO: Now you related the sermon as an author telling the reader what Leland had said at a particular point in time, past time. If you could have figured some way of making him do it in the present, stir a crowd with it, it might have helped.

CHAPPELL: If, *if* I could have done it. I thought of everything for the book. I even went so far as to consider him keeping a journal or a diary. And that was . . . well, who wants to read a diary, a fictional diary? It's fun to read a real diary. Like, "When I was at Chickamauga I got a miniball in my left side." Those are fun. But, you know, a guy making up a diary, it doesn't work out for me. It works for Gide, I guess, but I feel false doing it.

SOPKO: That was one problem that I found with *Dagon*, that it depended too much on the myth for its whole purport.

CHAPPELL: Right. I invented the myth, though. So I feel like the myth is what is; that's what's real. But it's a horror story really. If you look at it, if you think about it for five or ten minutes, you think, well, *really* it's a pulp horror story from about 1930-something.

[*Carr joins the conversation.*]

SOPKO: What is the basic premise of *Dagon?* I didn't plug in to the myth, unfortunately. I never did really grasp the myth.

CHAPPELL: There's a quotation very early from Bradford's *Plymouth Journal*, the history of the Plymouth colony. The myth is that this was a real religion. Dagon was worshiped at one time in America in Merrymount—well, at what became Merrymount later; it was called Mount Dagon first. The myth I use is just that there was a secret cult that still worshiped him, that went on all through American history, and that Dagon himself, this terrifying idol of disfigured fertility, of really of—I don't know whether it makes any sense; it does in terms of the book; I just don't know if it does talking about it logically—of impotent, unceasing fertility, is still being worshiped in America. And obviously, the secret cult is a metaphor for the whole of Detroit, Gleem toothpaste and that whole business. You know it's Protestant, Puritan ethic and money. For some reason we want to produce, produce, produce even when we don't need half the stuff, 10 percent of it.

CARR: Have you ever thought the great old Marxist implications of that book? That you have ceaseless production sustaining itself for the sheer sake of production?

CHAPPELL: Yeah, I have. As a matter of fact I think the book that influenced me most when I was thinking about that, and it all came together in my mind, was a book by R. H. Tawney called *Religion and the Rise of Capitalism.* Everyone was telling me I should read Max Weber, but of course by the time they were telling me, I'd just finished the book and it wasn't any help.

SOPKO: The ending of the book is where the myth is supposed to come together with the story in some kind of remarkable revelation.

CHAPPELL: Yeah, well a lot of people object to that. I don't know—

SOPKO: I think I do. I just didn't think the ending came off.

CHAPPELL: Peter Taylor hates it. On the other hand, I didn't have it in me to just leave it just in such a black, horrible shape as it was left at first, you know.

SOPKO: I understand that point. It's a very good point. But the attempt there to just weld the whole Dagon thing with this last chapter seemed to be artificial.

CHAPPELL: It is. On the other hand—I don't want to defend the son of a bitch, it ain't that great—but I just couldn't think of no other way of doing it. If somebody else can do it—I mean do the novel and make it work dramatically, to make it work personally, to make this huge thing we know about society and history work—personally, I would love very much to see him do it.

CARR: Here's an interesting thing, as long as we're talking about the ending. Well, first—the book does have three sections: it goes from straight, formalistic, liturgical religion, or as liturgical as Methodism can be, to a kind of paganism which is still a religion of materialism and objects. Objects in the sense that the penis and the god are objects. And in the third part, the chapter that everybody seems to have trouble with, there is a complete mystical fade-out.

This student said the last section reminded him of Zen Buddhism. I don't know whether that's what you think or not, but from chalices and liturgy to the worship of lesser objects, we do move into mysticism.

CHAPPELL: Yeah, I think—I don't want to sound pompous—but I think the human spirit can surmount its materialism. After all, materialism is really just an invention of the spirit. Anything we can invent we can get over. I hope. We got them bombs and that germ warfare. I don't know . . .

SOPKO: You really think so?

CHAPPELL: We *can.* Whether we *will* or not I don't know.

SOPKO: The next question which I have written down here—which I came down here all prepared with—is "What is the connection between morality and literature?"

CHAPPELL: For one, literature *is* moral—that sounds like old-fashioned and terrible and nobody likes to say it anymore—but the act of literature, it seems to me, is a moral act. I don't think literature should preach about morality. That's one of the faults of *Dagon*, but the act of literature is a moral act. It's a criticism of the human mind, one way or another, like it or not.

SOPKO: One way or another?

CHAPPELL: Right. One way or another. And any criticism that is made is made, hopefully, with the desire to improve.

SOPKO: This next question comes out of a statement that William Harrison's made on one or two occasions. Quote: "The artist is a god who walks about the earth sprinkling life upon it." What do you think about that?

CHAPPELL: I don't believe it.

SOPKO: What my question is, what I'm saying is, aren't all writers, whether they like it or not, propagandists? Preachers? If literature is a moral act.

CHAPPELL: Preachers, yeah. Propagandists, yes. I guess. In the very, very broadest sense of the word—and in the broadest sense of the word preachers, too. I'm willing to accept that. As long as you're willing to put in he's also a lot of other things as well as being a propagandist and preacher. Which he is; he's also an artist.

If you want to look at some preaching, I just . . . Bill Root happened to bring a book over to the house the other day, Picasso's *Erotica*. They were preaching things, you know. They tell you how good sex is, what a wonderful thing life and love is. "It's just a joy," he says. But when you think about it, when you look at those engravings, you don't think, "Now, Picasso's trying to preach to me here." That's the last thing you think.

SOPKO: I have been taken altogether by the sense of the grotesque in your writing. I was just wondering . . . why?

CHAPPELL: For the simple reason that, to me, it doesn't seem grotesque.

CARR: Fred said once—and I agree with him . . . I think Fred's an interesting writer for the simple reason that he maintains that what is real to a person is the only reality you're dealing with. Especially when you consider artistic, structural things, viewpoint. You know, what difference does it make if you're in a loony bin and think that purple monsters come and pitch camp on your golden locks? And if this guy thinks that the god Dagon hops up on the table, that's his reality.

CHAPPELL: For him, it's for real.

CARR: Therefore it's not grotesque.

CHAPPELL: It takes an awful lot of nerve to say that the guy is really out of his mind: "Normal people like me, man, we know better." I would never be able to say that about anybody. I get along well with guys who think they're Napoleon. There he is, man. This is all exaggeration and hyperbole, but it is pretty good scientific theory too. You find this in the works of Whitehead and Russell.

CARR: Do you worry that Southern writing is getting more and more grotesque? Shelby Foote had this thought, and he's also in this book of interviews—that Carson McCullers is so grotesque she reads as a parody, an unwitting parody, of the Southern tradition.

CHAPPELL: "Grotesque" is only a literary term in that sense. I mean what possible grotesqueness can you have in a Southern novel or any novel that can possibly match the grotesqueness of Chicago last summer? Of the assassination of King and Kennedy? There's nothing as grotesque in literature as what we have in American life right now. Biological warfare and all that stuff, man. The Southern novel . . . may look grotesque to some guy who commutes from Westport to New York every day and goes to PTA meetings and all that. But the majority of the population of the world doesn't do that. When you think the median income in this country is not much over $4,000.

CARR: Yeah.

CHAPPELL: You know, our old notion of what is real ain't got nowhere to go.

SOPKO: Tell me your Campbell Soup can story.

CHAPPELL: It's not really a Campbell's Soup can. It's a Carnation Milk can. Didn't you hear that?

SOPKO: Yeah, I did.

CHAPPELL: You just want it on the tape? O.K. I'll have to do the whole thing. Cowboys never drank milk 'cause they couldn't milk them ole long-horned cows. They were wild, really wild. They were worse than bears. They lay out there in the rain. They never went in no sheds or nothin'. They didn't know what to do with them. So what the cowboys had to drink, when they drank milk at all—sometimes, not very often—was canned milk, and the brand they drank was Eagle canned milk and the slang term for it—or what the cowboys called it, was—the milk was called "bird juice" cause of the eagle on the can. So later on—I can't remember when, sometime around the turn of the century—Carnation Milk Company wanted to move in on this huge Texas territory that had always belonged to the Eagle, so they ran a contest in the newspapers. They wanted people to write jingles about Carnation Milk. They offered prizes. So this ranch lady who lived way out by herself—way out in the wilds somewhere—wrote a little couplet which goes:

> Carnation Milk, the best in the land,
> Comes to the table in a little red can.

And a cowboy friend of hers—she, of course, way out there lonesome, she never got into town—this cowboy friend of hers passing through, she gave him this thing to send off in the mail, just a postcard. Three or four months passed and she got a letter from the Carnation Milk people saying they were not using her jingle because it was "unfit for print." So she knew what had happened, that the cowboy had added something to it. And cowboys, being very gallant people, always gallant, had tremendous respect for a lady. That's one of the true things about them. All that shyness you see in the movies is true. But he was ashamed when she asked him, 'cause he didn't know he'd said anything wrong. And she finally wormed out of him what he'd put down. It was:

> Carnation Milk, the best in the land,
> Comes to the table in a little red can.
> No tits to pull, no hay to pitch;
> Just punch a hole in the son of a bitch.

"Son of a bitch" was the most common slang word among cowboys. They had a stew they made from veal called "son of a bitch stew." They put a piecrust on top of it and called it "a son of a bitch in a blanket." The name was so common they often substituted names of local politicians, and their buddies knew what they meant.

CARR: Where'd you learn all that stuff about cowboys?

SOPKO: Yeah, what about that?

CHAPPELL: I don't know why I got interested in it. I think George Garrett showed me a book at his house one night that looked real interesting. I remember it was about the West. I went to the library and got all those books about Western stuff and started reading. I read Wyatt Earp's testimony about the O.K. Corral fight and all that. It's fun to read.

SOPKO: My point in asking that question about the grotesqueness—there's no point in arguing about it, there're a whole lot of things going on around here that are frightfully grotesque—but writers today just don't write about it, for the most part.

CHAPPELL: Well, it depends on what you have a talent for and what you're drawn to. I think John O'Hara is a perfectly fine writer. It's just that I'm not drawn to his subjects in any way whatsoever. That is, to write about. In the first place, I don't have the information he does. In the second place, my favorite writers are often fantastic writers—Jorge Luis Borges, for example.

SOPKO: Do you have any particular long-range goals at the moment, Fred?

CHAPPELL: Well, I have a novel that I should finish, if I can ever just make myself sit down and finish it. It ought to be out next year sometime and then I'm going to write verse for a while. I like verse. I like to doodle with it. I like to play with it and things. And I want to get away from all this awhile and see if I can't open a new door. Well, I have always done verse, but for the last two years I've just done it the way a prose writer writes verse: "Well, this don't seem to be going good, I guess I better write a poem." And now I'd like to do it seriously, see what's there, to get some variety in my life. I live the most restricted life imaginable. You get tired of writing prose, you want to write verse. I'd also like to write nonfiction, essays, just to see what's what. I've never done any seriously. I'd like to try.

The Lumbees, the Klan, and . . . Hollywood:
❧ GUY OWEN

Interviewed by JOHN CARR

Those who read The Flim-Flam Man *or saw the movie version (although I hope that hasn't been most people's only exposure to the story) saw at first glance that Guy Owen had created a Southern type: The Lovable Thief, The Thief with Righteousness on his Side, an aging Pretty Boy Floyd gone cynical and hunting smaller game. But wait, there's something else going on here: the men who criticize Southern letters damned it with faint praise and went their way, but still, no doubt about it, something's going on here—and it is, simply, the transposal of myth into humanity, nevermind that it's a very provincial humanity.*

Every folklore has a character like the flim-flam man. The Indians had Laughing Coyote, the trickster who always came out on top, whether by fair means or foul. European fable had Reynard the Fox, and in the Childe collection of ballads many of the ballads deal with Robin Hood.

Guy Owen's swindler, an aging crook, is that myth made flesh. But it could have stopped there, could have turned into a story whose protagonist, like Ellison's Invisible Man, was as much allegorical as real. Owen went a step beyond, with a poet's audacity, and made this pigeon-dropper (which is what the underworld I'm familiar with calls men in that racket) a character in a realistic fiction, a man as crooked and as violent (although in a more spiritual way) as Bigger Thomas. Hmm, says I, after reading the book and seeing the movie (although that was an unfortunate experience, to say the least), this fellow can flat-out write.

Then, to my pleasant surprise, I became aware of Guy Owen the poet and editor. It is refreshing and encouraging to report that in a nation and an age that almost enforces *specialization, Guy Owen and others like him refuse to be tied to one form, even to one role in the game-at-large. By not only writing verse* and *fiction, but by editing* Southern Poetry Journal *and* North Carolina Folklore (*in addition to his duties as professor of English at North Carolina State*), *Owen has gained something as an artist and a man that less committed, less authentic men are losing, or have already lost.*

Guy Owen was born in 1925 in Bladen County, North Carolina, and grew up in the Cape Fear River tobacco country. Besides a number of short stories, he has written four novels: Season of Fear (1960), *which was both a critical and a popular success;* The Ballad of the Flim-Flam Man (1965); Journey for Joedel (1970), *which won the Sir Walter Raleigh Award for fiction; and* The Flim-Flam Man and the Apprentice Grifter (1972). *His poems have been published in more than thirty magazines and anthologies, and have been collected in* Cape Fear Country and Other Poems (1958), The Guilty and Other Poems (1962), *and* The White Stallion (1969). *He has also edited several books of essays and poetry.*

He was interviewed in Charlotte in March, 1970.

OWEN: My situation, John, is a little bit different from these other people you've interviewed. I think of myself primarily as an editor—and teacher.

INTERVIEWER: Who has somehow written four damn good novels.

OWEN: I'm working on my fifth novel now, but I still think of myself as an editor and teacher rather than as a writer.

INTERVIEWER: All right, let's begin at the beginning. You started *Impetus.*

OWEN: [*Laughs*] Or *Impotent.* Right. Ten years ago, at Stetson.

INTERVIEWER: In your basement, right?

OWEN: Yeah, and I paid the costs of the darn thing. It wasn't very much, though. I think by the time I left Florida I was five hundred dollars in the hole. I'm about a thousand dollars in the hole right now.

INTERVIEWER: From *Southern Poetry Review?*

OWEN: Yeah, yeah.

INTERVIEWER: How do these magazines live?

OWEN: Oh, just a hand-to-mouth existence, mostly. But we've been very fortunate with *SPR*: we get grants. I recently got a grant from the National Council of the Arts; and the North Carolina Arts Council, headed by Sam Ragan, has given me several grants; and one of our poets recently won a five-hundred-dollar award in the National Council of the Arts contest.

INTERVIEWER: Weren't you one of the first ones to publish Richard Dillard?

OWEN: Well, not really the first, but I published Dillard, and that whole interesting crowd up there, as a matter of fact. His wife Annie, and Julie Sawyer—oh, any number of times—and George Garrett.

INTERVIEWER: It must be a lot of fun doing that.

OWEN: Well, it's very rewarding, and you know, it's a good way of keeping in contact. And, as I say, I had very selfish reasons for editing a little magazine: this was one way I could educate myself as I went along. Also, I've been teaching for twenty years so I have students scattered all over the country. Many of them are writing and it's kind of a thrill for me to get out an issue of the magazine and see three or four of my old students in there.

INTERVIEWER: Do you literally not have any help doing that magazine?

OWEN: Well, we have a secretary. We get about a hundred dollars a year from North Carolina State, but we do have a secretary. And I'm not knocking the college. They give eight thousand dollars a year to an undergraduate magazine; that's where they're putting their money, and they should. Really, I'd just as soon not have a great deal of money from them, because then I'd be pressured to publish students—and teachers.

INTERVIEWER: People who run magazines, little magazines, *are* pressured to publish undergraduates and teachers if they're running a college magazine, are they not?

OWEN: That's right.

INTERVIEWER: I suppose there is no freedom in little magazines anywhere, though, unless you have a million dollars and are sitting in an apartment on the Upper East Side in Manhattan, doing your thing.

OWEN: Right, right.

INTERVIEWER: Speaking of New York, as I don't believe we were, you're not too happy with the New York literary scene, are you?

OWEN: As a matter of fact, that's one of the reasons I help edit a little magazine. And also, from time to time, we publish books. We have published a fine book of Paul Ramsey's poetry and we are getting ready to publish, as you probably know, an anthology of recent North Carolina poetry. That's how we're using the grant. We're publishing people like—well, not only Charleen Whisnant, but other young people like this Negro poet here in Charlotte, T. J. Reddy, and Julie Suk, from here in Charlotte, and others. But you can see why I'm not happy with the New York scene. In the first place, I think it's a very unhealthy situation when you've got one area that virtually monopolizes publishing. I think you can see what's happened to Broadway. I look on Broadway as just a damned disease or something of the sort. As far as I'm concerned, they're going downhill, and, you know, I resent the fact very much that when I write something I have to send it . . . to an editor in New York. I think we need more regional publishers, we need more active college presses. In North Carolina we have a regional publisher like John Blair in Winston-Salem. He published my book of poems, *The White Stallion*. It won't sell many copies outside the South, but it has been widely reviewed, from Boston to California.

INTERVIEWER: But doesn't regional publishing eventually break down because we don't have as good a system of distribution as the New York publishers?

OWEN: That's true, so most of the copies of this book Mr. Blair sold were to individuals who just wrote in for a copy, and you know that most of us are rather lazy about that—we go into a bookstore and *then* we want to buy this book or that book.

INTERVIEWER: Is there any firm that serves strictly as a distribution house for smaller magazines?

OWEN: Yes, but you see, they take their cut off the top and it's a high percentage and it makes it almost impossible for you to do it.

INTERVIEWER: Have yall ever thought about forming a co-op?

OWEN: Yes, there is a kind of co-op being formed. This was, I think, one of Carolyn Kizer's ideas when she was with the National Council of the Arts. For example, this association has its own house organ and there are traveling displays of little magazines going from campus to campus. There are all kinds of new ideas about this.

INTERVIEWER: You have to work very hard to get distribution outside your immediate area?

OWEN: Oh yeah, very hard, very hard. And so hard, John, that you wonder if it's really worth it. You've got to spend all that extra energy to do it and—frankly—most of us aren't interested in reaching a very wide audience. There really aren't that many people who are going to be interested in reading the kind of things we're interested in printing, so rather than devote an enormous amount of energy trying to pick up ten more subscribers in Washington, I think my time could be better invested in trying to write a new chapter of another novel.

INTERVIEWER: That's a problem, when you're a writer and also want to be an editor.

OWEN: That's right. Well, I want to invest my life as creatively as possible, and editing has a way of eating into it and, as you know, teaching is a creative thing and drains your energy too. I save the Christmas holidays and the summer. That's when I get my writing done.

INTERVIEWER: Have you found that that's about the only time you can write?

OWEN: Yes, really. You're writing a novel, too, and it takes big chunks of uninterrupted time to write a novel.

INTERVIEWER: Is "uninterrupted" the clue?

OWEN: Right. I write like a fiend during the summer—and write, I'm afraid, very badly: first drafts and whatnot. But I find that I *can* revise during the school year, so this is a pattern I'm working on now, and I think it's working out pretty well for me.

INTERVIEWER: How did you first get the bug to write?

OWEN: Gosh, I think I've always—as long as I can remember—wanted to lead some sort of creative life, and being a child of the Depression, I didn't take violin lessons and we didn't have a piano in the house and there were not many people around me who were sculptors or painters. I was born in Clarkton, North Carolina. Five hundred people—five hundred citizens, counting the doctor's cow. Somebody said our population remained the same because any time a young lady had a baby, a young man had to slip out of town. Gone to Texas.

INTERVIEWER: Where'd you go to undergraduate college?

OWEN: University of North Carolina. Chapel Hill.

INTERVIEWER: Were you there the same time as Shelby Foote, Walker Percy, and Max Steele?

OWEN: Well, Max Steele. Yes, I was there the same time, as an undergraduate, when Max Steele was there, and I knew him. I think Walker Percy is a little older than I am, and Shelby Foote had probably already graduated, but he was around at that time. Yes. There were quite a number of writers there and I think, by the way, that this helped me because—well, Noel Huston was there and Jimmy Street, and of course the ghost of Tom Wolfe. I didn't talk to Mr. Street or Shelby Foote; I chatted sometimes with Mr. Huston, but I think it's important for a young writer to see that here's a writer who's also a fellow human being and to say to yourself, "Well, if he can make it, maybe I can too." I think the situation over there is probably a little more healthy than it was when I was a student. When I was a student, and in the English department, anything creative was distrusted. So I had to take creative writing not in the English department—you know now they have a very vital program over there—but I had to go to the journalism department to take a creative writing course under Phillips Russell.

INTERVIEWER: You took a creative writing course in college and now you teach one. How good are they?

OWEN: I suffer a great deal about this and I suppose we all do, although I must admit I don't agonize as much over it as I used to. Frankly, I used to feel that creative writing courses were not very helpful, but I find now—well, you know there are two kinds of writers: there are talking writers and there are writing writers. And this is a course that separates the two. You give them a deadline and they have to do some writing and I just play the role of a friendly critic. They know and you know that there are no friendly critics in New York; they're hard-nosed people, they won't finish your manuscript, or before they even see it some bright little Vassar girl with a recent B.A. is rejecting it, so I try to be a friendly reader, and I try to encourage them as much as I can and I try desperately, lean over backwards, to keep them from writing the way I do.

INTERVIEWER: Well, I think you write very well myself, but maybe what you mean is that you're wary of imposing your style.

OWEN: That's it, exactly. For example, I feel that John Crowe Ransom, when he was teaching at Vanderbilt, God bless him, a grand old man and a marvelous poet in many ways, but if you'll look at some of the poets that came out of there—well, as a matter of fact, if you'll look at some of the first issues of the *Fugitive*, when the poets didn't sign their own names—they had these fantastic pseudonyms—almost all of the poems could have been written by John Crowe Ransom.

INTERVIEWER: Yeah, William Harrison said something about that, that the Vanderbilt poets were in the same stream, all the way through. I think there's a distinct danger—well, students, or people, sometimes even some critics and editors, read you and say, "Well, he's making it, and it must be because of his style." What *is* style?

OWEN: I think all of us try to find our own voice, and this is a great struggle. It's not just a matter of different style with me, I find that every novel I write demands a new style—part of it, as you know, because of the new subject matter, but also because the writer's changed: he's ten years older, the tempo, the texture of life has changed, and his own sensibility—and all of this comes into style.

INTERVIEWER: Your style is not like your fingerprints, in other words.

OWEN: That's right, that's right.

INTERVIEWER: It goes on and grows, hopefully.

OWEN: Yeah, hopefully. And I don't know if this isn't one of the reasons I'm not writing very much poetry right now: I look at it and I don't find the kind of growth I want there. And I think if you can't grow, it's best to stop.

INTERVIEWER: How did your first novel come about? Did you start off with an image?

OWEN: Well, I usually do, as a matter of fact. The impetus for this one was that I'd just finished a very dull and incredibly stupid dissertation—I did an M.A. thesis on Thomas Dekker and my dissertation is a long study of Thomas Middleton's plays. I'd just finished that when I picked up a newspaper in Chapel Hill and read about a terrible murder. And I got an image: a picture of a haunted and lonely man, even a mentally retarded man, who is looking out a window, a torn window shade, at a sixteen- or seventeen-year-old blonde girl on a swing across the way. And out of this little story—I guess Henry James would say that's the *donnée*, the starting point—well, it haunted me so that I felt for the sake of my own sanity I'd have to write about that.

INTERVIEWER: Did it really obsess you? The idea of a murder? And that you could see the murderer?

OWEN: Yes, and the girl of course was not the victim. The victim was a young man who was about to marry the girl and this poor man, looking at her was so obsessed by her, he was so much in love with her—although she was unaware of it—that he sneaked over and put dynamite in the young man's car and murdered him that way.

INTERVIEWER: You were saying that most young writers would sweat and strain and give it their all to really get the blowup in there. And you said you went on and wrote around that scene when you got into difficulty with it.

OWEN: Oh yes. I find that—this won't work for everybody—but my technique is pretty much what Tom Wolfe did. Now this is because I'm writing fairly loosely; *The Ballad of the Flim-Flam Man* would lend itself to that, loosely structured as it was. But the method is this: I might be writing on one day something that will go in chapter three, and on another day, the next day, I might be writing something that will finally wind up in chapter fifteen. And then the next three weeks I might be writing something that will end up in the wastepaper basket.

INTERVIEWER: That's rather liberating, though, to know you don't have to struggle straight ahead through a plot line, or whatever less workmanlike term you might prefer.

OWEN: It is, and I think that's the reason I stress that. I think that problem is one of the big hangups of young writers: they don't have very much confidence; they haven't completed anything. And I've seen so many writers with talent come along who'd want to write a novel, and they'd write three chapters, and at the end of the third chapter they wouldn't be quite sure what was going to happen . . . . And my feeling is that if they could just take a leap, go around, that all the time, the unconscious mind is helping solve these problems. And then you come back and it's not the same old traumatic experience of facing a blank sheet of paper and having to go from page 41 to page 42. Ah, that can be murder.

INTERVIEWER: Before we get into novels, do you like to write short stories, as well as novels?

OWEN: No, I find that I'm not very good at the short story. Frankly, I don't write well enough to handle the short story. As you know, today the short story is very skillfully done in most cases. They've become like poems, and it takes much more artistry, and devotion to minute details, and reiterated motifs and so forth. I find that I'm perhaps too impatient with that sort of thing, but . . . but perhaps I'm too much in love with the texture of the world's body and the details and whatnot, and I get a big bang out of rendering background fully, for example, and handling the kind of detail that would get in the way of a short story. And I like a more leisurely pace, so I find I work more comfortably over the long haul than I do over the short one, but I hope that one of these days . . . Oh, I've written a few short stories, published two or three here and there, but I find it easier to publish novels than short stories, primarily because of the market. The market for the serious short story—and we're not talking about the formula short story—has simply dried up.

But today, with the situation as it is, if you write a novel and give it everything you've got and it's turned down by seventeen or eighteen publishers, that's not the end; some paperback house may take it, or, heaven knows, we have a number of regional publishers, like Mr. Blair . . .

INTERVIEWER: Plus, even if it's turned down by seventeen or eighteen publishers, that leaves about thirty more that are publishing hardbacks, doesn't it?

OWEN: Right.

INTERVIEWER: Might be the Buddhist Press, but—

OWEN: Right. Oh, we all hear hard luck stories, such as Mac Hyman's *No Time for Sergeants* being turned down by seventeen houses, or William Faulkner's *The Sound and the Fury* being turned down by about that many and being published by a company that promptly went bankrupt, so . . . I've run into this myself: I've turned down poems at *Southern Poetry Review* and three months later seen them in *Harper's Magazine*.

INTERVIEWER: [*Laughs*] Does that reflect your taste or *Harper's?*

OWEN: [*Laughs*] No, it's just that so many things are involved. It's just like the discussion on style we were having a minute ago; personality is involved here. It might be that here's a poem dealing with the subject which we've just covered, so to speak, in the last issue, a poem dealing with about the same thing. So many things enter in, seriously, that it need not be a reflection on anybody's taste or judgment. Especially when you've got a board, as I do. I'm the editor in chief—I wear that particular hat—but I have three or four editors who help me, and we have a policy that if a poem gets one negative vote—unless the others want to really argue for it—it goes back. We come out twice a year, and we can afford to be very selective, and this is the only way I can keep the editors happy, you know. If I were to consistently publish poems that one or two of the editors could say they weren't happy about, then I'd have to look around for somebody else to help me read the manuscripts.

INTERVIEWER: Do you think little magazines are serving any aesthetic or social purpose nowadays?

OWEN: Oh, by all means. I would say that almost any breakthrough that you look at in the history of modern letters in this country has been spearheaded by little magazines. Today, the neosurrealism movement, concretism . . . Well, we know the story of the Beats. They tried to get their poems published in *Poetry* and some of the established magazines—they had to go and found the *Big Table* and so forth. Look at John Crowe Ransom. The only way he and the Fugitives could get into print, to begin with, was with their own little magazine.

INTERVIEWER: It's almost a miracle they never had more than three hundred paid subscribers.

OWEN: I should also mention the *Dial*, edited by Emerson and Thoreau and Margaret Fuller, because they never had more than five hundred paid subscribers. So the history of little magazines in this country goes back a long way.

INTERVIEWER: It sounds like a history of poverty.

OWEN: Right, but big magazines are not really interested in making breakthroughs in aesthetics, coming up with new modes, nor are they really interested in expanding the range of possible subject matter for poetry or for fiction. They are interested primarily in ads. On the other hand, the editors of little magazines are much concerned about, for example, racial problems—you heard me ranting and raving last night about the Indians. Well, I'm much concerned about the Indians—although today it's very fashionable to be concerned about the Indians, I guess. And practically every little magazine editor I know was opposed to the Vietnamese war a long time before there was a big stir about it anywhere else. . . . Well, look to Bly, who was one of the editors of *The Sixties*. When he won the National Book Award, he took the money and gave it to help the Resistance. And that's just a symbolic gesture. You think of all the editors scattered all over the country who were saying, "Yeah, man, amen to that."

INTERVIEWER: Right on . . . Let's take a different tack for a moment. Novels and novelists. You knew Mac Hyman, didn't you? He died very early.

OWEN: Yes, in his early forties. Tragic. However, I never met him.

INTERVIEWER: He wrote *No Time for Sergeants* and then, people tell me, it was such a huge success that Hyman felt stifled by it.

OWEN: That's true.

INTERVIEWER: Afraid that he couldn't top it?

OWEN: That was part of it.

INTERVIEWER: Is that a problem when you start to play the game? You don't realize that once you make the first move, you have to make an even bigger move to keep up?

OWEN: Yes. Mac had a unique problem, one that certainly doesn't bother me. In the first place, I haven't had a huge success, but his problem was that his first—incidentally, it wasn't his first novel, but his second novel—that was a huge success. It was a comic novel and he did not want to be labeled a comic writer. He was sort of like Mark Twain, you know, who didn't want to be known as simply a humorist . . . . But these pressures face us all, I think. This is part of the whole damn American system. This drove Thomas Wolfe up the wall, nearly killed him. You write a book and in America, it's a factory system: a year later somebody says, "When's your next book coming out?" Or, "What are you doing now?"

INTERVIEWER: Or, "When's that book we been hearing about going to be run off the presses, young fella?" Like you were making pots, or something.

OWEN: Right. Have you got another pot on the wheel? Throw on another pot. This is very unfortunate, and this is not true, or it's not as generally true, of a writer in, say, France. But in America, you've got to not only write a book this year, but next year, too. You've got to have a book or you're not a writer, you see, so that very often pressures us to publish before we should.

INTERVIEWER: Just anything.

OWEN: Then, you have to be a success. You have to be a financial success. Very often there is this little nagging pressure to get the next book out and the next book, and the next book. And I think perhaps very often we ought to risk lying fallow for five years.

INTERVIEWER: I think it's good, too. I think you're familiar with people we all know and love, but who have published too much.

OWEN: Oh, yes.

INTERVIEWER: And the next thing they publish is not even looked at, even if it's the greatest thing since *War and Peace*. Because it's by old Joe Schmoe who publishes every year.

OWEN: Right. Too much. And then the bookstores know this and won't even order the books. The books won't be there, and the reviewers won't review them. But it's sort of like being a fighter, I guess. He's used to fighting, and even if he's over the hill and punch-drunk, he thinks, "I'll go into training. I'll train a little harder. I'll stay off the booze and next time, I'll get a sneaky punch in." And so we keep hoping the next one will be a sneaky-punch. We'll get by the *Saturday Review*, for example.

INTERVIEWER: Is it a writer's superstition or a publisher's superstition that your second novel is going to be a bomb-out? Whose superstition is it?

OWEN: I don't really know but, yeah, it is a problem, and it bugs a lot of people. It bugged Tom Wolfe, you know. He got out *Look Homeward, Angel* in 1929 and the next year everybody was saying, "Well, he's a has-been." And it takes him eight years or so to put together *Of Time and the River*. I think there's some truth to it, though. I think very often a beginning writer who is fortunate enough to get his first novel published . . . You know as well as I do that most first novels that are published are not first novels. Very often they're third novels. For example, Mac Hyman published a second novel, a serious novel, that was published after he died, that was a bomb, just an utter bomb, but it was the first novel he had *written*. The first novel is published, which is to say a second or third novel, and then that one's successful, so a publisher that's already turned down novel number one and novel number two will go back and pick one of those up. But now that's not enough to explain what we were just talking about. I think it has something to do with this: Very often a beginning writer's first novel is autobiographical and he can really make it authentic. He brings everything to it, he gives it everything he has, and very often I think uses himself up and uses up the material that he knows best. The second time around, he has to depend more on his imagination. It might be better written, but it also might be a little thinner.

INTERVIEWER: Do you think some people have the kind of imagination that lends itself to short stories, while other people have the kind of imagination that loves a novel?

OWEN: Oh, I think this is definitely true. Some people have the kind—I don't have this kind of mind—that likes to deal with little moments, the moments of epiphany. They, for example, may not like to handle huge blocks of description. Or they'd much prefer to deal with two or three characters. And another kind of mind likes to handle big, big blocks of narrative. And I think it really is a kind of . . . it's a difference and it's almost as much of a difference as the one between a novelist and poet. I hate to go back and repeat myself, but I think that the writer of the short story today is in some ways much closer to the poet than he is to the novelist.

INTERVIEWER: Maybe because poetry is dying out, and that kind of talent starts out with short stories today instead of poetry?

OWEN: No, I don't think that is true. It is true, as I see it, that modern poetry is moving much more in the direction of a highly charged and energized prose. The short story is moving further and further in the direction of the poem, where we get the kind of control, the kind of self-conscious manipulation of rhythms, images, of symbols—where we become aware of the ramifications of words and the texture of language. I think that what I'm trying to say is that the short story writer today emphasizes control, form, technique, texture of the language, all of these things, in a way that just two generations ago, or one generation ago, we never demanded from the short story. We would only demand that kind of control and self-conscious manipulation of the language from the poet. And of course that's going over into the novel, too, when you deal with a novelist like James Joyce, who is obviously concerned with this image and then picking it up a little later on, manipulating it and stitching it together.

I think, as a matter of fact, that one of the things that's wrong with some novels and short stories I read is that the writer just hasn't made up his mind whether he's writing poetry or fiction.

INTERVIEWER: Back to you. Your third novel's come out now.

OWEN: Well, we can say it's the third. It's actually—well, I have one novel that I haven't been able to sell yet.

INTERVIEWER: How do you feel about the unsold one, kind of like you would towards a bastard child?

OWEN: [Laughs] Kind of like an illegitimate child, or maybe one that's bowlegged and has a harelip, but it's beautiful to me.

INTERVIEWER: The one that's out now, though, is about the Lumbees?

OWEN: In part, yes; it deals with the Lumbees.

INTERVIEWER: Journey for Joedel is about a Lumbee boy?

OWEN: Joedel is a thirteen-year-old boy who really doesn't know what he is because his mother is a Lumbee Indian and his father is a white tenant farmer. Not too much has been done with the Lumbees, other than Paul Green's The Lost Colony, which deals in part with them, and I think he's done a one-act play dealing with the Lowrey gang; but the Lumbee Indians are really the Croatans, and they got their name from the one word that was carved on a tree—incidentally, misspelled—that's part of the irony of it, you have the one word carved on a tree, and it's misspelled.

INTERVIEWER: Did the Indians kill those people, or take them off?

OWEN: The colonists vanished into the wilderness. The theory that the Indians have come up with is that they did not kill the whites—but took them as captives and intermarried with the Lost Colonists. And, as a matter of fact, the Lumbees today have an impressive number of the same names that were in the Lost Colony. Now some historians will not buy this because there's too much of a space between the disappearance of the colonists and the time we meet the Lumbees—there are missing links. But I'm disposed to accept the word of the Lumbee Indians.

They had to give up the name *Croatans* because they ran into a lot of racial prejudice from the whites, who called them Crows —not like the Crow Indians, but like Jim Crow—so they gave up the name. Then they called themselves Cherokees, but then the "real" Cherokees went on the warpath, so they had to go back to the legislature once again, and now they're called Lumbees. They'll admit there was never a tribe of Indians called the Lumbees. They got the name from the river that runs through the area where they've settled. And, by the way, the river's name has been changed now to the Lumber River, but it was once the Lumbee. At any rate, that's the story.

INTERVIEWER: The whole Southern hangup about the connection between name and thing.

OWEN: Well, also, to me, that search for a name is symbolic of the search for identity, and a feeling of dignity and a sense of belonging. I was down there about three days ago—because I'm writing a comic novel about the great Lumbee Indian uprising against the Ku Klux Klan. You know, this incident, to the outside world, is not important, but it's *very* important to the Lumbee Indians, because this is one thing that has unified them and it is one thing that they can look back on which gives them a real sense of pride, and it's something that made the other Indians look up to them. They got wires from the Seminoles in Florida, when Catfish Cole started bringing his white-sheeted boys in there, saying, "If you need help, count on us."

INTERVIEWER: What happened that day?

OWEN: I forget when it was, exactly. It was in the winter of 1958. It was cold as hell, and I remember that Catfish Cole and his Klansmen had come in to intimidate them, and he'd burned a number of crosses and they'd had a number of little marches and he was preaching his usual hatred of Negroes, and Indians—who he said weren't really Americans. I guess maybe he wanted to send them back to Asia, where they came from. And he'd called for an open meeting of the Klan in a pasture there, and about a hundred of them showed up. The Indians were tired of being pushed around, so they just got organized, and there were about three hundred armed Indians who sneaked up there—some of them even had feathers on. They were very carefully organized, and at a signal one rifleman, just one Indian brave, stepped out, took one shot, and knocked out the big light over the spot where Catfish Cole had already started speaking. I wish I could have been there. I've talked to some of the people who were there, and it was just fantastic.

Now, these Indians had them completely encircled at that moment, so these brave Klansmen dropped their guns, took off to the woods, and left their wives and children to be scalped by the Indians. Catfish Cole did, as a matter of fact. Some of the Klansmen stayed and one got conked over the head and a TV man was shot, and one Indian was shot in the foot. It was a miracle that some people didn't really get hurt.

INTERVIEWER: Nobody was hurt?

OWEN: Not seriously.

INTERVIEWER: Any casualties we don't know about?

OWEN: I think Catfish Cole was really mortally hurt. He died two years later of a heart attack. He was so humiliated that I think this was the end of him. But there's good comic material there —but although I'm writing about it in a comic vein, there are very serious themes here. I don't know whether you know the history of the Lumbees during the Civil War or not, but I look at the Klan attack as a second rising.

INTERVIEWER: What happened?

OWEN: It was a very famous episode. These Indians obviously did not want to fight or serve in the work force. They were not slave-owners; they had been treated like Negroes themselves. So the authorities came out at the beginning of the war, when they found out these Indians were not going to fight to maintain slavery, and they took one family, the Lowreys, and made them dig their graves, and then they shot the men right on the spot.

Two of the Lowrey boys who remained organized a guerrilla force, led by Henry Berry Lowrey. The took other Indians and went back into the swamps and raided the whites all during the Civil War. Before it was all over, all of the Lowrey boys had been killed. As you can see, it's kind of a romantic legend. The Lowrey boys, Ben Lowrey especially, have become authentic folk heroes. Ben Lowrey is the Nat Turner of these Indians. Paul Green has written a one-act play dealing with the mother of the Lowreys, the last few years of the running battle, her last two boys coming to say good-by to her, then we hear a shot outside at the end and know that's the end of the Lowrey gang. The Lowrey family is still in Pembroke, and I look on this last Indian uprising against the Klan as one more thrust of the kind of guts and determination these Lowrey boys typified. "We'll be pushed just so far, but you're not going to wipe everybody out; we'll go back into the swamps and fight." No Wounded Knee for them. I don't want to harp on this . . .

INTERVIEWER: I think you should.

OWEN: And I don't want to give the impression that I'm obsessed by it, but I was horrified when I learned that the first example of biological warfare committed by American soldiers or American government officials was the selling and trading of blankets to the Indians that came out of smallpox hospitals. It was deliberately done.

INTERVIEWER: I think something like that happened to the Mandans.

OWEN: Well, I can't recall against what tribe, but this has been authenticated. As far as that goes, the selling of whiskey was a kind of biological warfare. They knew what it would do to the Indians. I'm told by Indians that they really don't have the capacity whites have, that it hits them harder, so that the sale of whiskey is biological warfare, for example. You know, John, the Pulitzer Prize for the novel this year was given for the first time to an Indian, Scott Momaday, who wrote a very fine novel, *The House of Dawn*. But in his novel, the Indians are not drinking alcohol, they're chewing peyote.

INTERVIEWER: What's going to happen to the Lumbees, here with us on the East Coast, surrounded by large numbers of white people and more and more enmeshed in the culture?

OWEN: It's really hard to say what the future for the Lumbees will be. Right now, of course, the government antipoverty programs are stepping in, and they're trying to disperse them. You know, there are a lot of them in Robeson County. Thirty thousand.

INTERVIEWER: Thirty *thousand?* Is that counting non-Indians who've become members of their communities?

OWEN: No, these are, according to the census, people who at least at one time were listed as Indians. And incidentally, some time ago—it wasn't the last census, but about twenty years ago, as I remember—in North Carolina we lost a lot of Indians according to the official figures. If you looked at the statistics, you might have assumed that smallpox had wiped them out again, but it was just that these Indians down there were not listed as Indians, but as "nonwhites." And they are about thirty thousand strong now. And they're poverty-stricken, a lot of them. There's no industry there, and they're boxed in.

INTERVIEWER: They're not on a reservation, are they?

OWEN: No, not on a reservation. They have never been on a reservation. One of the hopeful signs I see now, and maybe I'm being too optimistic about it, is that now the Indians are beginning to cooperate with the Negroes, something that they've never done before because they've been anti-Negro.

INTERVIEWER: The dog kicks the cat.

OWEN: That's right. If they could combine forces with the Negroes, though, then they could take over the political machinery of the county, and I think they could make themselves a much better life. They could certainly begin to take, as they need to, a more active part in political life. And there are other groups of Indians. There are the Melungeons, for example, in West Virginia and Kentucky, and the Brass Ankles, for example, down in South Carolina. There are thousands and thousands of them, many of them in the South, groups that—

INTERVIEWER: And we've overlooked them in the great black-white conflict.

OWEN: That's right. We've overlooked them. And these people now are beginning to make news. They're not saying red power or mulatto power or whatnot, but they are . . . learning something from what the Negroes are doing for themselves, organizing, making certain demands, and they're getting more attention, as I indicated, just from the antipoverty programs, which tend to take them where there are jobs. And their schools are being upgraded. And just in time, because they have been the most backward people, far more backward than the Negroes, because they refused to go to school with the Negroes and for a generation or two kept their children out of school.

INTERVIEWER: They didn't even go to school.

OWEN: Didn't go to school. And do you know the life expectancy for Indians in this country? Well . . . it's somewhere in the mid-forties. And, as you know, the total Indian population was down to almost half a million at one time. Now it's coming back.

INTERVIEWER: What's been the economic history down there in Lumbee country? Were they in peonage to the big landowners, for example?

OWEN: No. As a matter of fact, until 1837 the Lumbees, or Croatans as they were called then, had the right to vote. Then they were suddenly stripped of the franchise.

INTERVIEWER: What happened?

OWEN: Free Negroes were not being allowed to vote, and suddenly we wanted to put these people out, too. They were very proud and they of course obviously disliked giving up their rights. But these Indians now are small landowners and their aim is to own land. Incidentally, the New Deal made it possible for them to own their own land down there.

INTERVIEWER: Do they believe in ownership in common?

OWEN: Well, not so much now. They're getting away from that. Their aim now is to own a small farm, a tobacco and cotton farm, a modest farm that will pay its own way. But now, as you know, the tobacco industry is going down, down, down and the allotments are being cut, so the prospects are not too good for them.

INTERVIEWER: Well, what are they going to do, move to the cities and there lose their culture?

OWEN: That's about what is going to happen, but they're very clan-oriented, so I think it'll be a slow process.

INTERVIEWER: I lived in Greensboro in 1964 on North Mendenhall

Street, by a house full of Locklears, who were Lumbees. There
are pockets of Indians all over that town, most of them living
in big two- or three-story houses, two or three families to a
house.

OWEN: I understand when they go there that one man is sort of
the chief, and he stays in the house and takes care of things
while the others go out and work.

INTERVIEWER: Some people in town then said they weren't Indian,
but part-white, part-black, part-Indians. Do you run into the
same criticism now?

OWEN: Oh yes. As a matter of fact, as I indicated a moment ago,
the Cherokees simply would not stand for their calling themselves Cherokees, because the Cherokee theory is that the
Lumbees are not Indians, but mongrels. Think of this, think of
the pressure of this marvelous legend—and if we don't accept
it as being authentic history, we can certainly look at it as
a beautiful legend—of their being descendants of the Lost
Colony. And then their being driven to repudiate all of that
and give up the name because it had become pejorative. And
to come back to the famous attack on the Ku Klux Klan, that
is the one thing, the one thing that helped unify them and
give them a sense of pride, give them a sense of identity,
because they can look around at the Negroes and say, if they
want to, "Look, the Klan came in, and you were intimidated,
and you closed the doors, and you didn't go out on the
streets. And they came to us, expecting to give us the same
kind of treatment, and we rose up and went on the warpath
and did everything but scalp them." Not only was the story
picked up in this country, but picked up in Europe, too. It
became . . . I suppose if the Russians hadn't sent up Sputnik
about two or three months earlier, there is no question about it,
that would have been the leading story that swept all over
America and Europe.

INTERVIEWER: Let me backtrack just a minute. How did they get
their English names—Locklear and Oxendine and Sinclair?

OWEN: Well, there's the point. That's one of the theories, you see:
that Locklear is nothing but a corruption of the name LeClair.
And those who believe the Lumbees, the Croatans, are the

descendants of the Lost Colony point to the names, you see. For instance, a number of them are named Taylor. There were Taylors in the Lost Colony.

INTERVIEWER: We've talked about the hiatus between the disappearance of the colonists and the first contact with the Croatans. What were they doing in the meantime, just keeping ahead of the frontier?

OWEN: Well, this is a real mystery. These Indians were already there along the Lumbee when the Scots people came in the 1720's and 1730's. Not only already there, but living in cabins and farming. There are histories done by the Lumbees, but they are very spotty and poor. The government—this is once again how the government is helping them—recently gave Dr. Dial, who is a Lumbee—Dial is one of the Lumbee names—a grant that will allow him to do a three years' study and come up with a history. Now, he is going around to talk to all the old Indians. There are quite a few who are very old, in their nineties, and what he is trying to do is get the total picture, the folklore, maybe the remnants of the Indian language. It has died out, you see.

INTERVIEWER: You're still co-editor of *North Carolina Folklore*. How is the Lumbee folklore different from the Cherokee?

OWEN: Frankly, I don't know that much about the Cherokees. My guess is that the Lumbees don't have very much unique folklore—from what I can learn from what has been gathered. They don't really have much folklore that couldn't have been picked up from the whites, mostly, and some from the Negroes. For example, I have looked at pages of Indian riddles, and they are the same things I learned from my grandmother, or that you could pick up in the area. A little Indian child would be asked, "What's green on the outside and red on the inside and filled with little niggers?" And the answer is, "A watermelon." That wouldn't be shared with the Negroes, of course, but it might have been picked up from the whites, you can't tell. They've been so totally neglected.

INTERVIEWER: Has contact with a semi-industrial society kind of wiped out their folklore?

OWEN: I think so, and there is the fact that for so long . . . You see, I think part of it has to do with the fact that they kept their people out of school, so that there was not much written down. Now we have to fill in in so many, many ways. I am going back to Raleigh in two weeks. We are holding our annual folklore meeting, and part of the program will be some Indian youngsters doing some Indian dances. Now how authentic will that be, you know? It might turn out that some of these Indian dances might be something they picked up in the movies. I can just see the possibility of Ruby Keeler influencing them. Not only that. I saw a picture of a Cree Indian who had come there to live with them, and there he is, beating on his tom-tom, with the Lumbee youngsters dancing around him. Well, how authentic is the dance they are going to learn from a Cree doing something he might have seen on TV? But, as part of the research for this novel, I tried to get some authentic Indian folklore.

INTERVIEWER: You believe in going through the motions of what your characters would have done, don't you?

OWEN: Well, John, you said you carried Mississippi around in your head. And I carry a great deal of this area around in my head. I went back in that novel to the thirties. Well, I don't remember a great deal about the early thirties, but my technique is, I'm sure, the technique I share with most novelists. By my second or third draft, if a scene seems thin to me, I am willing to go down and sleep under the tobacco barn, just as I am willing to go down and talk to some of these Indians, to go to the experts rather than just depend on sociological studies and tables of statistics having to do with the crime rates of the Lumbee Indians and so forth. And I even try to get the weather right, and the birds. I wouldn't want a Baltimore Oriole there in the wrong time of the year, or a red-winged blackbird. And these little minor details, they are part of . . . It is hangnails very often, but they are part of the joy of writing. And you know we are not writers twenty-four hours a day. We are human beings first and writers next, I think . . .

INTERVIEWER: Some people have that reversed.

OWEN: At any rate, that is the way for *me* to work as a human being. It is going, as I intend to, and living with the Lumbees a while. It is going back and reliving an experience I had as a boy when I slept under a tobacco barn.

INTERVIEWER: For *Journey for Joedel?*

OWEN: Right.

INTERVIEWER: That's an interesting structure you worked with. It all takes place from the time he gets up till the time he goes to bed, on one day.

OWEN: Yes, one day. With just two flashbacks, and I'm a little worried about the flashbacks but, at any rate, that's the structure of it. You see, with a structure like that, if I get up and I don't feel like writing chapter three, then I can deal with something in the afternoon, or I can deal with noon.

INTERVIEWER: Who is Joedel? Is he a teen-ager?

OWEN: Yes, he's a thirteen-year-old half-blood boy and . . . Well, I can't summarize it for you, but this is kind of . . . this is a geographical journey for Joedel, but it is a kind of spiritual journey for him as well. I am not trying to fall back on the old cliché of after this one day my boy becomes a man, passes over that watershed, because I think that if I were to say that this story is about Joedel growing to manhood, why everybody would immediately assume that during it Joedel must have his first sexual experience, or something of that sort, and that's not so. I think all of that is an oversimplification anyway. I think it takes a little more than sleeping with a woman to carry you into manhood. What takes place in the novel is an awareness on the part of the boy of the moral ambiguity in the world around us, and, at first, a kind of repudiation of it. And then a realization that we have to live in this world and maybe even compromise with it. And, at the end, we see him not just turning away from this, but kind of accepting it and going on, the way we have to accept reality around us and learn to live with it.

INTERVIEWER: And your next novel will be a Lumbee novel, too?

OWEN: Yes. Well, that will be this comic novel. This will not be an historical novel. I'll simply take this confrontation with the Klan that a lot of people know about. And I was wondering what I could do to set the tone, how I could get myself into it. I was thinking in terms of dealing with the antiheroic.

Maybe having the Klansman, Catfish Cole, who incidentally came up to North Carolina from South Carolina, where he'd been frightening the Negroes, come over and just put up this little sign saying "Ku Klux Klan Meeting" or "This is Ku Klux Klan Country." You've seen those signs.

INTERVIEWER: Especially the last one, on billboards welcoming you to North Carolina, a guy on a horse wrapped in a white sheet and a blazing cross somewhere in the picture. Nothing cheap about it.

OWEN: Right. At any rate, I had this image . . . Once again, you know, I like to start with an image, something concrete. *The Flim-Flam Man* started with an image of an old, old man, dressed in a dark suit, being booted off a boxcar and being picked up by a young, green kid. And out of that image came the whole novel. I just had an image of an antiheroic Indian, riding along on a mule, an old swayback mule, and maybe the Indian's drunk. But his reaction is not the reaction we've seen rippling through the community to begin with: a little bit of fear and hesitation. No, he takes one look at the sign and sort of staggers off his mule and urinates all over it and then gets back up on his mule and rides off, and out of that we begin to get the friction that will bring us to the huge confrontation and to the very comic trial scene, the two-day trial in which Brother Catfish Cole got a two-year sentence and some of his other leaders checked in their hoods and gowns for a pair of striped pajamas. Not striped anymore, I guess.

INTERVIEWER: No, they're green now. Does it bug you to think about trying to get inside the mind of a Lumbee Indian?

OWEN: Yes, it does, it does. And that's why I cheated a little bit on Joedel, in *Journey for Joedel*. Had I known enough . . . You see, I grew up in an area where we did have some Lumbee Indians. Had I known enough, or maybe had I been bright enough, John, I would have gone ahead and dealt with an altogether Lumbee family. But I felt that I couldn't do that justice, that I would be cheating. I'm not sure that I've done this justice, but I thought perhaps I could handle a half–Lumbee Indian, and the mother I was careful to keep pretty much in the background.

INTERVIEWER: Is she dead?

OWEN: Oh no, she's not dead, but this deals with a journey, so the boy is getting away from his mother, and most of the day he's away, and then he comes back. So the mother plays a very minor part. The three main characters are the half–Lumbee boy, his father, who is a white tenant farmer, and a landowner who's white and, incidentally, my grandfather.

INTERVIEWER: I think some people say one of the greatest things a novelist gets to do in a novel is pull in old girl friends and old enemies and old heroes and let them mix it up.

OWEN: Oh yeah, I do that all the time, and I'm sure you do, too. I use all my uncles and aunts.

INTERVIEWER: [*Laughs*] But you've got to be clever about it.

OWEN: [*Laughs*] Right, disguise it a little bit, so that your kin will still speak to you occasionally.

INTERVIEWER: Oh, mine gave that up years ago.

OWEN: I think maybe this kin bit, the fact that we do use our aunts and uncles and cousins, I think this is in part responsible for what some Southerners . . . But I don't want to get off on regionalism, because I don't consider myself a regionalist. I write about the South because I grew up in the South. I sent my nerve ends out, and they didn't encounter icebergs or igloos or ivory hunters. They encountered tobacco patches and cotton fields and tobacco barns and Negroes and—

INTERVIEWER: Isn't the South merely your effigy?

OWEN: Right. That's the way I look at it. God knows, most of us are not writing about moonlight and magnolias anymore. We are trying to tell it as it is.

INTERVIEWER: The execution of the Lowrey brothers by a glorious Confederacy, for example.

OWEN: And I think that many of us are in the same boat that Tom Wolfe was in after writing *Look Homeward, Angel*. You know, we are probably not threatened, but I have never been invited back to the high school where I graduated, for example.

INTERVIEWER: Because you were doing it for the Yankee dollar. Speaking of the Yankee dollar, how did your second novel come to be sold to the movies?

OWEN: It happened, ironically enough, on April 1. I got a phone call saying, "Look here, we've just sold your novel *The Flim-Flam Man* to Twentieth Century Fox." And I started to hang up, and then I thought I would play along, so I just said, "Oh yeah, sure you have, sure you have." It took my agent some time to convince me that this really had happened. I had nothing to do with it being sold to the movies. This is all done in New York. Agents handle all of this. I had very little to say about it, but it was a very interesting experience for me. And I think it is inevitable that when I saw the movie, even though I had read the script and worked with Bill Rose . . . I think he's a fine screenwriter, one of the best. I had worked with him three or four days and made some suggestions I thought would improve the film considerably. Even so, when I first saw the film, I was naturally somewhat disappointed because, after all, I spent four or five years struggling with the idea of the book—it took me two years to sell it after I had written it, so I was about five years living with it. And then Hollywood comes along and in three months they do a film. And inevitably you look up there and these people on the screen are not the way you saw them, not really the way you visualized them, but that's inevitable. You write about lower middle-class people and you suddenly see that Sue Lyon does not want to be, her image will not let her be, another *Tobacco Road* girl, you see.

INTERVIEWER: And so she gets a bigger house.

OWEN: She gets a bigger house and she also plays maybe a lot larger role. . . . I don't think any of us write aiming toward Hollywood. For example, I was very disappointed when one of the reviewers right here in Charlotte said my novel was obviously aimed for Hollywood. Well, they don't know the facts of life. In the first place, I wrote the novel *The Flim-Flam Man* with a tremendous sense of despair all the way through it because I know the facts of life. I know . . . by the facts of life, I mean that I knew the possibility of writing a novel in Southern dialect and even getting it published was bad. You know what the chances are against it, because this is virtually taboo today. I knew, for example, that *No Time for Sergeants* had been turned down by over fifteen publishers, and I also knew that only one novel out of a hundred is ever bought by Hollywood, and that a lot of those are just optioned, and never filmed. Then somebody says this is a novel obviously aimed toward Hollywood.

INTERVIEWER: It nauseates you a little bit, I take it.

OWEN: Yeah, a little bit. Oh well . . .

Waiting for Joiner:
❧JAMES WHITEHEAD

Interviewed by JOHN CARR and JOHN LITTLE

James Whitehead was born in 1936 and raised in a little town in Missouri and in Hattiesburg and Jackson, Mississippi. He played football for Vanderbilt University and now teaches at the University of Arkansas, where he is part of the university's creative writing program. His poetry has appeared in the little magazines and in 1966 Domains, *a collection of his poems, was published. In late 1971, his novel* Joiner *(originally entitled* The Revolt of Sonny Joiner) *was published. He is now working on a second collection of poems.*

This interview took place in the last week of April, 1970, in the basement of a faculty member's home just off the campus of the University of North Dakota in Grand Forks. A conference on Southern writing had been arranged and those invited were Jesse Hill Ford, Peter Taylor, Fred Chappell, Jim Whitehead, George Garrett, and me. The man who gets most of the credit for organizing the conference is John Little, who is an instructor in English at the university and is from Raleigh, Mississippi, and was in my class at the University of Mississippi and one of Whitehead's students at the University of Arkansas, where Little earned his M.A. There was a party upstairs and a blizzard outside (we reacted to that with deep shock; it was April) and people came and went, but it was mostly just the three of us talking, nobody trying to take the lead, until we got Whitehead to talk about his work.

CARR: Your poem "The Floaters" is written about the time when you were a little boy and going down to your granddaddy's place south of St. Louis. How much did that background as opposed to, say, the Mississippi background, have to do with forming your mind?

WHITEHEAD: My grandfather's family was from southern Missouri. Not all the way down, not Penobscot County, but the lead belt area. *That* part of the family, the family this Southern-Midwestern river patriarch established, was terribly important to me; it was a kind of Eden to me during my childhood and during the war, when I stayed there for a while because my father was overseas. It was a family in which my grandfather was the head and my grandmother was kind of the queen, you might say, and there were thirty or forty people who would sit down to family Sunday dinner. In the church, a little Presbyterian church, at least half the congregation seemed to be our family. Then there was just the fact of the river, and the rock creek which ran around behind my grandfather's house and spilled into the Mississippi. And the little town of Kenswick and the little town of Windsor Harbor, where the beach was, and where the floaters were, occasionally. That was a great time, a wonderful time.

Now when I was in Mississippi first, in the first grade, I remember rather positively our maid, whose name I think was Helen. It was a good time. I have rather profound, rather heavy, whatever you want to call it, memories of Hattiesburg in those days. The pine trees, for one thing, stuck in my mind.

But my initiation into Mississippi, for what it's worth, was after the war, when I was in the fifth grade and we moved down there. Now my family had always been a mix of Southern sensibility and Midwestern sensibility. My mother was born in Springfield, Missouri, and they were kind of Midwestern or Ozark, and my grandmother, my father's mother, was from Van Buren, Arkansas, and was very much a Southern lady. The wife of one of my great-uncles was from South Carolina. Now I'm not suggesting that you have to account for the Southernness. I never really thought about that very much. The thing that was largest in my imagination was the river, the Mississippi River, and that's *really* big. *Tom Sawyer* and *Huckleberry Finn* were my best books, and *Huckleberry Finn* continues, and I mean *continues*, to be a book I'm passionate about. And right after that, *Life on the Mississippi* is one of the great books of my life.

But when we were going back to Mississippi, and at this time I was in the fifth grade, as I've said, I heard some ridicule of the place in my family from a couple of my cousins who were the most Midwestern of the cousins; and I felt that my mother was a little nervous about going back to Mississippi. My father wasn't. My father was going to be working for the state, in the Health Department. He eventually became superintendent of milk and foods, in charge of the standards for dairies, meat plants, and chicken plants and that sort of thing. The family was sort of agricultural-once-removed. My great-great-grandfather had been a farmer and then my great-grandfather had been a cattle and wheat broker in southern Missouri and southern Illinois. I felt that we were going home when we moved back to Mississippi, but the truth is that when I got to Hattiesburg, all hell broke loose. It was the wound; it was the absolute trauma.

LITTLE: I meant to ask you about that. In your novel, a little boy is tied to a tree and stoned.

WHITEHEAD: Yeah, there's a scene in the novel in which Boykin is tied to a tree and stoned for being a smart aleck and also kind of smart. Well, I was tied to a tree in Hattiesburg and stoned.

CARR: A guy your size?

WHITEHEAD: Well, I was big, but I was a little soft, and I was not at all conditioned to violence, because in my family, my grandfather's family, it was a love feast. For a child. There were tensions I learned about later, real problems in that household, but for a child it was a love feast. We were tended to, we were loved, we were taught to be expressive, it was *great*. But when I got to Hattiesburg, I had an accent, not even a Yankee accent, an Ozark accent, and I got the *shit* beat out of me. And I got tied to the tree, and I was stoned, and I was humiliated again and again. And I didn't really know how to cope with it. Oh, I cried a lot. But, fortunately, there was a football league for fifth-graders in Hattiesburg—this is somewhere around 1947, 1948; I can't remember exactly—and my daddy said, "Why don't you play in the Cub Scout football league?" And I did, and I put on my equipment and ran out on the field and began to leap on people and drag 'em to the ground and everybody began screaming and yelling and here were all the bastards that had been beating the hell out of me, and under the legalized ritual of the game I was tromping the hell out of them. And they left me alone.

And Jesus, did I want to be left alone. That's the most important thing in the world, just . . . to . . . be . . . left . . . alone. Well, that was the *rite de passage*, that was the union card, that was how I could survive and go on being a kind of bookworm, and . . . and sentimental and tender—in a way.

LITTLE: In *Domains* you do explore violence on several levels. There is a racial violence, and there are violent deaths—

WHITEHEAD: Yeah, there may be too much of that, except—

LITTLE: What I'm interested in is that you're still dealing with this in your novel. Do you think all this violence in your work is a result of that wound?

WHITEHEAD: No, shit no. That's a *reductio.* No . . . *Domains* does have many instances of violence, but they're pretty much at a distance, and there's a lot of love poetry. I'm trying to understand why men lose control, I'm trying to understand whether losing control is always bad or not, and I'm trying to understand to what extent it is sometimes the only way to understand ourselves. The novel I *had* to write is admittedly a *Bildungsroman* of sorts, a kind of *Wilhelm Meister* for rednecks . . .

CARR: And that's a kind of traditional thing young writers do.

WHITEHEAD: Yeah, I know that and I'm appalled by people saying, "Yeah, you're writing a standard first novel, Whitehead." I'm not. I wrote this book, in a way, when I was twenty-one. It was an insane novel—not insane, just really bad. I sold a little chapter of it to a magazine as a short story, and that was the end of it, because I hadn't really learned to look at other people, to create other characters. This book is a monologue, a first-person book, yet I'm convinced there are other characters in it. Sonny Joiner, the protagonist, is something of myself, but not autobiographical—not really consistent with me. But to speak to the point of violence, I think it's not really so much that it has bothered me that there is violence in the world. What has concerned me is the business of balancing emotion and what is called reason, mind and body, the intellect and passion, the humors; it's almost a question of trying to understand the humors. So this still amazes me. If there's anything in my own personality that is in the book, it's that I'm oversized and Joiner is oversized and that we've always . . . I've always been conditioned to be gentle, and I really think I wish I were five eight and could be a *mean* son of a bitch.

CARR: Well, what a lot of people don't realize is that even in football you're not allowed to let your raw temper overwhelm you.

WHITEHEAD: Right. And by the way, I'm not suggesting that I was a great football player. I think that if I hadn't gotten hurt in college, I would have been a fair-to-middling country tackle. No more, no less. I wish I had not gotten hurt, because I did love the game. I loved the pacing, the ritual, the almost mystic drift that you experience on a good night, very much like an evening of good writing, a session of good sex, a conversation with just the right amount of booze, or what have you. I love ritual, I love to feel that my mind and my body are totally functioning together—and I don't really believe in mind and body.

CARR: As functioning together, you mean?

WHITEHEAD: Yeah, the unity.

CARR: Well, I would think that this novel about Sonny Joiner is going to say something, eventually, about the union of mind and body, from what you say.

WHITEHEAD: That's what I'm fighting for it to do. But the curious thing about Joiner is that being from Mississippi, meaning the Mississippi River really . . .

CARR: You think of it *that* way.

WHITEHEAD: I think of it *that* way. The lower valley. But not being native to the region. And somebody did say, "You son of a bitch, you weren't really *born* there." Tough titty. Maybe my relationship to Mississippi is like Frost's relationship to New England. And I think he got them as well as anybody. I think I was much involved, and not only just in participating in that wretched childhood that we experienced in Mississippi: I was emotionally involved. But when I finally had my papers in order as a football player, I was left alone, I was accepted. Even though in Hattiesburg I was called "Yank."

CARR: That was your nickname?

WHITEHEAD: Yeah, I didn't even know what the word *meant*. Because my family certainly didn't think that way. Half had fought for the Union, half for the Confederacy, and that all didn't mean anything; but once I got into football, the nickname went away, and by the time we moved to Jackson a year later, it was gone, and I was given a little more breadth. But about Mississippi, the only thing I hope is, the only thing I know is, that I'm not only *in* it, but I've got a little distance *on* it.

CARR: Maybe it's . . . Well, I started to say that maybe it's better to be born outside a region and move into it at an impressionable age.

WHITEHEAD: Actually, my father's home, on the river there at Windsor Harbor, was not radically different in any way from that of a Delta planter's, except for the absence of the Negro.

CARR: There were no blacks where you lived?

WHITEHEAD: Oh, very few. And though my great-grandfather had married into a slaveholding family, a big Southern family, and he was kind of a Snopes character on the make . . . He was a very aggressive cat, a very tiny man, by the way. And he got control of the Waters business and turned it into the Whitehead business—with the help of some other men. Anyway, if I were to state my literary heritage, it would be Twain—whom I consider a Southern writer, by the way—and, after that, Faulkner or Carson McCullers or Flannery O'Connor. Now I'm just talking about people I read fairly early who made a strong impression on me.

Camus was the big thing in the middle and late fifties. I was a Camus nut. I was out of my mind for Camus. It was Camus, Sartre, Kierkegaard, Marcel—

CARR: You were interested in Marcel?

WHITEHEAD: Oh hell yeah. I was a philosophy major at Vanderbilt. I preached the gospel as a teen-ager—in the Presbyterian church—

CARR: Were you what we would call a lay reader?

WHITEHEAD: No, in the Presbyterian church you are a candidate for the ministry, and this allows you to have preaching privileges like an elder and a preacher, but not sacramental privileges. And I did that for a couple of years.

CARR: At Vandy?

WHITEHEAD: After high school, and a year or so at Vanderbilt, and then I quit. And I started a flirtation with the Catholic church.

CARR: Why?

WHITEHEAD: Well just because I was so deeply and terrifyingly committed to the necessity of Christianity. Like I believe in *hell*, man. And joining the church seemed to me the only reasonable thing a man could do, if *hell* existed, like a real place. It was terribly simple-minded.

LITTLE: Before Gen?

WHITEHEAD: Oh yeah. I was in and out of my flirtation with the Catholic church before I met her. When I was in college, we'd stay up all Saturday night and drink and read poems and talk and then we'd have six o'clock breakfast and then we'd go to this wonderful old cathedral in Nashville. Spanish cathedral. I loved it. You went to mass with the milkmen and the maids and the nurses from St. Thomas Hospital—I think it was St. Thomas—and we went six months to a year, every morning. But I couldn't make it, because I knew something was wrong, if not with the logic of the church, with its imagery, with its language.

CARR: Was this before the new mass?

WHITEHEAD: Oh yeah, you know, to hell with the new mass. I want Latin.

CARR: Really?

WHITEHEAD: Well, yeah, I say that flippantly. But I loved the Latin. But it was such a soppy, sentimental, sort of fifties Christian existentialism, which I was ass-deep in.

CARR: Due to what? Marcel?

WHITEHEAD: No, due to wanting to be a Christian, wanting to have that sort of relationship to the created world.

LITTLE: When you use that word *Christian*—I've heard you define it before, and it's not in the usual sense of the word as taught by Southern mothers.

WHITEHEAD: No, or by the Presbyterians or Baptists, or as it's found in any of the Southern Protestant versions. I don't know whether

I'm a Christian or not. George Garrett and I and some others like to kid around about it—this is getting into a heavy philosophical thing, and I'm not really interested in talking about it, because there's a literature that has a skein of this sort of thing in it.

CARR: It's important if you're talking about a writer's background.

WHITEHEAD: My college career was like the brief performing of four centuries of history. I entered college as a sort of fairly sensitive sixteenth- or seventeenth-century mind; by my sophomore year, I had gotten to be an eighteenth-century mind, and by my junior year, I had moved on the nineteenth century, and by my senior year, I was convinced I had entered the twentieth century and was a completely comfortable, liberated agnostic. And that was all super-dandy. But now we're about things that, in a curious way, don't get into my literature.

CARR: But don't you think your understanding of the world as a Christian is implicit in your work?

WHITEHEAD: I'll state a paradox, or say something confusing—I'll say something confusing: I think probably that to profess and push the Christian doctrine, which says that we are resurrected and that there is an afterlife, is a pernicious thing to do in this day and time. We must not believe there is afterlife, because this in a way gives us license to kill. Garrett and I were talking about the idea of dying before one becomes aware that he probably goes into oblivion. We were talking about a medieval hanging where, to really kill the guy, you keep him from being shriven by the priest. Because you hang him, and the people come up and they sing hymns and the banners are out and he confesses to sin. He had to die—

CARR: Like the Elizabethan story of the man who was shot at the instant he was made to blaspheme God.

WHITEHEAD: Right, or like the story in Huizinga's *Waning of the Middle Ages* where a guy really wanted to kill another one, so he rushed up and knocked the priest off the scaffold and tripped the trap door himself. So that guy was really *dead*. Like Hell City. But I don't think you go around talking about heaven these days. I think what we need to do is to live in our politics and our social behavior and our social morality as if oblivion were the fact. But as private men, knowing we have to live in our bodies and comprehend mysteries, and knowing that death is almost impossible to comprehend, we have to live as if Christianity were so. I tend to believe it probably is, but I'm not sure. Oh, the psychologists can get into this and they can analyze it, and I've read my Freud, I've read my Jung, I've gone that whole route. Some of my best friends are psychologists and they help me from time to time—I get shrunk now and then and they explain all these things to me. But I guess in a way I'm a kind of secret Christian.

CARR: You sound like a stoic.

WHITEHEAD: No, there's nothing stoic about it. The Christian thing has to do with original sin and it has to do with the fact that, man, you gotta live in your flesh and you want this flesh to endure, but it's always rotting off your body and we don't want to die. I want to drink whiskey with you a thousand years from now and I believe that Gen and you and John and all the people I love—we ain't gonna die, man, I gotta believe that with part of my mind. I've got to act as if that were true in one part of my being and then I've got to act as if the other thing were true to be sane socially. And the curious thing is that I'm sounding like one of those goddamned Anglo-Catholic rightists that I detested so much in the fifties, whereas I'm essentially a socialist politically.

CARR: You remind me of the stoics' blind faith in good moral acts.

WHITEHEAD: I'm not interested in good moral acts. What I want is the resurrection of the body.

CARR: The *physical* resurrection of the body?

WHITEHEAD: Hell, yes. To believe otherwise is heresy.

CARR: Well, I'm a pretty good heretic.

WHITEHEAD: Well see, I don't believe it, but I want it. What else is worth anything? He is risen! My redeemer liveth!

LITTLE: You want to talk about the poems in *Domains*? I want to ask you a question or two about them. The title first. How'd you come by the title?

WHITEHEAD: What I knew about the book when I was writing it was that I was writing about sex and politics.

LITTLE: What about "In the Country Where Only the Deaths of

the Aged Were Clear"? Wouldn't that have made a nice title?

WHITEHEAD: Well, I offered it to Charles East, my publisher, and he liked it but when he showed it to the guy who designs the dust jackets, he freaked out. It was just too long. And *Domains* struck me as nice because the book is partly about the domains of politics and sex. I'd written a poem I'd given that title to kind of intuitively, and I thought that would be a nice short title, and one of my friends, whom I admire very much, said, "That's a *very* nice title." How do you like the title *Reckonings?*

CARR: Nice.

WHITEHEAD: I think that's what I'll call my second book of poems. "Reckoning" is a good, moral-sounding word.

LITTLE: It suggests also a kind of reflective quality. Your poetry is reflective.

WHITEHEAD: Some of my detractors have called me anecdotal. I would say my poems are the essence of dramatic situations. [*Laughing*]

CARR: What got you started on poetry?

WHITEHEAD: [*Very dramatically*] Oh, I was an *introverted* kind of little *boy.*

CARR: Yeah? Couldn't that have produced fiction just as well?

WHITEHEAD: Listen, when I started writing in high school—a little bit—I started writing sermons, short stories, poems, essays. Then when I got to college I got confused and went through all this foolishness . . . I played ball, and I stuck to the books mostly, had an erratic career, lost my first girl friend and my religion and all that. I just wanted to write, and I *still* just want to write. I don't want people to come up and say to me— as they have always done in Iowa or Mississippi or North Dakota—and say, "Well, what are you, *really?*"

CARR: You could say, "I raise bats."

WHITEHEAD: I'm working at whatever I can do, I really like to write, in every way I can. I really like to be a writer. You know, like who are my heroes? Hardy—obviously; Robert Penn Warren—not because he's a Southerner, but because he's a hell of a poet and a hell of a fiction writer.

LITTLE: Why Hardy?

WHITEHEAD: Hardy was one of the first people I read and loved.
CARR: Don't Southerners like Hardy?
WHITEHEAD: Yeah, well, they keep telling you that, because you're a Southerner, you like so and so, and I'm not really interested in this Southern thing. Because it was such a pain in the ass to me, and so I have written a novel that's set more or less in the piney woods section of Mississippi—mainly because I've lived there on two occasions and I know it pretty well and because I cruised timber there in high school and college, worked in the lumber mill. That's John's part of the country, but I know it pretty well.

However, I don't think of that as Southern, I think of it as a place I know, in which characters appear that I love and understand and hate. It fires off something in my imagination and intellect and reason and my body, and that's what I understand.

But this business of the general term *Southern*—I think we all understand that there are thirteen or fourteen Souths, and in some ways I feel closer to some Vermonters or New Hampshiremen I've known, or some guys from Iowa or some poor Finn in Brockett, North Dakota. I guess the greatest distance in my sensibility is between me and guys from Southern California.
CARR: Are we talking about not Southern writing, but writing that springs from a writer's contacts with the country?
WHITEHEAD: Well, I was raised in a small city, Jackson, and my main contact with the "soil" was in the timber business.
CARR: Okay, but I'm not talking about actual contacts so much as growing up in a country of the mind, a country of the heart, that corresponds to a real place, which happens to be controlled by an agricultural economy.
WHITEHEAD: I grew up in North Jackson, and it was so far north of Jackson it wasn't even that, really. There were woods a block away, and I spent all my time—my best friend and I, Ed Stuart, a broker, hunting rabbits and fishing crawdads. It was like being a country boy, but yet when we walked up the hill we were in a subdivision. What you get is just a little more schizophrenia, I guess.

CARR: Peter Taylor had a good question for you last night and I think I'm obligated to ask this question, because I do think you couldn't mistake something written by a Southerner for something written by a New Englander or a Nevadan or—

WHITEHEAD: I disagree. I think we have many things in common with a place like New England. Well look, here we are at a Southern writers conference in North Dakota, and we were riding around out there today, and we know it looks like Washington or Sharkey counties, Mississippi. Oh, there's something strange about it, but . . .

CARR: Okay, but look: with all the social and historical *donnée*—

WHITEHEAD: *Donnée*, is that like *de rigueur*?

CARR: Yeah, and *cum grano salis* and *ipse dixie* and all that. But . . . given all the givens, why has a little poor place like Mississippi produced good writers and a place like North Dakota—and I'm not picking on our hosts—not produced as many good writers?

WHITEHEAD: Yeah, well, we've had this tradition of laziness and slothfulness—and a little decadence here and there, and a real affection for bullshit and rhetoric. We're people of the word. Oh, this is like a conversation I heard in Nashville in—

CARR: Yeah, you always hear this conversation. Let's change it.

WHITEHEAD: No, let's don't, because I'm really curious, puzzled, and angry every time I hear it, and also a little insecure about how to answer it.

CARR: Are you a Southern writer because you've stuck up over the years for something you have discerned about the South, or are you a Southern writer because you were born there—or through the grace of God and your parents moving, brought up there. And I think it's a real question, because one attitude would mean a *sympathy* with it, instead of just the accident of having that material to work with.

WHITEHEAD: Yeah, it's an interesting question, and it's also one that's impossible to answer. Anyway, I'm glad I grew up in *god-damn* Mississippi. I'm glad I'm a Mississippian. I'm glad I got the wound there. Okay. *But* . . . I'm not saying that's better than being raised as a college professor's son at the University of North Dakota. I don't *know* absolutely. There's a mystery in that kind of judgment. I'm not going to presume on that. I love to wrestle with trying to be reasonable, if at all possible, with trying to manipulate forms of literature, if at all possible. I like the sense of tension in the South between the classical education and the gut-bucket, down-home, honky-tonk raunchiness that makes your balls cringe. There's a terrible tension between those two traditions. Look, you know the Delta pretty well, you and I consider ourselves sort of populists, but still we like to sit down by the swimming pool in Leland or Rosedale and have our toddies.

CARR: Well . . . once a summer is enough with some of them.

WHITEHEAD: But I think probably some Sioux one of these days is going to walk into Grand Forks, North Dakota, and hand in the great Sioux novel. And it'll have—ta ta rah ta da—*universality!*

CARR: Don't you think that one thing that helps the Southerner is that he has a different viewpoint on America?

WHITEHEAD: We shouldn't have to justify ourselves as Southerners.

CARR: I agree.

WHITEHEAD: Don Justice is one of the finest American poets, and you can see that in his first book. He also translates French very well. I think he's a Southerner, but he avoids talking about it all the time. So does Bill Harrison.

LITTLE: What about Peter Taylor?

CARR: Peter Taylor will stick up for it.

WHITEHEAD: I stick up for it, god damn it! You heard me stick up for Hank Williams last night. You heard me—I was delighted by the fact that here at the North Pole we find Hank Williams on the juke box.

CARR: And Kitty Wells.

WHITEHEAD: And Kitty Wells. And that's great, but also maybe they need to have studied their Latin.

CARR: Don't you think that a lot of that so-called classical tradition in the South is confined to a number of neo-Ionian porticoes those fools put up after they made a fortune during World War II?

WHITEHEAD: Yeah, well, I'm sure that a lot of it is phony and bullshit, but that tradition taught love of language. It made you not only enjoy the etymology of words, but the whole rhythm and spool of a phrase, of a paragraph . . . Grammar is a way *into* sensuality. The excuse for grammar and rhetoric is that it helps you perform language more sensually.

LITTLE: I want to ask you a question about poetry. I don't think it's accidental that *Domains* won the Robert Frost Award.

WHITEHEAD: Yeah, well I think I deserved to win that award, not because I'm any good, but because I . . . really . . . love . . . Frost. And I tried to learn something from him.

LITTLE: There's a word you use in that book over and over again. I'm sure that one of these days, some graduate student is going to count how many times the word *common* appears in that book, and he's going to come up with something like ninety-seven times.

CARR: Which leads me to think that you've done it already.

LITTLE: One poem in there is entitled "Common" and you explained that the other night by saying that it was a word you had heard your parents use a lot—

WHITEHEAD: Not my parents. Not my parents. They were almost totally without prejudice, God love 'em.

LITTLE: Well, I want to make two observations on that word. First, I want you to elaborate on what the word means and why it held such interest for you, and—

WHITEHEAD: Because I learned quite early that there were some people who did in fact condescend to people who were poor and who belonged to different racial groups. That's very common, that's very corny stuff, but it shocked the hell out of me.

LITTLE: Were you ever concerned that you were overusing it?

WHITEHEAD: No, not very much, because that's just one book of poems, and I don't know how much it'll appear in the first novel. I'm a young man, I'm going to write, hopefully, God help me, more books. I don't know how many more times it will appear from here on in, and I'm going to try not to think about it because if it's an obsessive word with me, it might be a good word, and I really don't like this line of questioning one bit.

CARR: [*Looking at Little*] Furthermore, deponent sayeth naught?

LITTLE: Well, I guess we'll go back to philosophy. I thought it was a good question.

WHITEHEAD: No, John, sure it's a good question. Sure, you have to watch out for the things you're obsessive about.

CARR: Since we brought Marcel into this a little earlier, I'd like to talk about one of the terms of his philosophy, *deponbilité*, or being at the disposal of other human beings.

WHITEHEAD: You are available to others and the experience accruing thereunto motherfuck. Right.

CARR: Is that the way that you would like to live? Well, here we go, more Boy Scout questions, friends, but I really can't help it.

WHITEHEAD: What I would like to be is a great writer who is also remembered for being a wonderful father and a loving friend. But Yeats is probably right. You choose perfection in the life or the work, and many of my friends, and probably my wife, would agree that, while my work is not too good, my life is worse. I don't know, there is always this hypothetical question, "Would you sell your wife into slavery if you could write a great book?" Thank God that question never comes up. I groove on writing. I really *love* to write.

CARR: Another thing we haven't brought up so far, maybe because we know you so well, is that it's very unusual for a varsity athlete to write poetry.

WHITEHEAD: Varsity athlete? That's very inexact to call me a varsity athlete in college, because I really played in very few college football games. I had a letter, but mainly because I worked very, very hard as the guy the second- and third-string tackles beat up on all the time.

CARR: But it is interesting that a varsity athlete, no matter how ritzy the college he played for—

WHITEHEAD: Or how bad the football team . . .

CARR: Or how bad the football team—becomes a poet.

WHITEHEAD: I was hell in high school.

CARR: You were All-American, weren't you?

WHITEHEAD: Well—I was All-State two years, All–Big Eight two years, All-Southern two years, and I was invited to play in the high school All-Americans game. I don't remember where they listed me or ranked me. I was captain of the South side in the Mississippi All-Stars game, and got my ankle broken on the third play. We beat the *hell* out of those Delta boys, 21 to 20.

CARR: Yes, I remember, Jim. It was a slaughter.

WHITEHEAD: Tommy Little from Meridian kicked that precious extra point. And it didn't go straight on in, it kind of slid up on its side, balanced ambiguously on the bar, and sort of *collapsed* on the other side for the extra point.

CARR: Sonny Joiner started off in your novel as a professional football player enamored of peanut butter, didn't he?

WHITEHEAD: No, he started off eating a lot of peanut butter, but he's come to eat less and less peanut butter as the book has gone through three drafts.

CARR: What happened to the peanut butter?

WHITEHEAD: Well, I got into the habit of eating less and less peanut butter. People keep telling me what this book means. My friends write descriptions of me, the book's not in print yet, and they—but anyway, it's *not* a book about a football player, and it's *not* about a peanut butter freak—it's about Sonny Joiner. And it's about Royal Carl Boykin, who is his best friend and ends up marrying his wife—the book begins, "My ex-wife is marrying a Jackson lawyer in a couple of days."

CARR: So it's not about Mississippi, or football, or violence or the South, and so that wipes out most of the er, ah, existential qualities of the book.

WHITEHEAD: It's about the instress of the inscape. Sort of the essence of resin.

It's an endless novel I have worked on with great confusion and fervor and, I think, *reason* for three years. I . . . don't . . . know . . . what . . . it's . . . about. I've got a character in the book, and a few other characters with him. And to me, a novel is character.

LITTLE: Are you going to write other books about these particular characters?

WHITEHEAD: I hope so. I have short drafts of a book called *Stream*, which is about Coldstream Taggart, one of Sonny's friends, and I've got a draft of a novel called *Boykin*.

LITTLE: *Joiner* is an internally created story. Are these others going to be done in the same way?

WHITEHEAD: I don't know. I suspect that *Boykin* will be a little more objectified and probably written in the third person. One of the great things about *Joiner* is that though it is written in the first person, it is lucid and has remarkable sense of objectivity and a great ability to create characters other than the protagonist, he said humbly.

CARR: All right, but why use first person and why use third person?

WHITEHEAD: Because Boykin, unlike Sonny Joiner, is a man who looks at *himself* in third person. When people knew I was writing the book about Sonny Joiner in the first person, they said, "My *God*, man! Don't write a *Bildungsroman* in the first person for your first novel. In fact, you're thirty-four years old, you should have *learned* better!" Well, I haven't. It happened to fit the character in this case. I'll do anything I can to gratify the character I'm writing about. It's his book, not mine.

LITTLE: Jim, along that line, I understand that when you started the book, it was going to be told from many first-person points of view.

WHITEHEAD: Yeah, right, I started writing it that way, and the final book would have been, like, 17,000 pages long.

LITTLE: But you didn't *really* have a 17,000-page novel in mind. You thought you could do it—

WHITEHEAD: In about 700 or 800 pages.

LITTLE: And one part just grew.

WHITEHEAD: Yes, in point of fact, one part did grow.

LITTLE: That's interesting to me, because your poetry is so very economical.

WHITEHEAD: This novel is *terribly* economical.

LITTLE: Yeah, but it's still 500 pages . . . big.

WHITEHEAD: Yeah, but it is short scenes—a few long scenes in some of the chapters, but it is still economical. Look, everybody says, "When you write novels you go *balooey* all over the place," and that's *not* so!

LITTLE: That's not what I'm saying, either! I have heard the novelist defined as someone who cannot get something said in a shorter form—but you have demonstrated you can, in *Domains*.

CARR: Some people think there is a difference in the kind of mind that works mostly with the poem or the shorter forms and the mind that goes to the longer form. What would you say about that?

WHITEHEAD: Poems aren't short. Listen, man, Hopkins' "The Windhover," though short in number of lines, is longer in many ways than Frost's "The Witch of Coos," which is a great narrative poem, because length is not defined in number of words but, often, rather in terms of the complexity of metaphor, in the amount of energy displaced on the part of the reader to understand said metaphor or metaphors.

CARR: We are talking about the intensity of experience? You can endure, for example, an intense short story, but you can't endure an intense novel. It's a long voyage.

WHITEHEAD: Yes, you can. You can endure a long, intense novel. Listen, *Absalom, Absalom!* is a long, intense novel. Let's try to write that kind of book. *Ulysses* is that kind of book. A book like *Under the Volcano* by Malcolm Lowry blows your mind from page one on.

LITTLE: Oh, it doesn't either. There are ups and downs. Take *Portnoy's Complaint*, that's a one-note novel, and it's not sustained; it fails.

WHITEHEAD: I can't say that *Portnoy's Complaint* fails. I read that book at one sitting, and I said, WHOOOOEEE! and it really turned me on, it was a great piece of absolutely brilliant porno, and porno can very well be art. Prurience is often art. I loved the book, and I understood all the flaws in it, and I say the last of the book is not consistent with the beginning or middle, and there are a couple of characters who are definitely walk-ons, and I was computing all this information as I read the book, and when I finished it, I said, WHEEE! what a great piece of work! and threw it up against the wall, and went on back to—

LITTLE: What influence has Miller Williams had on your poetry? And your life as an artist?

CARR: And, we might add, your life as a human being?

WHITEHEAD: Miller Williams. Art and life and er, ah . . . He encouraged me when I was a youth and I've always appreciated that.

LITTLE: He picked you out as a likely lad, did he?

CARR: For the record, who is Miller Williams?

WHITEHEAD: Miller Williams, poet, novelist, *bon vivant,* and currently lecturer in American Studies in the university at Mexico City. He's of the agrarian, neosocialist, syndicalist, anarchist, sensualist fugitive movement à la . . . à la 1960's. He's got a beer-drinking soul. Look, John, I overreacted to your question about Miller because people don't like to be asked their opinions on their close friends, who happen also to be good writers. I don't like this business of let's-knock-down-the-competition. And let's don't praise them, either. That might hurt as much as knocking them down. All right, look: Miller and I are dear friends. He's very good, but I want to share *and* keep my distance.

CARR: Hey, I got an off-the-wall question for you. What are we all doing teaching college?

WHITEHEAD: *Love* to teach school.

CARR: Oh, yeah, right.

WHITEHEAD: It's an art, it's an art.

CARR: What harm does it do, what good does it do?

WHITEHEAD: If you teach well, it does good.

CARR: And it doesn't take away from your writing time?

WHITEHEAD: Sure, everything takes away from your writing time.

LITTLE: All the writers, or a great many of them, are caught up in an academic environment. They are not cruising timber, they are not out having experiences—

WHITEHEAD: They never . . . have . . . been—while they were writing.

LITTLE: Do you ever feel that this is a restriction?

WHITEHEAD: Used to, if you were a writer, you had to work for the duke. Right? And boy, you had to eat some shit to work for the duke. But now our patron is the dean. And he is about as good as the duke was, no more demanding and no less. So I feel that had

I been a sonneteer in the Renaissance, I could have worked for my duke. And I can work for my dean. I happen to have a good dean.

LITTLE: But regardless of how much liberty your academic environment gives you, there is a restriction on the subject matter that's available to you and that you respond to. And your book about Sonny Joiner is not set in any classroom. You go outside the classroom when you draw on the stuff of Sonny Joiner.

WHITEHEAD: I'm only in the academic environment when I'm teaching school. I have a very loose relationship to it. I don't serve on committees, I don't go to many faculty parties, I don't see many faculty members.

LITTLE: All right, do you feel you have access to the materials you deal with?

WHITEHEAD: I don't have to worry about it. I've got three more novels to write out of my past experience and another book of poems. If I wake up some morning and say to myself that I've got to start writing villanelles about teaching freshman grammar, then I might cop out and go do something else. But I'll be forty before that happens.

LITTLE: Have you ever wished that you could get back to things like cruising timber?

WHITEHEAD: No. I might take off during a sabbatical year and drive trucks. I was a commercial truck driver—I had my license until a few years ago—and I liked that.

LITTLE: I'm interested in this because a girl at a party says a line like "I just can't help feeling sentimental about Jesus" and she says it in front of seven writers, and it appears in seven books.

WHITEHEAD: Well, we were all in the room at the same time.

CARR: What? What is this?

WHITEHEAD: This is with Harrison in '58, back in Nashville. We were all in a room drinking beer and talking religion and she pops up and says, "I don't care what you boys say with all your schoolin', I still feel sentimental about Jesus."

LITTLE: Yeah, and it ends up in seven books, and that's what writing is today.

WHITEHEAD: I think it's out of mine, I'm not sure. It may be the last line of the novel in an early draft, I don't know. It happens that

I'm an artist, and teaching is an art form. At this point in my life, it is my second favorite art form and it subsidizes my first favorite art form.

I love teaching school. Theodore Roethke, who I think is the greatest American poet we've had in the last twenty years, made it as a great American poet, and he is remembered *also*, in the subordinate clause, as a great teacher. And I honor that tradition. Had he made a lot of money, he might have quit teaching, but as long as he taught school, he taught it with the passion of an artist. That is not evasive. Listen, I have to take tranquilizers at the first of every semester, because I teach school like it was going out of style. Which it is, in most places.

LITTLE: If you didn't have to teach, would you?

WHITEHEAD: Yeah, I'd teach a little bit. And I'd teach like hell.

LITTLE: Creative writing?

WHITEHEAD: Now and then. Next year, I think I'm going to get to teach undergraduate Shakespeare. I'm a pretty good Shakespearean, and I love it. I'd like to teach Shakespeare, I'd like to teach Chaucer, modern poetry and fiction, anywhere they will let me, with my inadequate academic credentials. He said, humbly.

CARR: But the point is, you can understand what you're teaching from a little bit different viewpoint than that of most academicians.

WHITEHEAD: Listen, I don't like this business of academic people taking out the whips and cords to flagellate themselves. It is an honorable tradition, it is an honorable art, and we are *not* worse than most people; we are better, probably. I have no apologies for the university and its traditions; I have no apologies for the teaching profession; and we are going to get ourselves in god*damn* hot water if we go around being obsequious about our tradition and about art.

LITTLE: You have written a book of poems while teaching in school about people who had never essentially been to school. You have written a novel about people who are very distant from an academic environment—

WHITEHEAD: No, that's absolutely inaccurate. Sonny has been to school, Coldstream has been to school—

CARR: Yes, but his point is that they're not academicians or what some
people would call learned men.

WHITEHEAD: No, Sonny's got a history major, Royal's got a law
degree, and Coldstream—

LITTLE: All right, you've written a novel about intellectuals, but Jim,
the stuff of the novel, the impetus, doesn't come from anything
in academic life, and—

WHITEHEAD: All right, John, listen: we also went to school, but we
also love to go to the National Tobacco-Spitting Championship
in Raleigh, Mississippi, and I'll tell you something, I think you
and I *dig* the National Tobacco-Spitting Championship as much
as any redneck there and maybe understand it a little better.

LITTLE: The thing is, the academic environment does not put you in
touch with the tobacco spit.

WHITEHEAD: Well you're talking like when you sign a contract to teach
for a year at a university, they lock you up in a prison. That's utter
bullshit.

LITTLE: Jim, how many years in your life since you started the first
grade have you spent outside the academic environment?

WHITEHEAD: Part of every day is spent out of the institution. Now
I'm being criticized for being an intellectual.

CARR: Hardly.

WHITEHEAD: Yes, you are, you're beating your breasts and flagellating
yourselves for being intellectuals.

CARR: *You* are an intellectual. Maybe. But never mind: how did
you react to the question I heard someone ask you upstairs about
our students being worried about overpopulation? I know they
asked you because you have seven kids, but how do you react to
the general attitude that the world is dying and what-are-we-
doing-to-justify-our existence?

WHITEHEAD: The world is—the world is *dying*? Gimme a cigarette before we deal with that piece of liberal bullshit. That's like landing
a 727 in an omelette . . . Let me tell you, baby, what I worry
about is whether the Mississippi River at Memphis is being pol-
luted by the Endrin Corporation pumping that shit down to
Louisiana and killing all the fish and putting 4,000 fishermen out
of business. I know that river; that's something I can write a letter
about, or use as a metaphor in a poem. I don't wake

up in the morning and say, "What can I *do* for the *world* today?" What I worry about is whether they're going to dam the White River in Arkansas—which they shouldn't do—and whether they're selling too much goddamn DDT in the Mississippi and Arkansas Deltas. But don't give me this abstract shit, because what we're involved in is solving the problem at first base, then at second, and then at third base. I'm for clean air and pretty people, too . . .

CARR: Time for one last word.

WHITEHEAD: The only trouble with the Midwest and the high North is that they didn't have the good fortune of being raised in a multiracial society. Let's hear it for the brave, miscegenated South. [*Bronx cheers by all*]

CARR: On the other hand, as somebody said today, maybe the three of us profited by that lost war, but what about the twenty million other crackers?

WHITEHEAD: They profited too, man. They understand that life is losing. The thing most people don't understand about life is that you don't win all the time. Being accustomed to loss can be a great virtue.

Biographical Notes
on Interviewers

JOHN CARR was born in Mississippi in 1942 and graduated from the University of Mississippi in 1960 and from Hollins College (MA) in 1969. He held an Etheridge Fellowship at the University of North Carolina at Chapel Hill in 1968 and was writer-in-residence at Phillips Exeter Academy in 1970–1971. He has taught at the University of North Carolina at Charlotte and at Loyola of New Orleans. His fiction, essays, and verse have been in *Folio, Red Clay Reader, Intro 2, Hollins Critic, Fly By Night,* and *Contempora.* He was an editor of *Underground* in 1966–1967, a reporter for the *Delta Democrat-Times,* and is an editor of *Contempora.* He now lives in New Orleans and is finishing his first novel. He is also co-author of a new book on teaching movies.

JAMES B. COLVERT, professor of English at the University of Georgia and past editor of *Georgia Review,* received his doctorate at Louisiana State University in 1953 and has taught at the University of Texas and the University of Virginia. He has published a number of literary essays in various journals and has written critical introductions for the University Press of Virginia multivolume edition of the works of Stephen Crane.

WALLACE KAUFMAN transplanted himself to the South to escape the "megalopolization" of the Northeast. He is a former scholar of New College, Oxford University, teaches English at the University of North Carolina at Chapel Hill, is vice president of the state's conservation council, runs an environmentally oriented real estate firm, and has published stories, poems, and articles in numerous magazines and anthologies.

JOHN LITTLE, from Raleigh, Mississippi, is on the staff of the University of North Dakota, where he teaches Southern fiction and creative writing. His stories have appeared in *New Orleans Review, Scopcraft, The North Dakota Quarterly,* and *Rhetoric 12.* He is a co-editor of the most recently published *Worksheet,* an anthology of student writing.

JAMES SEAY is now teaching English at Vanderbilt University. He is a native of Mississippi and graduated from the University of Mississippi in 1963. He earned a master's degree at the University of Virginia and later taught at Washington and Lee University and the University of Alabama. He is the author of *Let Not Your Hart,* a volume of poetry published in 1970.

JOHN SOPKO lives in Irvington, New York, but commutes daily to Bridgeport, Connecticut, to cover city news for the local paper. He was born in April, 1943, and earned a master's degree from Hollins College in 1970. His current project is a novel about a guilt-ridden teen-aged killer.

GEORGE WOLFE, a native of Columbia, Mississippi, graduated from the University of Mississippi in 1964. He has received a master's degree from the University of North Carolina at Chapel Hill and is there now, working on a dissertation on Lawrence Durrell. He was in Vietnam while in the Navy. He has published fiction and essays in *Roanoke Review* and *Red Clay Reader.*